28.54/70

PROF. DR. H. D. BETZ
329 WEST SEVENTH STREET
CLAREMONT, CAL. 91711, U.S.A.
PHONE: (714) 624-2275

STUDIA POST-BIBLICA

VOLUMEN VICESIMUM PRIMUM

STUDIA POST-BIBLICA

INSTITUTA A P.A.H. DE BOER

ADIUVANTIBUS

T. JANSMA ET J. SMIT SIBINGA

EDIDIT

J. C. H. LEBRAM

VOLUMEN VICESIMUM PRIMUM

LEIDEN
E. J. BRILL
1973

RABBINIC LITERATURE
AND
GRECO-ROMAN PHILOSOPHY

A STUDY OF EPICUREA AND RHETORICA
IN EARLY MIDRASHIC WRITINGS

BY

HENRY A. FISCHEL

LEIDEN
E. J. BRILL
1973

ISBN 90 04 03720 9

Copyright 1973 by E. J. Brill, Leiden, Netherlands

All rights reserved. No part of this book may be reproduced or translated in any form, by print, photoprint, microfilm, microfiche or any other means without written permission from the publisher

PRINTED IN BELGIUM

*In loving memory
of my parents*

TABLE OF CONTENTS

Preface IX

PART I. The "Four in 'Paradise'" (*Ḥagigah, et al.*): Anti-Epicurean Stereotype, Biography, and Parody in the Portrayals of Tannaim 1
Epicureanism in the Ancient Near East 1

PART II. An Epicurean *Sententia* on Providence and Divine Justice in the Midrash 35

PART III. *Epicurea* and *Rhetorica* in the Midrash of Ben Zoma   51
   1. An Heurematological Oration 51
   2. An Oration on Table Manners and Gratitude . . . 65
   3. Stoic *Paradoxa* 70
   4. An Anti-Epicurean Sorites 74
   5. A *Chria* on Absentmindedness 78

PART IV. APPENDIX. *Epicurea* and *Rhetorica* of Ben Azzai?   . 90
   1. The Meaning of Sacrifice 90
   2. Laughter at Death 90
   3. The Sage's Death 90
   4. Two *Bona* and Two *Mala* 91
   5. Celibacy 92
   6. Education of Women 92
   7. Endorsement of Controversial Books 92
   8. Man in God's Image and *Imitatio Dei* 92
   9. Avoidance of Sin 93
  10. The Sage's Asceticism 93
  11. *Memento Mori* 95
  12. Inclination and Fate 96
  13. Man and the Cosmos 96

TABLE OF CONTENTS

Epilogue 98
Notes to Part I 99
Notes to Part II 128
Notes to Part III 138
Notes to Part IV 161
Notes to Epilogue 165

Bibliography 166
Index of References 167
Terms and Keywords 182
General Index 186
Index of Modern Authors 198

PREFACE

This is the first of a series of inquiries emanating from a larger research project "Studies in Bureaucratic Phenomena in Classical Civilizations". This particular study was made possible by a 1969-1970 Fellowship of the John Simon Guggenheim Memorial Foundation the instrumentality of which is hereby gratefully acknowledged. For several years preliminary studies had been faithfully supported by the Office of Research and Advanced Studies of Indiana University to whom likewise long overdue gratitude is herewith expressed together with grateful acknowledgment of their contribution to the printing costs of this volume.

Furthermore, I desire to express many thanks to Dr. J. C. H. Lebram, the editor of *Studia Post-Biblica*, and to Mr. F. Th. Dijkema, the Oriental Editor of E. J. Brill, for their decision to include this work in their series, their valuable assistance, and their suggestions for the final title.

Thanks go to my colleagues in the Classics Department of Indiana University, Professors David L. Sigsbee and John R. Wilson, for useful hints and, above all, to Professor Paul D. Eisenberg of the Department of Philosophy who read parts of the manuscript and offered valuable criticism and corrections.

The three parts of this study had originally been written as three independent essays. It is hoped that the traces of their former independent existence have been eliminated and that the reader will find repetition only where the argument requires it.

In many instances, the interdisciplinary character of this inquiry has made it necessary to quote in detail the title, edition, and purpose of a standard work or basic text which is only too well-known to the expert in one field but novel to that in another, be it Classics, Judaic Studies, Patristics, Philosophy, or Religion. The uses of literary terms peculiar to this inquiry, however, have not been burdened with extensive definitions but explain themselves by their application. Similarly, terms of classical rhetoric have been used according to their most simple definitions without complex distinctions and mention of controversial points which abound in ancient criticism.

It seemed practical to use three different systems of transcribing Hebrew and Aramaic:

1. Wherever intrinsically philological problems are under discussion, the technical spelling prevalent in Ancient Near Eastern or Semitic philology has been used.

2. Recent books in Hebrew, especially Israel publications, are quoted according to the quite serviceable system of the Library of Congress, Washington, D.C., the only inconsistency of which, that of writing *biyeme* instead of *bime*, has been corrected.

3. The rendering of talmudic authorities and works has been slightly simplified and vowel length, aspiration of d, g, and b (the latter is common practice) as well as initial and word-end '*ayin* and '*aliph* have not been indicated so that fairly familiar names would not appear in too exotic a garb. All these systems are, of course, overruled by the actual spelling which a publisher or author prefers on his English title page whenever reference is made to such a particular edition: thus *Seder Eliahu Rabba*, ed. Friedmann, but elsewhere *Seder Eliyahu Rabba*.

For the convenience of the reader, brief Latin quotations embedded in an English sentence are frequently italicized. In some few instances, the italicized names of authors have been used instead of the titles of their works in order to simplify quotation and avoid confusion with other works of the same title; thus *D.L.* for Diogenes Laertius; *P.-W.* for Pauly-Wissowa; *Ueberweg*; and *Usener* (details in the notes). Literature is listed only if it has actually been consulted.

Appreciation must also be extended to the Library of Indiana University for their continuous additions to the Classical and Judaic collections, frequently aimed at fulfilling the needs of this particular research, and to the Interlibrary Loan office whose efficient aid proved indispensible. Among the libraries supplying materials to the latter, the collection of the University of Illinois in Classics deserves special mention, and the Library of the Hebrew Union College in Cincinnati must be acknowledged for their prompt and generous service as well as their inexhaustable collection of Judaica.

Frequent and thorough treatment in contemporary scholarly works made it unnecessary to introduce the scene and events which produced early Palestinian Rabbinic literature (tannaitic literature), the New Testament, and early Patristics. For the same reason no introduction is given to Philo of Alexandria. The Near Eastern presence of Epicureanism, however, and its Roman phase, had briefly to be recapitulated owing to less frequent treatment.

It is fortunate that at this stage of scholarship no further defense has to be made for the assumption that Greco-Roman situations were well-known to the creators of the Midrash, i.e., the literature that modifies the word and the world of Scripture by interpretation, explicitly or implicitly. Rather, the problem is how far this knowledge went, how much of Greco-Roman academic procedure and philosophical quest was used in that on-going process in which the culmination of the tannaitic culture, *c.* 200 A.D. (the codification of the Mishnah) and that of Palestinian amoraic culture, *c.* 400 (Jerusalem Talmud) were important stages.

The present inquiry is thus in line with recent trends of sholarship but goes farther in a number of points. Perhaps for the first time parallels to Greco-Roman orations and important rhetorical *topoi*, basically intact as to structure and stylistic devices, are laid bare in well-known Rabbinic literary items the later interpretation of which, especially the mystical one, had obscured their original meaning. Examples of other literary genres of Greco-Roman rhetoric are analyzed in the tannaitic material which occasionally preserves not only their literary form but also their ethical or philosophical-religious content. The use of the philosopher biography in its popular rhetorical garb is claimed for the portrayal of leading Tannaim, as is the use of the Sage anecdote or *chria*, the parody, and a number of shorter forms and coinages, all vehicles of philosophical polemic and satire. Perhaps for the first time, the entire midrashic output of a specific Tanna is shown to be of Greco-Roman rhetorical provenance.

All claims of Greco-Roman patterns are made solely for the Midrash or author under discussion and cannot be generalized or extended, although in this volume only a segment of the adopted Greco-Roman corpus can be treated. Even this task could only be performed within limits: finer distinctions had occasionally to be omitted for the sake of revealing the dimensions and ramifications of the entire phenomenon.

The ever on-going adaptation of a single Greco-Roman literary unit to the indigenous needs and moods of the talmudic culture, a process which unfolds in the constant reuses of such a unit, in its combinations with biblical prooftexts, and in the choice of its final location in talmudic codes, make the task of recognizing and reconstructing an originally Greco-Roman item quite precarious. However, to assume that literary units have a rigid, unchanging life of their own, and that the state in which they are found is the original and only valid one, is an equally, if not more, precarious method. By the same token the tannaitic stage of talmudic culture cannot be fully reconstructed by assuming that it resembled the amoraic one in all respects, just as the latter cannot be fully understood by making medieval situations the norm.

Although we live in an age of continuously changing fashions and emphases even in scholarship, an inquiry which probes into the interaction between cultures, professional classes, and systems of values and beliefs, needs no further justification. The by-product alone would justify the attempt: a better understanding of texts and episodes that have always been mysterious.

In spite of strong ethnic, religious, and other areas of independence of ancient cultures in many parts, there was thus a general context in late antiquity the representative and ideal of which was the *sophos - sapiens - ḥakham*, the Sage, i.e., this special brand of scholar-believer-bureaucrat, who under the precarious and often tragic developments of late antiquity strove mightily to uphold rational and emotionally balanced positions in many aspects of civilized life, who was loyal to native aspirations and traditions, yet also devoted to an intercultural context which had its own momentum and its own ethos.

August 1971
Bloomington, Indiana

Henry A. Fischel
Department of Near Eastern
Languages and Literatures
Indiana University

PART ONE

THE "FOUR IN PARADISE"

ANTI-EPICUREAN STEREOTYPE, BIOGRAPHY,
AND PARODY

Scholarship on Epicureanism, always lively and abundant,[1] has rightly emphasized the fact that a renewed vitality of Epicureanism became manifest from approximately 150-250 A.D.[2] Much of this Epicurean resurgence was located in the Eastern part of the mediterranean world including the Near East.

Epicureanism had reached an earlier high water mark in its Roman phase: in Rome, Naples, and Herculaneum,[3] and without this important phase in the history of Epicureanism the Near Eastern phase cannot be understood. It was in Rome that the Epicurean Amafinius, an older contemporary of Cicero (106-43), wrote the first Latin work of philosophy of any kind. Among the highlights of the Roman Epicurean movement are, above all, the great poem *de rerum natura* of Lucretius (c. 94-55),[4] the literary activities of Philodemus of Gadara (c. 110-40/35),[5] second in importance of all "technical" Epicureans,[6] and the varying involvements with Epicureanism of Julius Caesar (c. 102-44); his father-in-law L. Calpurnius Piso; Cassius, the tyrannicide; Titus Pomponius Atticus (109-32); the Augustan poets Vergil (70-19) and Horace (65-8); and, still later, Seneca (c. 5 B.C. - 65 A.D.) and, perhaps, Petronius (d. 66 A.D.).[7] Even Ovid (43 B.C. - 17/18 A.D.), Maecenas (d. 8 B.C.), and Juvenal (c. 50 - c. 128) have been called mildly affected by Epicureanism.[8] The Roman activities of the Epicurean physician Asclepiades (d. c. 40 B.C.) whom Sextus Empiricus praised, also belong to this development.[9]

Cicero who at one time had heard the Epicurean teachers Zeno of Sidon and Phaedrus in Athens and who counted many Epicureans among his friends may —according to some opinions— have passed through a brief Epicurean period in his earlier life but finally became the leading critic of Epicureanism in his time and a model to many of its later opponents.[10] Nevertheless, even in his most critical period he occasionally still showed praise for Philodemus and for Vergil's friend Siro(n) as well as for Epicurus himself and he frequently admitted —or complained— that Epicureanism had "occupied all Italy" and was ubiquitous even in the barbarian provinces.[11]

Occasionally, Pliny the Elder, 23/24-79, is considered to have been in sympathy with Epicureanism, especially on the grounds of his vehement and detailed denial of afterlife, *naturalis historia* VII. lv. 188-190.[12]

Renewed support of the Athenian school which had carried on since the time of its founder, Epicurus (342/341 - 271/270), was obtained by the widow of Trajan (98-117), Plotina, under Hadrian (117-138) and continued by Marcus Aurelius (161-180).[13] These pro-Epicurean measures coincide with a vehement though mostly literary and oratorical opposition, such as Plutarch's extensive anti-Epicurean works composed in Greece and his lectures in Rome, *c.* 90,[14] the diatribes of the moralizing Epictetus (*c.* 50 - *c.* 135; he left Rome in 89),[15] and the Jewish historian Josephus' (37/38 - after 100 ?) critical statements written during his active years in Rome.[16].

The century from *c.* 50-150 could thus be considered a transitional period in the history of Epicureanism between the Roman movement and the reassertion of both Epicureanism and anti-Epicureanism in the East, from *c.* 150 to 250.

There had always been Epicureans and Epicurean "events" in the Near East, from the time of Antiochus IV (d. 164 B.C.) and his "conversion" effected by Philonides [17] and the short-lived Epicurean tyranny and reform in Tarsus by one Lysias [18] to the anti-Epicureanism of Nicolaus of Damascus, Aristotelian court historian of Herod (*c.* 73-4 B.C.) in Jerusalem.[19] In Hellenized Egypt, too, Epicureanism was active since the days of the first Ptolemies when Epicurus himself had sent Colotes to the Egyptian court. Philo of Alexandria (*c.* 30 B.C. - 45 A.D.), the foremost Hellenistic-Jewish philosopher, belonged to the camp of the anti-Epicureans, quoting, paraphrasing, alluding to, refuting and allegorizing Epicureanism some thirty times in his extent works [20] and displaying a considerable knowledge of technical terms, even of Epicurus' theory of cognition, but also relapsing into the popular-rhetorical abuse of Epicureanism as mere enjoyment of pleasures.

From the second century on, Epicureanism and, with it, anti-Epicureanism, again grew apace.[21] It was thus *c.* 150 in Asia Minor that Diogenes of Oenoanda erected his stone inscriptions of the Epicurean philosophy in the forum of his native town.[22] Apuleius

(b. c. 129), the famous author of the "Golden Ass", was apparently proud to play the Epicurean while active in Egypt and Carthage.[23] Lucian, the Syrian wit, writing his *Alexander, The False Prophet* (of Abonuteichos) in c. 180, endorsed wholeheartedly the contemporary Epicurean attack on superstition in general and the Paphlagonian form in particular.[24] Some time before 165 Justin of Palestinian Shechem (Nablus) had opened the patristic opposition continuing where Paul had left off.[25] Origen, head of the catechetic school of Caesarea of Palestine for approximately twenty years (c. 232-252), who had studied Hebrew under Hillel, brother of the Patriarch Judah II, accused his opponent throughout most of his *contra Celsum* as an Epicurean and in the more than twenty passages of this attack reveals a considerable knowledge of Epicureanism.[26] Eusebius of Caesarea of Palestine, *fl.* 300, who preserved important Epicurean materials in his works, quotes fragments and anti-Stoic polemics of an Epicurean Diogenianus (c. 200) of uncertain nationality.[27] Approximately in 250, Diogenes Laertius, although perhaps not a thorough Epicurean, concluded his *Lives of the Philosophers* with the climactic and personally colored tenth chapter on Epicurus and marks the end of Epicurean expansion and creativeness both in the East and the West.[28]

Equally important were the media which Epicureanism now employed. Disregarding the Master's hostility to rhetoric, Philodemus popularized the use of the diatribic-rhetorical tract and abandoned the terse Aristotle-patterned style of much of the work of Epicurus.[29] The letters of Epicurus and his immediate successors —charming personal ones as well as technical-dogmatic ones— reached a peak in their general distribution in collections and epitomes and seemed to have influenced Seneca's epistular style.[30] Collections of aphorisms, i.e., gnomologies,[31] some anonymous and thus concealing their Epicurean origin, increased in number and, dealing frequently with the ideal philosopher-sage (*sophos, sapiens*) as they did, seemed to have become acceptable in the Near East where especially in the early talmudic civilization the ḥākhām (sage) occupied a similarly central position. The shortest of these gnomologies, the *Kyriai Doxai* with their 40 *sententiae*, may go back to Epicurus himself [32] and lend themselves to easy memorization.[33]

Furthermore, condensations —epitomes— of the whole Epicurean system flourished, likewise initiated by Epicurus himself.[34] The counter-arguments, tirades, satires and parodies of the anti-Epicurean opposition, such as found in the works of Cicero and Plutarch,[35] which also furnished excellent summarizations in spite of their symposiastic form, became commonplace in the Greco-Roman rhetorical tradition, probably both, oral and literary,[36] in an infinitely less systematic, but diatribic or anecdotal, form, such as found with Epictetus or Aelian (170-235 ?).[37] This rhetorical material as well as anthologies and handbooks of various kinds, including doxographies,[38] diadochies,[39] and popular *bioi* or *vitae*, i.e., biographies of the philosophers[40] which ancient culture produced in increasing numbers were the quarries exploited by the ubiquitous orator after they had served him as aids in his education.[41] Epicureanism thus survived, after the disappearance of the Athenian school and centers elsewhere, in the form of literature and oration, being apparently still quite potent in spite of Emperor Julianus' over-hasty announcement of its near-demise.[42] The foreground of the stage, however, was increasingly occupied by anti-Epicureanism, especially with the expansion of Christianity.

The later Palestinian Tannaim[43] and earlier Amoraim,[44] between 150 and 250, must have been exposed to some of these media, since talmudic literature shows parallels to several popular items of both Epicureanism and anti-Epicureanism in this period.[45] A fresh investigation into this phenomenon recently undertaken by the present writer suggested that certain novel themes and values in mishnaic-talmudic culture seemed to be of Epicurean origin both in content and formulation.[46] The occurrences of these Epicurean bits surpassed in number by far the items which have been discovered to this date[47] and even anti-Epicurean statements seemed to be more numerous than the passages known previously.[48]

In the course of that investigation it became apparent that a considerable number of utterances of the Tanna Shime'on ben Azzai (first half of second century, henceforth b. Azzai), a younger contemporary of Akiba (*c.* 50-135), resembled Epicurean stances. B. Azzai, as is well-known, is one of the "four who entered Paradise" in the famous passage *Ḥagigah* 14b of the Babylonian Talmud and its parallels.[49] A further analysis of this item and its problems seemed to indicate that *Ḥagigah* 14b may originally have been another piece of anti-Epicurean polemic and, as to its literary form, represents two popular typologies: the first referring to four types of Epicureans and the second to four types of fate destined for Epicureans. These typologies are separated from each other by a parody of Epicurean pseudapocalypses uttered in form of an admonition (*paraenesis*). Once the original meaning of this passage was no longer relevant in amoraic culture, it was conceived of as an anti-mystical statement, as its location in *Ḥagigah* —the longest talmudic sequence dealing with mystical or theosophic speculation— indicates. Finally, *testimonia*, i.e., biblical proof texts, had to be added to some of the statements in consequence of their re-interpretation. The details of these observations and these claims are offered herewith in the following.

The other three sages involved are Shime'on ben Zoma, a contemporary of b. Azzai; Acher (Achor or Elisha ben Abuyah, *fl. c.* 130-150), heretic and renegade *par excellence* in talmudic tradition, and (Rabbi) Akiba, martyr of the Bar Kokheba revolt, one of the great figures of Jewish tradition who became, subsequently, the "patron saint" and model of the mystics.[50]

The version of our passage which, as we believe, preserves most of the original features of the item[51] is represented by BT *Ḥagigah* 14b,[52] reproduced below. The translation offered here in conjunction with the unaltered text of BT projects the traditional understanding of the passage. A fresh understanding will be developed in the progress of the discussion, to be summarized, in the end, in form of a paraphrase.

.—.—.BT *Ḥagigah* 14b—.—.—.

תנו רבנן	1	Our Masters taught:
ארבעה נכנסו בפרדס	2	Four entered "Paradise"
ואלו הן	3	and these they are:
בן עזאי ובן זומא	4	B. Azzai and B. Zoma,
אחר ורבי עקיבא	5	Acher and R. Akiba.
אמר להם ר״ע	6	Said to them R. Akiba:
כשאתם מגיעין אצל	7	"When you reach
אבני שיש טהור	8	the stones of pure marble
אל תאמרו מים מים	9	do not say 'water, water.' "
[שנאמר	10	[for it is said:
דובר שקרים	11	"The speaker of lies
לא יכון	12	will not persist
לפני עיני]	13	before mine eyes". Ps. 101:7].
בן עזאי הציץ ומת	14	B. Azzai looked and died.
[עליו הכתוב אומר	15	[On him Scripture says:
יקר בעיני ה׳	16	"Dear in the Lord's eyes
המותה לחסידיו]	17	is the death of his saints". Ps. 116:15]
בן זומא הציץ ונפגע	18	B. Zoma looked and was stricken.

עליו הכתוב אומר	19	[On him Scripture says :
דבש מצאת	20	"Honey you found (or : "If..."),
אכול דייך	21	eat (only) your fill
פן תשבענו	22	lest you loathe it
והקאתו]	23	and bring it up". Prov. 25 :16].
אחר קיצץ בנטיעות	24	Acher [53] cut among the plantings.
רבי עקיבא יצא בשלום	25	R. Akiba [54] left in peace.[55]

The literary structure of the passage is as follows :

Line 1	Introduction.
Lines 2-5 :	First typology.
Lines 6-9 :	The parody (as *paraenesis*).
Lines 10-13 :	*Testimonium* (of later date ?).
Lines 14, 18, 24-25 :	Second Typology.
Lines 15-17 :	*Testimonium* (of later date).
Lines 20-23 :	*Testimonium* (of later date).

The first typology consists of four names (which, as we shall presently suggest, represent four well-known types of Epicureans or four well--known components of Epicureanism) : b. Azzai, b. Zoma, Acher, and Akiba. It is highly improbable that the later Tannaim or the Amoraim who created or edited the wording of this item recognized the Epicurean shadings of some of b. Azzai's ethical teachings and on these grounds identified him as an Epicurean, since the total system of Epicureanism was hardly known to them.[56] More probable is the assumption that they still knew or believed that he had some —or too many— dealings or discussions with Epicureans.[57] Most probable however, is the suggestion that the basis of b. Azzai's classification is a unique fact which made a strong impression on his contemporaries as well as on posterity : he is apparently the only teacher-sage in the talmudic tradition who, according to the dominant version,[58] never married, or according to the other versions, never consummated his marriage, practising either continence or not completing the marriage ceremony. In talmudic tradition, various harmonizations have been attempted in order to reconcile these contradictory reports.[59]

Whatever talmudic version we would trust most —celibacy, continence, incompletion of legal procedure, or divorce— his behavior is most unusual if not unprecendented in talmudic culture. It is, however, paralleled by the life and example of Epicurus [60] which were well-known and often quoted in ancient literature.[61] This Epicurean model of celibacy was reinforced by the teaching of Epicurus regarding love, marriage and child raising, equally well-known and often repeated in antiquity. They are somewhat more cautious and conditional than the caricature which quickly developed in anti-Epicurean literature.

Among the formulations that survived regarding Epicurus' teaching are: "... the sage will marry and produce children, as Epicurus (says) in the *Diaporiai* and in *Peri Physeōs*; he will marry—(but only) according to the circumstances of his life".[62] Epictetus-Arrian, *Disc.* I. xxiii, exclaims: "Why do you (Epicurus) dissuade the sage from rearing children? Why do you fear that because of this he will get into sorrow?" [63] and adds that Epicurus dared to say "Let us not raise children". Clement of Alexandria (c. 150-211/216) preserves a fragment that seems to state the reason: Epicurus rejected marriage and child-raising "because of the many unpleasantnesses that derive from them and the distractions [64] from more necessary things". A stern view is formulated in this fragment: "They (the Epicureans) do not think it proper that the Sage fall in love;" [65] and according to Cicero and Plutarch the Epicureans held that there was no natural relationship between parents and children.[66]

Epicurus' opinion was increasingly simplified and satirized with the writers of rhetorical literature. This is the characterization of the Epicurean in a diatribe of Epictetus-Arrian: "... can you visualize an Epicurean state? (For one Epicurean would say) 'As to me, I do not marry'. (Another:) 'Neither I; marrying is a thing not to be done' ".[67] The brief witty anecdote or *chria* was a still more effective medium since it lent itself to oral transmission. According to such a *chria* Arcesilaus [68] once explained to an inquirer why so many adherents of other schools converted to Epicureanism and why the opposite was never the case by the witticism that men become eunuchs but eunuchs never men.

These examples may suffice to demonstrate that the celibate Epicurean had become a stereotype in rhetorical culture. Even the epitaph shows traces of it.[69]

The thematic association of b. Azzai with Epicureanism, however, may still go further, since the biographical bits ascribed to him show a certain relationship to those of Arcesilaus who, in turn, seems to have been portrayed after the pattern of Epicurus, being another "impious" Founder-Sage, i.e., the initiator of the skeptical phase within the Platonic Academy.

Arcesilaus and b. Azzai have thus these features in common:

1. both are important and popular (*D.L.* IV, 37; Plutarch, *Mor.* 1121 Ef., Bacher, *Tannaiten, passim*);
2. both are unmarried and childless (*D.L.* IV. 43);
3. but both ingeniously castigate the unmarried;[70]
4. both are "in love" with aspects of learning, b. Azzai with Torah, Arcesilaus with Homer, see חשקה נפשי and ἐρώμενον, *D.L.* X. 31;
5. both quote or read their canon, i.e., Bible or Homer, when going to sleep, *D.L.* X. 31; *Midr.SS* 5b;
6. if the version of our basic story is preferred according to which b. Azzai was "stricken" (i.e., became insane) and b. Zoma died, another parallel emerges: both became insane.[71]

The portrayals of Arcesilaus and Epicurus have these features in common:

1. both are well liked, attractive, admired;
2. both are also sharp, argumentative (E.: beginning of *D.L.*'s *Vita Epicuri*; A.: *D.L.* IV. 28, 30, 33, 37);
3. both are unmarried and childless;
4. both live with courtesans (*hetaerae.* E.: *D.L.* X. 5f.; A.:*D.L.* IV. 40);
5. both are concerned with their friends and students (E.: *D.L.* X. 9ff., 16ff. A.: *D.L.* IV. 30, 37, 38, 40);
6. both shunned politics, lived retiredly (E.: X. 10 and explicit teachings. A.: IV. 39).
7. both made careful wills for those close to them. Three letters (E.) and three wills (A.) are prominently mentioned (*D.L.*, end of their *vitae*);
8. both are accused of living lavishly (probably untrue for E., *D.L.* X. 6f.; A.: IV. 41f.);
9. both are accused of inconsistency: E. especially in popular anti-Epicurean sources: preaching austerity and living lavishly; or denying the involvement of the gods and attending public worship,[72] A. implicitly: calling the Epicureans eunuchs, being childless himself;[73]
10. both died after drinking unmixed wine (E.: X. 15; A.: IV. 44).[74]

To make b. Azzai a mystic on the grounds of *Ḥagigah* is not justifiable in view of the lack of any other indications of mysticism on his part. On the contrary, we do have indications that he had no mystical inclinations. He was, e.g., of the opinion that "even the angels do not see the Glory itself",[75] and in Ps. 29:3, "the voice of the Lord over the waters", he saw fairly rationally its function as guiding and assigning courses to the waters.[76] In either case a mystic would have been inclined to engage in speculation. According to Lev. Rabba XVI. 4 on 14. 2, he expressly denied, upon the appearance of fire which surrounded him, that he was dealing with *Merkabah* speculation, typical of mysticism, but declared that he was merely engaged in finding parallel phrases in Torah, Prophets, and Hagiographa, a fairly rational occupation. This required great acumen of which the fire apparently became the symbol or, rather, the concomitant.[77]

The classification of b. Zoma as an Epicurean is somewhat mysterious. It is true, there are a few Epicurean-colored items in his name.[78] Yet almost his entire aggadic creation is non-Epicurean and shows a strong affinity toward other aspects of Greco-Roman philosophical rhetoric.[79] Ultimately, the opposition to his activities and the anecdotal portrayals which show him in an unflattering light may have been based on his closeness to the Greco-Roman culture in general. This does not explain, however, the precise meaning of his inclusion in the story of the Four, i.e., his characterization as one of four typical Epicureans.

The anecdote of his absentmindedness [80] gives us perhaps a clue: whether true or not, he was imagined to have over-occupied himself with speculation about heavenly phenomena and the closely related fields of cosmology and cosmogony. The anecdote of his absentmindedness makes him allude to a particularly absurd Epicurean cosmological detail.[81] We must assume, however, that no one specific detail but rather the occasional occupation with such extreme or "foreign" matters may have given him the name of a speculator in cosmology. The best known prototype of the *Sophos* who went to extremes in matters of "physics", however, was for both the philosophical expert and the popular rhetorician. Epicurus. They all ridiculed Epicurus' *intermundia* and the "void", the apparently arbitrary kinetics and *clinamen* of his atoms, his foot-sized sun, and other instances of his non-conformist physics.

Strange speculation —or merely speculation which was strange to b. Zoma's Palestinian contemporaries— may thus have been instrumental in his characterization as an "Epicurean" speculator.

There is, however, another less likely but closely related possibility of explaining b. Zoma's classification in the story of the Four. His contemporaries —or subsequent generations— may have assumed that his speculations which occasionally focused on the first chapters of Genesis were close to Gnosticism.[82] According to a nomenclature peculiar to late antiquity such a suspicion would likewise have made him an "Epicurean" speculator, for it is a well-established fact that the Church Fathers and the apologetes of earlier Christianity as well as some secular philosophers called the gnostics "Epicureans". This was eventually done in a purely pejorative sense as all heretics werefinally called Epicureans. There seems to have been, however, a transitional stage in this development at which the systems, or merely important detail, of gnostics and Epicureans were compared more rationally.[83] There was ample justification for such a comparison.[84] Both gnostics and Epicureans devaluated and depersonalized the cosmos, the latter by their atomic theory and through gods who were —to paraphrase Aristotle— unmoved non-movers, the former by their doctrine of a demonic demiurge who had created a cosmic realm of unredeemed matter. Providence, in the Stoic or Judaeo-Christian sense, was, of course denied by either. Both were "asocial", e.i., rebellious toward prevailing social standards, and withdrawn in their conventicles,[85] and suspicious of the state. Consequently, both were soon accused of sexual license.

Plotinus (c. 205-270) thus named Epicureans and gnostics in one breath.[86] Tertullian (c. 150 - c. 230) made Marcion, the gnostic, go to school with Epicurus, as it were, and called the latter "consiliarius Marcionis".[87] An anti-gnostic work, somewhat sophistically, does likewise in regard to their cosmologies, using the term $αὐτοματισμός$ for both.[88] Irenaeus (second century) already, in his polemic against Gnosticism, had reproached Anaximander, Democritus, and Epicurus as the originators of the "God of the Philosophers"[89] and he compared the void, $κενός$, of atomism with the gnostical Pleroma.[90] Soon, however, detailed reasoning gave way to a vituperative use of the term "Epicurean" both in the Church and in talmudic civilization.[91]

Thus, either the suspicion of "peculiar", foreign, or extreme speculation or of gnosis-like pre-occupation with Genesis —perhaps both, reinforcing each other— may have led to b. Zoma's classification as the speculating Epicurean.[92]

The nature of the heresy of Acher, the third sage of the typology, was an enigma to talmudic tradition. This is evident from the existence of fairly numerous and often contradictory legends, anecdotes, and mere notes on him of various origins and uncertain historical value.[93]

His heresy has remained an enigma ever since. Modern scholarship has offered a wide range of solutions, all more or less unsatisfactory, many of them unduly influenced by a mistaken interpretation of our very *Ḥagigah* passage.[94] The task to be undertaken here is not a historical-biographical inquiry which would attempt to contribute to a solution of the problem but rather an effort to ascertain whether there was a literary tradition available which could have encouraged Acher's classification as an Epicurean in our passage.

Among the recurring themes dealing with Acher's heresy which show some coherence and consistency, is his denial of the existence of divine providence and of divine justice, i.e., of reward and punishment, either in this or in another life. Of particular interest is an anecdote which represents one among several other attempts to explain why he lost his faith in divine justice.[95] According to this anecdote Acher saw once how a man climbed a palm tree, took a mother bird together with her chicks —against the biblical injunction of Deut. 22 : 6f.— and descended unharmed. The next day he saw how another man climbed the same tree, took young birds and released the mother —in accordance with the biblical commandment— and descended, only to be bitten by a snake and to die. Whereupon Acher exclaimed, bitter and sarcastic, "where is that man's 'well-being', and where his 'length of days' ",as promised in Deut. 22 : 7.

This incident recalls a story of similar structure and meaning in Athenaeus' *Deipnosophistae* XIII. 593 B-D concerning Danaë, the daughter of Metrodorus, Epicurus' deputy and confidant, and Leontion, famous Epicurean woman philosopher and hetaera.[96] When Danaë, a hetaera herself, was led to a precipice for execution she said that "rightly do most men think little of the divine,[97] since, for instance,[98] I who once saved my former 'man' receive such recompense from the deity, Laodice who killed hers is deemed worthy of such great honor."

The two items have these features in common :

1. the death of the innocent, the gain of the transgressor ;
2. the complaint of the victim or onlooker which includes
3. an antithetical formulation of the ironic facts and the denial that divine justice exists ;
4. the previous moral deed of the victim and the previous transgression of the survivor ;
5. utmost economy of words in the narrative framework ;
6. utmost economy of words in the formulation of the antithesis.

To be sure, the Greek item deals with the execution of a heroic victim, i.e., with martyrdom,[99] whereas the Hebrew item deals with accidental death. However, in JT the story of the palm tree is immediately followed by another episode which, indeed, *does* involve martyrdom: Acher saw the tongue of R. Yehudah the Baker —a martyr of the Hadrianic persecution— dangling from the mouth of a dog. Here, too, an antithetical exclamation castigates the irony of fate: "This is Torah and this its recompense?"![100]

It is difficult to decide whether the Danaë episode did indeed affect the Acher anecdotes. The stories of the beautiful, witty and learned hetaerae, companions of the ancient sages and celebrated in *chriae* of their own, were well-known in antiquity.[101] The Epicureans, in particular, were frequently protrayed in the company of hetaerae, partly in the vulgarized accusation of hedonism [102] by anti-Epicurean rhetoric, parly because they, indeed, corresponded with and even admitted women, among them hetaerae, to their inner circle including Leontion who was famous for the beauty of her literary style.[103] It is thus not impossible that even the hetaera motif, either of the Danaë or any similar story of this type, is represented in the cycle around Acher, in a *chria* involving him and a harlot.[104] After a heavenly refusal to receive him even when repentent, Acher dedicates himself to an evil life (Epicureanism?): "He went forth, found a harlot and demanded her. She said to him: 'Are you not Elisha b. Abuyah?' When he plucked a radish from its bed [on the Sabbath][105] and gave it to her she said: 'It is someone (or something) quite different (*acher*).'"

The nucleus of the story is the witticism of the hetaera who uses a *double entendre*, since the equivocal *acher* also indicates that he is now quite a different man as well as quite shocking;[106] in addition, he acquires on this occasion his new by-name Acher —actually a *triple entendre*. A certain type of pun in the *chriae* and *apophtegmata* of courtesans reported in Athenaeus' *Deipnosophistae* is very close to our specimen. One item involves Leontion herself. In many cases the courtesans either give equivocal nicknames to their lovers or use their old nicknames in a novel and witty application.[107]

Another interesting but elusive item in both literatures must be mentioned here: special provision is made for the daughter of Leontion, i.e., probably Danaë, in Epicurus famous last will, *D.L.* X. 19: οὔσης αὐτῆς εὐτάκτου καὶ πειθαρχούσης Ἑρμάρχῳ, "... being well-behaved (or "on condition that she be...") and obedient to Hermarchus", the final heir of the Epicurean Garden. In BT Ḥagigah 15b, Acher's daughter appears before Yehudah ha-Nasi [108] to ask for support and, in the face of his doubts regarding the progeny of the wicked, she begs him to "remember his Torah, not his deeds".[109] Perhaps a popular cycle of Epicurus' life or rhetorical mentions may have included bits of Epicurus' moving last will and probably more on Danaë, the daughter of his friend. The motemes, i.e., the smallest thematic units, in this instance: provision of support and the condition of merit (obedience to a guardian and faithfulness to a father respectively) as well as the legal setting indicate in all probability interdependence of the items in spite of the important differences in other detail.

Yet another item may likewise suggest a possible connection between Greco-Roman *Epicurea* and the talmudic material on Acher. The JT version of *Ḥagigah* adduces the *hapax legomenon* that Acher's mother, while pregnant with him, "passed by pagan temples and smelled that kind (of odor) [110] and that odor penetrated into her body like snake poison". This has to be compared with an anti-Epicurean item in *D.L.* X. 4: "when young he with his mother went around to the cottages to read purification rites". This allegation of involvement in vulgar rites as an impressionable youth was apparently designed to explain the "lowness" of his later teachings and had to be countered by Epicurus' brother Neocles who declared "that their mother had in herself a combination of such atoms as would produce a sage".[111]

The parallelism of motemes is as follows:

Hebrew:	embryo	mother	pagan temples
Greek:	child	mother	cottages of the superstitious
Hebrew:	sacrificial odors		explain heresy
Greek:	purification rites		explain baseness of doctrine

According to the often observed displacements of thematic bits, Epicurus' incantations may have reappeared in one of our context stories on Acher in which he "said words" over the school children and terminated their studies.[112]

Whether or not use has actually been made of chriic-rhetorical and biographic anti-Epicurean items in the talmudic Acher material, his denial of providence alone —which is strongly emphasized and often repeated— must have been crucial in classifying Acher as an Epicurean. This denial, indeed, must have been a much greater threat than. hedonism in a population that did never command much wealth.

There was, further, the example of the earlier Sadducees whose influence was on the decline after the catastrophies of 70 A.D. The Sadducees, too, rejected post-biblical concepts of an afterlife, although they may have believed in compensatory justice in this life in accordance with biblical precedents. In addition, what seems to be the oldest and clearest tannaitic mention of אפיקורוס, the Hebrew loanword and equivalent of "Epicurean", in *Pirke Aboth* 2.14 (2.18 Taylor) [113] still has the actual Epicurean as a denier of providence in mind (in the name of Ele'azar b. Arak) :[114] "Be alert to learn Torah so that you know what to answer the Epicurean, and know (then) before whom you toil and who your (heavenly) employer is (var. : who will pay you the reward of your work)." [115]

Although the denial of divine retribution is dominant in Acher's portrayal the motif of hedonism is, as we have seen, not entirely missing in the incident with the courtesan. These motifs are found also in Christian anti-Epicurean polemics with the by far strongest stress on the denial of retribution.[116] Dante still singled out Epicurus in his Inferno because of this denial, and his fate in Hell was an ironic refutation of his belief.

The claim that Akiba was included among the Four may seem preposterous if the ever increasing veneration which his memory commands is erroneously considered to be the basis of his entire biography. But of legends on vital aspects of Akiba's life there is no end,[117] and this biographic legendarization may have begun before he became the pattern and "patron saint" of mysticism.[118] Moreover, the anti-Epicurean interpretation of the story of the Four suggested here will sound more plausible if one considers that Akiba had formidable opposition in his lifetime, not only on single decisions but on vital aspects of his activities : his quasi-political messianism —he supported the Bar Kokheba revolt [119]— his aggadah,[120] his use of the minutiae of Scripture for legal decisions, and his theory of the Oral Law.[121]

Important for our issue is the fact that all his ancient biographers apparently agree that there was a period in his life in which he was completely remote if not violently hostile to the wold of law and learning. Whether or not this be historical, the details adduced for this claim are legendarizations : a period of forty years,[122] his life as a servant shepherd,[123] his beginnings as a proselyte or ignorant boor,[124] the astronomical numbers of his students,[125] and others. It seems that the details of his early life were actually unknown and the vacuum was filled with various imaginative guesses.

Akiba's classification as an Epicurean must have reference to this period of obscurity and seems to be such an interpretation of it. According to some sources he was not only ignorant but utterly hostile to the talmudic sages and to any form of talmudic education. This hostility is never described in terms of historical Sadduceeism but in terms of his belonging to or acting like the *Am ha-Areṣ*,[126] the class of the uneducated which was hostile to talmudic culture. He was supposedly willing to bite any representative of Rabbinism and did not know a single halakhah.[127] In a famous story, BT *Berakoth* 27b, he was considered without prestige.[128] These details may give us the clue to his classification as an Epicurean. One of the all-pervading characterizations of Epicurus, from his lifetime to his latterday denigrators, was that of a total ignoramus, $\dot{\alpha}\nu\alpha\gamma\omega\gamma\acute{o}\tau\alpha\tau os\ \zeta\omega\acute{o}\nu\tau\omega\nu$, the most uneducated of all mortals.[129] Even if Caesar appoint an Epicurean as arbiter in matters of culture, he would possess no authority according to Epictetus' diatribe against the Epicureans.[130] Likewise the Church Fathers, among them the "Palestinians", have a great deal to say on Epicurus' ignorance.[131]

These denunciations had a basis in fact: Epicurus exhibited a studied *apaideusia*, rejected the $\ddot{\epsilon}\gamma\kappa\upsilon\kappa\lambda\iota os\ \pi\alpha\iota\delta\epsilon\acute{\iota}\alpha$ —the conventional curriculum of disciplines of learning—[132] and deemed all cultural aspirations as an obstacle to the true life of the Sage (being in reality, of course, quite a learned individual).[133] This stricture determined his portrayal and that of all Epicureans with the rhetoricians and the Church Fathers in spite of occasional relaxations of this extreme attitude on the part of the later Epicureans.[134]

Furthermore, Epicurus used a style of his own which anti-Epicureans considered to be uncultured.[135] Unlike other philosophers he rarely [136] quoted from the national canon, i.e., Homer, Hesiod, or the earlier tragedians, and, to make matters worse, he claimed to be an autodidact (in spite of evidence to the contrary).[137]

No wonder, then, that among the unflattering epithets which Epicurus and the Epicureans reaped were frequently the adjectives "vulgaris", and still more often "indoctus", a fact which must have been known to practically the entire ancient world, learned and unlearned alike.[138] The classification of Akiba as an Epicurean must have been on the basis of his ignorance. It is interesting to note, in conclusion, that of no other Tanna or Amora do talmudic sources report such abysmal ignorance, not even in the instance of the farmer's son Eli'ezer b. Hyrcanus (*c*. 100) or Shime'on (Resh) Laḳish (*c*. 200 - *c*. 275), a former bandit.

The first typology in our item could thus be freely rendered as follows: "There are four types of Epicureans: the celibate, the wild speculator, the denier of divine retribution, and the intentional ignoramus".

The second typology concerns the fate of the Four: one dies after his Epicurean adventure. This may be purely Judaic: the belief in heavenly punishment for heresy; but then, in the Greco-Roman tradition, some of the best known Epicureans were said to have died young or suddenly, among them the three brothers of Epicurus himself.[139] The sudden death of another Epicurean was famous in the Near East, i.e., that of Antiochus IV Epiphanes, who had been converted by Philonides. There is no evidence, however, that it was generally known in Judaea that he belonged to this school of philosophy.[140] It is not known, either, whether Caesar's erstwhile Epicurean relations or those of Cassius who committed suicide were known outside Rome. The same is true for the suicide of Titus Pomponius Atticus or an obscure Epicurean Diodorus whom Seneca mentions.[141]

More important, then, is the view of rhetorical literature on Epicurus' death. Several passages contribute to this question. Cicero, aroused by the Epicurean denial of providence, addresses Piso, Caesar's father-in-law: "he (Caesar) will see that they (the gods) both do feel and have felt anger towards you (Piso)" and are not dispassionate towards man. Punishment, including the veiled threat of death, is here used ironically, i.e., not only as punishment but as a spectacular refutation of the very position of the Epicureans.[142] Aelian claims that Epicurus' impiety brought down upon him the anger of the gods.[143] To Plutarch the punishment of the Epicureans is non-security —another irony, since security was one of their principal aims—[144] as well as ill fame and oblivion.[145]

According to the credulous who are made vocal in Lucian's *Alexander* 25 (written *c.* 180 A.D.) through the mouth of the false prophet himself, Epicurus will sit in Hades "with leaden fetters on his feet in filthy mire..." Aelian, finally, contributes the story of the punishment of a sacrilegious Epicurean by a horribly slow death in this world, fr. 10, possibly reflecting the well known tragic illness and slow painful end of Epicurus himself.[146] Although this material presented here does not show a dominant death motif with *all* Epicureans, it is, still, all-pervading and could easily have colored the native Judean expectation of punishment.

The talmudic mention of the second type of Epicurean fate involves a somewhat arcane formulation. i.e., ונפגע. Although the *niph'al* (passive) formation of this root may have the general connotation "stricken", its use in our *Ḥagigah* passage and its parallels has at all times unanimously been given as "insane".[147] This meaning must be accepted, not only because of the Arcesilaus biography in which we found the vocable παρακόψας[148] but also because of additional supporting material in the Greco-Roman tradition on the Epicureans.

(A) *Epicurus and Epicureans called insane*. The strongest of such denunciations occur with the Christian writers Jerome, Lactantius, and Augustine. *Dementia. stultitia, delirium, furor*, to name only the major Latin nouns, abound for both Epicurus and Lucretius.[149] This outburst, however, merely continues a previous non-Christian habit which Lactantius and Augustine with their classical-rhetorical background could easily apply to their Christian polemics. Thus Cicero already calls Piso *furiosus, mente captus, dementior*, etc. (46f.). Epictetus, in diatribic fashion, asks Epicurus καὶ οὐ μαίνῃ, "and you are not insane either?" (II. xxiii. 22), implying that he behaves as if he nearly was. The same diatribic style element is used by Plutarch, *Mor.* 1123f., where the denunciation of Colotes waxes into a general statement on the Epicureans who although not insane (παρακόπτοντες cf. the Arcesilaus passage, *D.L.* IV. 44), nevertheless, make one wonder whether, in the last resort, they are. The beginning of this passage, 1123 B, too, suggests delirium and loss of contact with reality for the Epicureans. Even Horace who perhaps never broke completely with Epicureanism called it once playfully *"insaniens sapientia"*, *Carm.* I. xxxiv. 2. After listing all the calumnies of anti-Epicureans, *D.L.* X. 9 begins his refutation with the words Μεμήνασι δ'οὗτοι, "but these are all raving maniacs," whereby he probably meant to return the compliment.

Invectives of this kind are, of course, characteristic of the clashes between the different philosophical schools of antiquity (as they are of modern times) and of diatribe, rhetoric, comedy, satire, epigram and other forms of ancient literature. They are intended to offend, to ridicule, to devaluate, to refute, and to create relief to their users. In the case of anti-Epicureanism, however, the use of these invectives is much more consistent, determined, and emotion-laden, especially in Christian polemic.[150] Furthermore, in the mouths of Stoics, the main antagonists of the Epicureans, the insinuation of insanity was particularly offensive, since according to their "paradoxes" the Sage was the only sane one in a world of madness.[151] Their epithets of insanity for Epicureans denied them thus the status of sagedom (*sophia*, *sapientia*). Invectives, are, as said before, emotional, not technical -clinical or historical-biographical. It seems, however, that this rhetorical use of anti-Epicurean invective implying insanity hardened in time into a somewhat more concrete belief that actually claimed clinical and biographical truthfulness.

(B) *Mentally ill Epicureans.* Seneca who spoke approvingly of Diodorus' suicide (n. 141, above), added the statement that "alii dementiam videri volunt factum hoc eius, alii temeritatem", i.e., this suicide was open to interpretation; some saw in it insanity, some recklessness. The noun "insanity" is here no longer vituperative but semi-clinical.[152] The biographical tradition of Arcesilaus, traces of which, as we have seen, survived in *D.L.*, is another instance of the progress of this theme. Here, too, death is involved, i.e., a semi-suicide after a spell of insanity. Diogenes Laertius, in his usual self-composed epigrams (quasi-epitaphs) on the philosophers whom he has discussed, mentions Arcesilaus' madness prominently.[153]

Items such as these could have created the necessary atmosphere by which Jerome may have invented (or made use of) a similar legend about the death of Lucretius in his continuation of Eusebius' *Chronicle* which he published 380/381, probably in Constantinople.[154] According to Jerome —entry for the year 94 B.C.— Lucretius "amatorio poculo in furorem versus... propria se manu interfecit...", i.e., demented by a love potion he killed himself by his own hand. (He wrote his poem during intermittent lucid moments, *ibid.*). This passage has evoked scholarly controversies which lasted for many decades.[155] The point in question is whether Jerome used a now lost work of Suetonius, *de viribus illustribus*, section *de poetis*, or whether he himself created a "pious" legend for his anti-Epicurean campaign.[156] Ziegler marshals arguments in favor of Jerome's inventiveness, overriding arguments of others who tried to demonstrate signs of actual mental illness in Lucretius (!) or who saw a starting point for the legend in the prominent use of "*furor*" in Lucretius —in IV. 1078 and 1117 on the passion of love— and in misinterpretations of his description of mental illness in III. 828f. Others saw in Statius' beautiful praise of Lucretius, *Silv.* II. vii. 76,

et docti furor arduus Lucreti

the arduous passion of the learned Lucretius,

a possible basis for such a legend. Regrettably in none of these attempts, Ziegler's included, are the two passages on Diodorus and Arcesilaus utilized or even mentioned, although the discussants were aware of the verbal abuse the Epicureans had to take.

The example of Jerome (unless he, indeed, did know some further development of the Diodorus-Arcesilaus pattern —an argument *ex silentio* and therefore not usable) shows, however, that this biographical-legendary "creativeness" was in the air when it came to Epicureans and it is this availability which may have led to the claim of insanity for one of the Four, unless the ordinary barrage of rhetorical invectives regarding insanity sufficed.

What was the fate of Acher? According to the text of all versions "he made cuttings (or scrapings) among the plantings (or shoots)," קיצץ בנטיעות. This phrase has found many ingenious interpreters both ancient and modern.[157] Most of them, however, assume a mystical meaning of the entire *Ḥagigah* passage, i.e., that the visit of the Four was involvement with dangerous esoteric teachings or even techniques and experiments, such as ecstacy, vision, and ascent. In doing so, however, these interpreters use talmudic and other proof material which is based on or influenced by our very passage mystically understood, i.e., they are using circular argumentation.

The cutting of the plantings is, of course, not an activity carried on in "Paradise"[158] but corresponds to the death and insanity of the two visitors, i.e., it is the consequence of the previous misdeed, a fate incurred because of it: it indicates what happened to Acher after he left. Furthermore, the strong metaphor of cutting must refer to more than a heretical view of some sort; it seems to hint at an activity as has been rightly understood by Jastrow who lists among some other suggestions "corrupt the youth".[159] This is, of course, an ancient interpretation already suggested in a brief insertion into our passage by *SSR*[160] and in several detailed stories following our passage in JT. In all these views it is implicit that נטיעות means children or young students. This usage is, indeed, attested to in JT *Yebamoth* 2b, I, beginning: "He planted five shoots" (i.e., sons), חמש נטיעות נטע, and in JT *Moʿed Ḳaṭan* 81c, III, beginning: "You permitted the one son (or "child")..."[161] According to the JT *Ḥagigah* framework narrative Acher "killed the greatest students of the Law", or, so JT continues, "put to death[162] any student whom he saw succeed[163] in the Law; indeed, when he went to the academy and saw the young men before the teacher, he said 'what are these sitting (and) doing here? The craft of this one should be a builder; the craft of that one... a carpenter, ... a hunter, ... a tailor'. And when they heard him thus, they quit the teacher and went away". *SSR* I. 4 asks expressly "How did he 'cut among the shoots?'" and answers that "he entered Synagogues and houses of study and when he observed children progress in the Law, he said words (or incantations) over them which made them close up (or: which intimidated them)".

When the Greco-Roman anti-Epicurean material is applied to this situation, it becomes clear that the original intention is, indeed, to portray Acher as a corrupter of youth, i.e., as one who persuaded the academic youth to abandon their traditional study. We have seen previously that Epicurus opposed the general curriculum of education. He and the Epicureans went further, however, by actively and persuasively advising the youth to abandon all culture. The most famous formulation is found in Epicurus' warning to Pythocles: "All *paideia*, young man, flee, readying the boat"; παιδείαν δὲ πᾶσαν μακάριε φεῦγε τἀκάτιον ἀράμενος.[164] This bold iconoclasm is frequently quoted, literally or as a paraphrase, by Cicero, Plutarch and Quintilian.[165] The Epicureans' praise of the mathematics-shy Apelles has been mentioned previously (*Mor.* 1094 D). Plutarch further elaborates in his major attack on Epicurean education that Epicurus implored Pythocles not to emulate "the so-called liberal education", τὴν ἐλευθέραν καλουμένην παιδείαν [166] and that the Epicureans turned off their disciples from the rapture and joy which, among others, mathematics is able to give (C-D). Upon enrollment in the Epicurean community the young student was exhorted to reject all other knowledge.[167]

This active interference with the conventional education of the young became thus notorious and with the increasing heat of polemic the Epicurean was marked as a destroyer of tradition, i.e., a nihilist. Indeed, the description of his destructive activities hardened into a near-terminology. Again and again terms of the word family *dissolvere* (ordinem rerum) and *dissipare* (patrimonium) are applied to him, and, strongest of all, *evertere*, i.e., to overturn, to raze to the ground. *Vetera voluit evertere*, "the old he, Epicurus, wished to demolish".[168] It seems thus that Acher's fate is described in the light of this stereotype of Epicurus as a nihilist and destroyer of culture.[169]

Akiba, the fourth and last of the quasi-Epicureans, left, according to BT, "in peace". In the opinion of most commentators both ancient and modern including the authors of the talmudic framework stories, this phrase "left in peace" indicates that Akiba was not affected by his adventure.[170] All these approaches thus date his visit in "Paradise", as they must —an ignoramus does not study theosophy— in the time of his later scholarly career. We have seen, however, that in all probability our passage refers to the period of his ignorance.

This claim can be further elaborated. Since we believe that it was his boorish ignorance which suggested Epicureanism to the author of our passage, Akiba's escape can only refer to his conversion, i.e., his near-miraculous entry into the world of study and scholarship. This decisive event in his life became, indeed, the focus of legendarization. According to one such report an oracle-like chance event led him to education.[171] According to another he turned to education on the initiative of his bride.[172] To consider the Akiba section of this typology as another such legendarization does then after all not appear to be too arbitrary an assumption.

The introduction of a fourth fate, for an Epicurean, i.e., conversion to a better way of life (as seen from the viewpoint of the anti-Epicurean) is, however, novel and fittingly the climax of the story. It may be an intentional refutation and a conscious reversal of the general belief of antiquity that Epicureans could not be converted to any other school of thought or faith, that their sodality was closely knit, their loyalty to the founder unshakable, their convictions dogmatic and arrogant and defended with skill and, if necessary, "siren charm".[173]

In the view of the talmudic and patristic sources, the Epicurean was thus not considered lost. In the framework stories to our passage we find the moving attempts by R. Meir to save his former teacher Acher, even against the latter's conviction that it was too late.[174] Likewise Origen who as we have seen considered Celsus an Epicurean held possible his opponent's belated conversion to the better, c.C. IV. 54, while Augustine, in an autobiographical passage, hints at his own successful effort to escape the strong lure of Epicureanism.[175]

Although Akiba's final peace seems thus to correspond to the expectations of the indigenous culture, a Greco-Roman concept may nevertheless have paved the way. The first half of the JT formulation, נכנס בשלום, usually rendered as "(Akiba) entered in peace", may have to be rendered as "(Akiba) entered in(to) the peace (of study)". This is grammatically possible in view of the fact that the verb plus preposition נכנס ב... in the beginning of our very story undoubtedly mean "(Four) entered into (Paradise)", i.e., the preposition ב indicated here direction. The continuation ויצא בשלום must have been added for rhythmic reasons or when the story lost its original meaning and became mystical lore. It is out of place in the original story, as explained in note 170, *supra*. A formula or motif resembling this reconstructed version seems to have been known in Greco-Roman culture. It indicated the peace that is tantamount to true philosophical study or follows the conversion to or initiation into philosophy. Thus concerning Parmenides whom a certain philosopher initiated into philosophy, the phrase is εἰς ἡσυχίαν προετράπη, "was turned toward peace", *D.L.* IX. 21, end. In Plutarch, fr. 143, Loeb, vol. XV, pp. 266-268 (from Stobaeus) *hēsychē* is the gateway to study and wisdom which make their owner godlike (cf. Plato, *Theaet.* 176 b). This is, of course, a theme also in the Socratic tradition and is related to Aristotle's purpose in the *Protrepticus*, to remain important in all Greco-Roman thought.[176] Lucian, in his *Alexander*, ch. 47, still speaks of the peace (εἰρήνη) which a certain work of philosophy (it happened to be by Epicurus) created in its readers. In other words, there is a remote possibility that the JT text offered once merely נכנס בשלום, "entered in(to) the peace (of a new life)". Yet even the BT formulation, יצא בשלום may have once meant that Akiba "left in (the) peace (of a new life)" and the entire thematic syndrome may not be entirely independent of the Greco-Roman concept of the peace created by initiation into philosophy.

The second typology, listing the different possible fates of Epicureans runs thus as follows:

death - insanity - nihilism - conversion,

the latter, in its application to Epicureanism, being represented only in Judaic and patristic hopes.[177]

On the grounds of the foregoing analyses the meaning of the mysterious *pardes*-Paradise explains itself quite easily. The cognomina of the ancient philosophical schools, frequently coined after the circumstances of their meetings, were as commonly known then as cognomina in politics are in our time, such as the White House, or 10, Downing Street. The Epicureans not only met but lived together at the famous κῆπος, the "Garden", acquired for the group by Epicurus himself and still visited by Cicero, Atticus and uncounted others. The epithet Garden (or *hortus*) for the entire movement[178] was thus considerably more apt than the terms Academy, Lyceum (*Peripatos*), Cynosarges, and Stoa, for Platonists, Aristotelians, Cynics,[179] and Stoics, respectively. Besides, the Garden remained the permanent abode of the group for at least two centuries. The school in Athens received a generous stipend from Marcus Aurelius but the Garden was no longer the property of the heirs of Epicurus.[180] In any case, the collective "the Garden", or "the men of the Garden" stuck to all Epicureans.

We must thus assume that the term *pardes* of BT Ḥag. 14b and its parallels signifies the *Kēpos* (*hortus*) or Garden, i.e., the School of Epicurus or the Epicurean movement in general, in accordance with the common use of the word in ancient literature. It so happens that, indeed, *pardes* in talmudic literature is used exclusively in a technical and secular sense, i.e., for gardens, parks, enclosures, most often in contemporaneous settings, such as pleasure or royal gardens (Sebaste, or in parables), deer parks and agricultural types, thus continuing the secular use of the word in late biblical Hebrew.[181] It was impossible to use the simple גן for garden in our passage, since this term had acquired the connotation Garden of Eden, both of the Beginning as well as the Hereafter.[182]

The initial sentence of our basic passage could thus be rendered freely: "Four entered [183] into undue trafficking with the Epicureans", or, perhaps, "Four had certain leanings toward the School of Epicurus".

Attached to the mentions of the fates of b. Azzai and b. Zoma we find biblical proof texts: after the mention of death we find Ps. 116:15, "Dear in the Lord's eyes is the death of his saints;" after the mention of insanity, Prov. 25:16, "(If) honey you found, eat (only) your fill lest you loathe it and bring it up", the latter apparently conceived of as a metaphor for insanity.[184] Both in Greco-Roman literature as well as talmudic culture the proof text from the literary canon plays a specific role. Skill and ingenuity were expected from the rhetor-philosopher, i.e., the Sage, in applying it. Most often the *testimonium* is used to legitimize a new value, idea or belief. In its application an inventive reinterpretation of the authorizing canonical text is most often necessary which gives it a slightly, or even considerably, altered sense, a novel "twist", which is precisely the essence of "Midrash" in its original and literary sense. This may be done in seriousness for vital legal and social reasons; it may also be done in "playful seriousness", or "serious playfulness", as in the Hellenic-Hellenistic *spoudaiogeloion* and its talmudic equivalents.[185]

In both cultures the same literary item may be found with or without the *testimonium*. In some instances the appearance of a *testimonium* in a later parallel of a given text may represent an addition undertaken for some specific purpose. This seems to be the case in our *Ḥagigah* unit. Both proof texts seem to be harmonizations introduced to mediate between the transgression —or reckless daring— of the two sages and their reputation as great pious leaders which finally became dominant in the mainstream talmudic tradition.[186] Besides, in amoraic times

—perhaps already in the late tannaitic period— the anti-Epicurean tenor of our item was no longer understood and even the expressly anti-Epicurean statements of tannaitic literature using the loanword *Apikuros* had to be reinterpreted as antinomian, while "mysticism" had become increasingly accepted. B. Azzai's fate (in JT : b. Zoma's) becomes thus, through the use of Ps. 116 :15, something dear, almost a reward. Through the use of Prov. 25 :16 b. Zoma is no longer reckless but merely did too much of a good thing.[187]

It is obvious that the two remaining sages, i.e., Acher and Akiba, do not require *testimonia* : Acher was fully wicked in later tradition and Akiba had converted (or was never affected) —no harmonization was required. If thus in some of the parallels to BT *Ḥagigah testimonia* are found also for these two sages, it may be for reasons of symmetry or/and, perhaps, to reemphasize their fate in consonance with later frame stories and other portrayals in amoraic literature. Thus "on Akiba", to begin with him, "Scripture says : [188] 'The King has brought me into his chambers' ", Cant. 1 :4b, apparently a legitimization of his (assumed) expedition into the realm of vision : the divine King himself had brought him into the most secret chambers.[189] On Acher Scripture says : "Do not make my mouth your flesh sin", Eccl. 5 :5a (all versions except, of course, BT). The לחטיא, "to make sin", of the *testimonium* thus connects him with the common formula, both biblical and talmudic, for heretics "who sin and make sin", (shades of Jeroboam !)[190] The *testimonia* on Acher and Akiba are likewise later proof texts, although not harmonizations of conflicting situations. They filled the needs of later periods which tried to face the presumed mystical efforts of these sages.

In its brevity and opaqueness Akiba's warning,

> "When ye reach the place of the pure marble stones do not say 'water, water,' "

has been a formidable challenge to all interpreters. One has seen in this item either mere theorizing or the reflection of actual ecstatic experiences : vision, ascent to Heaven, or dream voyage ; and it has been classified variously as gnostic, apocalyptic, (neo-)Pythagorean, theosophic-esoteric, or mystical(-"Kabbalist").

Strangely enough, this warning is found only in the version of the Babylonian Talmud, thus evoking the question whether it has ever been an independent unit or, having always been a part of the original passage, was merely discarded by the Palestinian transmitters once it was no longer understood. A comparative analysis, however, employing, as previously, Greco-Roman situations, will reveal that we are dealing here with a brief anti-Epicurean parody which forms a literary unit of its own.

Paraodies and related literary genres abound in Greco-Roman culture in which wit played a vital role, not only as entertainment or comic relief but as a requirement for the ideal Sage who was expected to excel in it, be it in court, the forum, or the academy. Furthermore the strong competition between contrasting philosophies and ways of life in the ancient world favored the development of parody. The Epicureans some of whose beliefs and actions were quite unconventional and who were quite aggressive themselves, became naturally the target of parody. Among the many aspects of Epicureanism that have been subject to various forms of literary ridicule —be it in satire, comedy, mime, epigram, parody, diatribe and others— we shall single out only what seems to be decisive for the understanding of our passage.[191]

Epicureanism which ancient objective observers have variously defined as a philosophy of materialism, rationalism, or empiricism, and hostile opponents as atheism and vulgar hedonism to boot, frequently used a style and a quasi-ritual which ancient critics felt to be incongruous with any of the preceding characterizations. This contrast was increased by the esteem in which Epicurus was held by his adherents. Condemned by onlookers and opponents alike as atheists who paid merely lip-service to public worship in order to escape trouble, the Epicureans' inclination to consider their founder as near-divine [192] if not actually so, drove anti-Epicureans to a shrill and extreme opposition.[193]

Moreover, much of the apotheosis of Epicurus is based on his own statements and actions and those of the early circle.[194] Epicurean groups, their *contubernium* and their common celebrations,[195] have been rightly compared to a cult, sect, or even organized religion by modern observers.

In addition, Epicurus seems to have been considered by his adherents an inventor or discoverer, i.e., a culture-bringing *heros*, one of those distinguished humans who perceived or achieved something for the first time in history for the benefit of all mankind, thus approximating the beneficent gods. He was the first of all mortals who by his insights and his philosophical system banned the fear of the gods and its concomitant, superstition, from the human mind, as Lucretius throughout his poem exclaimed again and again in hymnlike adulation.[196]

As a near-god, founder hero and benefactor of mankind as well as a perfect Sage, Epicurus was described by a fitting vocabulary in which —among others— terms recur which reveal a leaning toward the diction of the mystery and the initiation rite. Among the more characteristic passages we find thus:

1. derivations of θεός, θεῖος, "God", "godly". Among others Plutarch contributes here θεόφαντα ὄργια, "god-revealed mysteries", as Metrodorus called Epicurus' teachings, *Mor.* 1117 B; cf. further *RAC, V,* 747.

2. ἄφθαρτός, "imperishable", *Usener,* fr. 141.

3. τελείως τέλειος, "perfectly perfect", as in the mystery initiations, Philodemus, *de dis* I, col. 24.11, Diels I, 93 (*RAC, V,* 752).

4. σωτήρ, "savior", used by Philodemus, Plotina, Diogenes of Oenoanda, Laertius and others, cf. *RAC, V,* 750.

5. μῦθος. Epicurus' life is, in regard to his goodness, a "mythos" according to *Gn. Vat.* XXXVI. Other items on and by Epicurus —to be discussed presently— resemble visionary and apocalyptic modes. Modern interpreters have seen in all this variously signs of apocalyptic catalepsy,[197] practice of communion with or at least contemplation of the divine,[198] and even a proclivity for magical formulae.[199] A more realistic analysis, however, will reveal merely the enthusiasm evoked by a liberating discovery and the certainty of rational intuition enhanced by poetic feeling.[200]

However this may be, the contrast between rational content and ecstatic literary form was soon a cause for hilarity with the anti-Epicureans and remained so to the Patristic Era. The main target of the sarcastic attacks, however, were the Epicurean pseudapocalypses. A few examples from the sources, Epicurean as well as anti-Epicurean, for this literary phenomenon will suffice to characterize them (essentials for the comparison with Ḥagigah italicized):

1. Possibly by Metrodorus, *Gn. Vat.* X (fr. 37, A. Körte): "... though mortal... through our discussions on Nature you have *ascended* the boundless and the eternal and *seen* the things that are, the things to be, and those before".

θνητὸς ὤν ... ἀνέβης τοῖς περὶ φύσεως διαλογισμοῖς ἐπὶ τὴν ἀπειρίαν καὶ τὸν αἰῶνα καὶ κατεῖδες τά τ'ἐόντα τά τ' ἐσσόμενα πρό τ' ἐόντα.

2. Lucretius, *de rerum natura,* I. 72ff., on Epicurus: "He *advanced* far beyond the *flaming bastions* of the world and *wandered* in spirit through the limitless cosmos...".

... et extra processit longe flammantia moenia mundi atque omne immensum peragravit mente animoque...

3. Epicurus, according to Seneca, *Epist.* LXVI. 45-47, Usener fr. 434, exemplified his own principles, among others tranquility of soul, which is "... like the heavens when they are *purified* to their fullest *splendor*..." (46),

4. Lucretius, III. 1043 f., on Epicurus: "... who quenched all (lesser lights) as the ethereal *sun*, once risen, quenches the stars..." ... et omnis restincxit stellas exortus ut aetherius sol.

Lucretius uses the word group *marmor, marmoreus*, "marble" (see שיש), several times in the sense of "resplendent"; so, e.g., II. 767. Although other Latin poets do likewise (usually in their description of bodies of water), the Seneca passage, above (No. 3) and Cicero's parody (below, No. 6) suggest that metaphors of splendor and purity (see טהור) were characteristic of the Epicurean style.

5. Lucretius, III. 16ff. (freely rendered): "... the *walls* of the world crumble: I see what comes to pass in the void: the holy godhead manifested and simultaneously the tranquil thrones..." ... moenia mundi discedunt, totum video per inane geri res, apparet divum numen sedesque quietae.

6. Cicero, *de fin.* I. xxi. 71, from the Epicurean's peroration:

"if then what I said is more *illuminating* and *clearer* than the *sun* itself..."

Quapropter si ea quae dixi sole ipso illustriora et clariora sunt...

7. Cicero, *de natura deorum* I. xix. 49. Velleius, an Epicurean, speaks in exaggerated diction so that the passage becomes a parody and reveals Cicero's sarcasm (cf. the preceding sentence, *ibid.*, where Velleius begins the more intricate part of Epicurean philosophy with offensive condescension):

"Epicurus, however, who indeed not only *saw* the arcane and utterly secret things in spirit but treats them also as if he had *touched* (them) by hand..." Epicurus autem qui res occultas et penitus abditas non modo videat animo sed etiam sic tractet ut manu...

8. The tone of the preceding is fully revealed through the introduction which Cicero gives to Velleius in I. viii. 18:

"Then Velleius, true to form, confidently, as is their (the Epicureans') custom, fearing nothing more than appearing in doubt about anything, as if he just then came down from the council of the gods and Epicurus' intermundane spaces..." [201]

Tum Velleius fidenter sane, ut solent isti, nihil tam verens quam ne dubitare aliqua de re videretur, tamquam modo ex deorum concilio et ex Epicuri intermundiis descendisset...

9. Cicero alluding to the Epicureans without mentioning them by name, *Tusc. Disput.* I. xxi. 48 : "... wondering at the extravagance of some philosophers who marvel at natural science and in the excess of their joy render thanks to its discoverer and founder and do reverence to him as a god..."

... mirari non nullorum insolentiam philsophorum qui naturae cognitionem admirantur eiusque inventori et principi gratias exsultantes agunt emque venerantur ut deum...

10. Seneca, *de beneficiis* IV. xix. 1f., not wholly negative. Although direct communication with the divine is here excluded, the lines show the same mood and key words:

"You Epicurus... have thrust him (*deum*) beyond fear. Closed in then by a *huge* and *unsurmountable wall* and cut off from contact and sight of mortals you have no reason for fear..."

Tu denique, Epicure... proiecisti illum extra metum. Hunc igitur insaeptum ingenti quidem et inexplicabili muro divisumque a contactu et a conspectu mortalium non habes quare verearis...

As expected, Plutarch joins this criticism of Epicurus in some decisive points [202] but his attack is preponderantly logical and merely bitter. His few flashes of contrived wit [203] do not include a parody of the Epicurean pseudapocalypse.

11. These allusions and parodies culminated finally in a famous piece that is geographically and chronologically quite close to Akiba's warning. It is found with Eusebius of Caesarea [204] who admits that he follows here Dionysius, Bishop of Alexandria :[205]

"Or did Epicurus *peep out* of the lower world and, *passing beyond* the heavenly *precinct* or coming through some secret *gates* which he alone knew (var.: *saw*), *behold* the gods in the void and bless them in their abundant comfort ?"

ἩH τοῦ κόσμου προκύψας Ἐπίκουρος καὶ τὸν οὐράνιον ὑπερβὰς περίβολον ἢ διά τινων κρυφίων ἃς μόνος οἶδεν ἐξελθὼν πυλῶν οὓς ἐν τῷ κενῷ κατεῖδε θεοὺς καὶ τὴν πολλὴν αὐτῶν ἐμακάρισε τρυφὴν ...

The parody concludes with the climactic mention of the divine banquet hall in the void and the nectar and ambrosia made of atoms. Since *Usener*, fr. 364, Heidel, *op. cit.*, and Reitzenstein [206] the prevailing opinion is that the central passage alludes somehow to Epicurus' own wording.

In any case, throughout most of the examples assembled here a certain sweep of style and certain key words are unmistakable, several referring to the arrival (after wandering in space, see כשאתם מגיעין "when ye reach") at a place (see מקום), to resplendence and purity (cf. שיש and טהור), and to walls or gates (cf. אבני, "stones").

12. Lastly, there is a remote possibility that the rhetorical tradition of criticizing Epicureanism in terms of their pseudapocalypses is found also in Hellenistic Jewish material. The particular difficulty of the passage in question, however, consists in the necessity of separating lively rhetorical-allegorical imagery based on a biblical story that deals with an ascent to Heaven, i.e., the Tower of Babel, from reminiscences of Epicurean pseudapocalypses (or criticism thereof with other anti-Epicurean rhetoricians). Philo, in allegorizing the boastful revolt of the builders of the Tower of Babel, Gen. 11:1ff.,[207] sarcastically castigates those "who stretch their sophistry (cleverness with words) unto Heaven", οἱ τὴν τῶν λόγων δεινότητα μέχρις οὐρανοῦ τείναντες, and, somewhat further on, *ibidem*, "... as they hoped to shoot up (soar) to Heaven in (their) imaginings for the destruction of the eternal kingship...", ... ἐλπίσαντας αὐτοὺς εἰς οὐρανὸν ταῖς ἐπινοίαις ἀναδραμεῖσθαι ἐπὶ καθαιρέσει τῆς αἰωνίου βασιλείας ...

The last passage seems to be inspired by more than a mere allegorization of the biblical story, as the sweep of its style and the verb ἀναδραμεῖσθαι indicate, the biblical text having no more than the hint that the top ("head") of the Tower was to be in Heaven (or the sky, Gen. 11:4) and surely no mention at an overthrow of divine government by unholy words (697-290 ἀνοσίοις λόγοις) or willfully constructed doctrine (696-285, τὸ οἰκοδομηθὲν δόγμα).[208] Even Philo's preceding phrase, "heaping attempt upon attempt (or "heave after heave") they built on high tower-like 'their edifice of unedifying dotrine' ",[209] ἐπ' ἄλλοις ἄλλα συνθέντες ἐπιχειρήματα δόγμα ἀδόκιμον οἰκοδομοῦντες εἰς ὕψος οἷα πύργον ἐξῆραν, has hardly a textual basis in that the biblical passage never returns to allusions of soaring and Heaven-storming. Another indication that Philo is not merely thinking of a building operation (and an allegory thereof) but of an apocalypse-like pattern is the mention of Plato's *Phaedrus* apocalypse with its Heaven-soaring charioteer,[210] a collation which is in line with Philo's habit of following such mental associations in his rhetoric.[211]

The presumptuous builders apparently are, for the most part of Philo's diatribe, Epicureans [212] who in disregard of their souls recognize only the world of senses, speak of (matter as) the pre-existent and imperishable [213] and deny the divine government of the world.[214]

Anti-Epicurean motifs shared by Philo and the Midrash are, of course, nothing extraordinary. According to both, Philo and the Midrash, the Serpent is, thus, an Epicurean, i.e., a hedonist and voluptuary,[215] and Cain and Abel exchange Epicurean and anti-Epicurean views in a dispute that precedes the slaying according to both Philo and four Palestinian Targumim.[216]

The mysterious twofold "water, water" may likewise be a parodying allusion to this enthusiastic pseudapocalyptic language of the Epicureans. Such twofold exclamations form, indeed, the climax of later Epicurean passages,[217] such as the famous apotheosis of Epicurus in Lucretius V. 8:

> deux ille fuit, deus, inclyte Memmi,
> a god he was, a god (Epicurus)...,

imitated in the climax of Daphnis' apotheosis in Vergil's *Eclog.* V. 64.

> deux, deus ille, Menalca,

and still echoing with Arnobius, the former rhetor, who knew Lucretius (and Epicurus) well:

> deus, deus (*adv. gent.* II. 60).

Similarly, again, Lucretius:

> aurea dicta, aurea,
> golden words, yea, golden (III. 12f.).[218]

Paul's inveighing against the "beguiling speech" of the Epicureans, Col. 2:4, and Laertius' note, X. 9, on their "siren"-like persuasion may be hints at this enthusiastic style. Cicero flings at Piso the words "man made for persuasion that you are...", ut es homo factus ad persuadendum, *in Pis.* 59.

The meaning of the formula "water, water", has been the subject of many a medieval and modern inquiry.[219] It seems that it has no intrinsic meaning at all. It merely parodies the style of the Epicureans but may, perhaps, also warn of the approaching "heretical" climax in the ecstatic speech of the Epicureans, which culminated in such doublets.[220] The *diplosis* "water, water", could thus just as well have been "light, light", or "truth, truth", even "atoms, atoms", a finish which Dionysius-Eusebius approximate in their parody:

> ἔκ τε τῶν ἀτόμων τὴν ἀμβροσίαν αὐτοῖς παρατιθεὶς
> καὶ προπίνων αὐτοῖς ἐξ ἐκείνων τὸ νέκταρ,

"... serving up to them (the gods) ambrosia of atoms and letting freely flow nectar of the same kind", *ibid.*[221]

Perhaps the choice of the twofold "water" over other possible items may have been influenced by the memory of similar, more serious apocalypses of this kind current in Greek philosophy and adopted by rhetoric, such as that in Plato's *Phaedrus*, 247ff., where some similar key words prevail.[222] Also combinations of such Platonic elements with Epicurean apocalyptic themes could have been the pattern since there are quite a few precedents for such a phenomenon, such as the origin of civilization, Lucretius V. 1395-1435, which combines Epicurus as in *Usener* fr. 207 with Plato's *Republic* 372a-d, and the function of the human organism, see Lucretius II. 1113-1142, and *Timaeus* 77c-81d.[223] Such Platonic reminiscences or Epicurean-Platonic items as patterns for our passage, however, may be limited merely to the choice of the moteme "water".

The resplendent stones of the Akiba warning must be reminiscences of the wall, gate, building or fortress which in poetry and ecstatic vision represents the celestial world in certain Greco-Roman traditions and which was appropriated in the Epicurean pseudapocalypse. Unless some of this Hellenic-Hellenistic imagery is merely poetic-martial language [224] —the walled-in stronghold on the mountain top— the earliest prototype of this *phantasma* may have been the Olympic banquet hall of the gods, or, perhaps, a heavenly temple, as Reitzenstein attempted to show.[225]

Akiba's warning could thus be paraphrastically rendered as

> "When (in your discussions with Epicureans) you reach (the point at which they speak of) 'the place of pure marble splendor', do not (be carried away by their enthusiasm and) say (like them ecstatically) 'water, water' (or whatever the dialogue may touch upon at this point)".

This warning hardly requires a *testimonium*.[226] Perhaps here again, for reasons of symmetry and uniformity, or, perhaps, in conjunction with the later esoteric-mystical understanding of the passage, Akiba's warning was given a testimonium: "The speaker of lies will not persist before mine eyes", Ps. 101:7 b, the meaning of which is quite general.

In view of the keywords of Epicureans and related "apocalypses" one could mistakenly see in the הציץ, "he saw", of the typologies a reflection of a visionary experience, and a parallel to the somewhat rare and whimsical προκύψας of the Eusebius text. It is doubtful, however, whether any visionary genres influenced the typologies. This "he saw" of the latter, indeed, seems to have an entirely different meaning. We have seen that the phrase "to enter Paradise" signifies "to go to the Garden", i.e., have intenisve dealings with Epicureans.[227] Our four sages are intellectually endangered [228] and even punished [229] because of their undue trafficking with the Garden but they are not accused of having visions. Even Akiba, in his independent warning, speaks of saying something or agreeing with something, but not of visions. It is therefore possible that *heṣiṣ*, "he saw", means here merely "he looked around",[230] "examined the situation", "got adjusted", similar to Caesar's *veni vidi vici*, "I came, *I saw*, I triumphed". The latter was apparently familiar to the Talmud. It seems to have been the pattern for the parodying וחמתה וחמדה ונסבה, "saw it, liked it, took it", in an early Palestinian amoraic anecdote.[231] The extended or concentrated seeing including the vision of the supra-terrestial in earlier talmudic Hebrew —unless an item is under the influence of our very passage conceived of as mystical— is usually represented by נבט, *hiph'il* (Jastrow, s.v. II) or סכל I, *hithpa'el*, or merely ראה. The verb *heṣiṣ* thus describes the sages as they begin their Epicurean adventure. They entered, they saw, they failed, except the fourth.

The fourfold division of our typologies may suggest to the unsuspecting that there were precisely four sages in history who exposed themselves to Epicureanism and incurred the fate of the Epicureans. Such an assumption would be somewhat uncritical in view of the nature of this type of material. The typologies could have listed only three personalities or with some ingenuity even five.[232] This is true also if near-contemporaneousness of the sages or mutual friendships are assumed to be the historical basis for the number of four. Non-ordination likewise is indecisive. It is well established for b. Azzai and b. Zoma.[233] Akiba may here be the third because of his late ordination, after the Epicurean adventure. Non-ordination for Acher, however, is not clearly, or not all, established.[234]

To be sure, uncomplimentary legends do not necessarily require a basis in historical fact,[235] and they are not necessarily the product of opposing schools.[236] It seems, however, that legendarizations whether positive or negative are attached almost exclusively to "Founder-Sages" who created new schools, trends, or ideas. As such they are related to the genres of heurematology, i.e., lists, typologies and legends on the inventors in Greco-Roman culture.[237] Our four seem to be close to these founder sages who are well represented in talmudic culture.[238] And yet even this possibility in conjunction with their "Epicureanism" cannot explain satisfactorily the limitation to four. Somehow five (or even more) Epicureanizing innovator-Sages could have been found.

It is evident that any literary attack on Epicureanism would have profited from involving as many characteristics of Epicureanism as possible, becoming thus somewhat of a parody even in the case of a typology. Now Epicureanism was, indeed, as well known for situations which involved the number four as, let us say, Hegelianism is known for the importance of the number three. A popular allusion to their school might include somewhere and somehow also a recognizable hint at this favorite number of four of theirs, especially in view of the fact that their most famous item, a quadruple maxim, was flung at their discussants or would-be converts on every occasion. It is the famous *Tetrapharmakos*, the "Fourfold Medicine", a brief summary of Epicureanism :[239]

ἄφοβον ὁ θεός
ἀνύποπτον ὁ θάνατος
καὶ τἀγαθὸν μὲν εὔκτητον
τὸ δὲ δεινὸν εὐεκκαρτέρητον

somewhat freely rendered :

God —not fearful,
Death —not riskful,
Virtue —obtained cheerfully,
Evil —endured steadfastly.

Hadrian, certainly not an opponent, used to call his favorite dish, which was prepared with four ingredients, parodyingly *tetrafarmacus*.[240] In the classical Garden, too, and subsequently in the mentions of it, the number four was important. Epicurus was joined by his three brothers Neocles, Chaeredemus and Aristobulus, *D.L.* X. 3, so that the four brothers formed the nucleus of the Epicurean sodality. Epicurus, Metrodorus, Hermarchus and Polyaenus are called the four καθηγεμόνες, i.e., authorities, "soul leaders".[241] The term is used especially in the period of Philodemus.[242] An epitome of their letters may have been available even before his time.[243] (A witty epigram by Philodemus himself, however, in which the number four is basic, may not be connected with any aspect of Epicureanism).[244] Even if the number four in our talmudic item be indeed dictated by historical facts, the effectiveness and subtlety of the passage must have been enhanced by its fourfold structure.[245]

In assigning the *Ḥagigah* passage to the anti-Epicurean utterances, warnings, and prohibitions of tannaitic culture, no denial of the existence of an early Jewish esoteric-mystical speculation is intended. Nor are the learned observations of so many modern interpreters of the passage less pertinent: our item, owing to its stylistic proximity to philosophical-rhetorical apocalypses, must have been early understood as mystical in talmudic culture and even its textual transmission tended in this direction. The anti-Epicurean interpretation attempted here has, perhaps, the advantage of utilizing more fully the literary form and what seem to be Epicurean "biographical" reminiscences within the text as well as the framework.[246] The explanation of the term "Paradise" is less forced. The fact that b. Azzai never was a mystic (perhaps not even Akiba) is accounted for. Furthermore, the ubiquity of parodies in anti-Epicurean literature and the probability that talmudic culture, in one particular stage, did employ cynicizing literary forms of Greco-Roman rhetoric, should strengthen the thesis proposed here.[247]

It is not asserted here that the tannaitic scholars read Epicurus' letters, recited Lucretius, went to school with the Church Fathers or had Herculanean papyri in their possession. It is claimed, however, that certain beliefs, maxims, habits and legends belonging to the academic lore of or on the Epicureans were common knowledge in the ancient world, that they spread abroad by popular media and personal encounters —whether employing Greek or Aramaic— and that they played a significant role in the academic tradition of scholar-bureaucracies which resembled each other to a certain degree and were in contact with each other in the classical, Christian, and Jewish worlds in the first two to three centuries of Roman Imperial times.

PART TWO

AN EPICUREAN SENTENTIA ON PROVIDENCE AND DIVINE JUSTICE

In this chapter an attempt will be made to demonstrate that in earlier sources the well-known talmudic-midrashic coinage

לית דין ולית דיין

there is no justice and there is no judge,[1]
is not only intended to characterize the belief of Epicureans but follows, in fact, a Greco-Roman rhetorical pattern used by and against Epicureans. This attempt involves a comparative structural analysis of the talmudic formula and of the Greco-Roman pattern, both within their respective contexts.

To be sure, Acher, when watching the extreme injustice of the death of an observer of Torah who dies while performing a biblical commandment (Dt. 22:7), does not use the coinage לית דין... but a similar one:

איכן היא טובתו של זה?
איכן היא אריכות ימיו של זה?

Where is the "goodness" (promised to) this one?!
Where is the "length of days" (promised) to this one?![2]

This somewhat different (but as we shall see, still closely related) formulation for the injustice of fate is here determined by the vocabulary of the pentateuchal commandment involved, which announces well-being and length of days to its observer. Likewise, Acher's exclamation at witnessing the martyrdom of Judah the Baker during the Hadrianic persecution[3] —according to a variant, of Huṣpith the Interpreter—[4]

זו תורה וזו שכרה?

This is Torah and this its recompense?!

is determined by the special circumstances of the case, i.e., the ironical fate of an eloquent teacher of Torah.[5] It is followed by yet another similar coinage in the mouth of Acher which is also uttered by Cain in several Palestinian Targumim :[6]

אין מתן שכר
ואין תחיית המתים

There is no recompense,
And there is no resurrection of the dead.[7]

Such a substitution by other coinages is also found in the exclamation of the Epicurean martyr Danaë who specifies similarly: "rightly do men think little of the divine since, for instance, I who once saved my former 'man' receive such thanks from the deity whereas Laodice who killed hers is deemed worthy of such great honor".[8]

All talmudic formulae present a related structure:

1. word repetition at the beginnings of "stichs":[9]

   לית... לית   איכן ... איכן
   זו ... זו   אין ... אין

2. additional word-plays:
   (a) etymological alliteration: דין/דיין
   (b) non-etymological alliteration: מַתן שכר/תחיית המתים [10]
   (c) approximation of rhyme: תורה/שכרה [11]
   (d) additional repetitions at end of stichs: שלוזה/שלוזה.[11]

In other talmudic-midrashic instances, however, the coinage לית דין... is used, with or without parallel formulae, for expressing this doubt in divine justice.[12] Perhaps the most significant occurrence of our formula is thus the well-known targumic passage which makes Cain utter it after Abel's sacrifice had been prefererd to his, during a fraternal quarrel "in the field" which led, according to the midrashic-targumic motif, to Abel's death. This passage is represented in four targumic versions on Gen. 4:8.[13]

The decisive section of Neofiti I, *ad loc.*, e.g., runs thus:[14]

1 לית דין ולית דיין
2 ולית עולם חורן
3 לית מתן אגר טב לצדיקיא
4 ולית מתפרעה מן רשיעיא

Cain to Abel, after an initial exchange of words and opinions:

1 "There is no Judgment and there is no Judge;"
2 And there is no Other World;

3 [And ?] there is no bestowal of recompense for the just;
4 And there is no reckoning for the wicked.[15]

Abel opposes this with ...אית, "there is...", using the very same words (and three times "and") with the final addition, found only in Neofiti I, לעלמא דאתי, "in the World to Come".[16] Fragmentary Targum (JII) adds two more lines:

5 ולא ברחמין איתברי עלמא
6 ולא ברחמין הוא מדבר

5 And not in mercy was the world created;
6 And not in mercy does He speak.[17]

By-passing the elaborate recent controversy as to the dating of this story of the fraternal dispute in general and its different versions in particular,[18] we must here subject the לית דין passage and its immediate context (lines 1-4) to the following considerations: it is highly probable that this passage, and within it, our coinage, try to make Cain an Epicurean. Even the additional "there is no Other World" (line 2) was a well-known and widely fought tenet of Epicurus who taught determinedly that there was nothing to expect after death, that body and soul, both composed of atoms, dissolved,[19] and that fear of an underworld and of punishment therein was groundless: the gods, as perfect, happy, and affect- and actionless beings did not interfere with man's world. The Sage did not expect any compensatory justice.[20]

That the extended targumic passages hint at Sadduceeism, as Vermès briefly suggested (p. 103), is rather unlikely. To be sure, the Sadducees did deny the existence of afterlife, resurrection, and final judgment. As conservatives and biblicists, however, they must have maintained the doctrine of just retribution in this life in accordance with the strong biblical emphasis on this belief.[21] Cain of the Targum, however, in most versions, denies any kind of compensatory justice, and the Philonic parallels as well as the Greco-Roman rhetorical patterns, presently to be discussed, make an allusion to the Sadducee-Pharisee controversy highly improbable.[22]

The anti-Epicurean meaning of our targumic passage, however, becomes most plausible once it is recognized that this is an item somehow connected with Greco-Roman rhetoric and that its anti-Epicurean content was anticipated by Philo.

The introduction of the targumic dispute between Cain and Abel is not necessarily provoked by a well-known difficulty of the masoretic text: "And Cain said to Abel his brother; (sic!) and while they were in the field Cain rose toward Abel his brother and slew him". (Gen. 4:8) [23] Obviously the verse fails to indicate what Cain said.[24] In most major versions the difficulty has been overcome by an insertion —or was non-existent owing to the availability of another basic Hebrew text— to the effect that Cain said to Abel "[Come,] let us go into the field".[25] An extensive dialoguic expansion, however, is found in Philo's Hellenistic homily *Quod deterius potiori insidiari soleat* i. 191f. (1ff.). It has no connection with this textual difficulty, since Philo used the fuller text of the Septuagint. Philo thus announces that Cain is drawing Abel into a dispute, the "field" of the biblical text being that of a rhetorical contest [26] and battle ($\delta\iota\alpha\mu\acute{\alpha}\chi\eta$), allegorically understood.[27] Whether or not this theme of a fraternal dispute in the field is of Hellenistic or Palestinian origin can no longer be determined but Philo's treatment of the ensuing battle of wits [28] is thoroughly Hellenistic-rhetorical. Although Philo does not reproduce the actual exchange of arguments, he contrasts Abel with Cain, going into a lengthy rhetorical description of two opposite types of men which Abel and Cain represent. The mood of the passage is in parts cynicizing-diatribic [29] in as far as Philo makes virtue-simplicity-poverty (Abel) clash with vanity-luxury-wealth (Cain). Abel resembles the lowly virtuous rustic, Cain the sophisticated and sophist urbanite.[30] Into this characterization, however, Philo mixes further details that may indicate his intention to give this non-virtuous *typos* Epicurean features:[31] (a) the mention of pleasures ($\dot{\eta}\delta o\nu\alpha s$ ..., 197; "... of all senses", 198); (b) arguments from the senses in favor of pleasures, fully spelled out; (c) the persuasiveness of the non-virtuous *typos*.[32] The only jarring feature in this portrayal of an Epicurean is the urge of the *typos* to hold public office and his hate of obscurity [33]. Philo's diatribe, however, may not be aimed exclusively at the Epicureans who are here only the most prominent representatives of misleading "fashionable" philosophies.

The core of Philo's homily on the two *typoi* which Cain and Abel represent (x. 197f.) is a structured unit which uses prescribed artifices of epideictic rhetoric: e.g., the "amplification", consisting of the basic moral statement and its opposite ($\dot{\eta}$ $\tau o\hat{u}$ $\dot{\epsilon}\nu\alpha\nu\tau\acute{\iota}os$ $\sigma\acute{u}\sigma\tau\alpha\sigma\iota s$),[34] preceded by six successive questions (197f.) —a diatribic device. *Parechesis*, i.e., repetition of sound in successive words, is represented here in the specific form of $\dot{o}\mu o\iota o\tau\acute{\epsilon}\lambda\epsilon u\tau o\nu$, *similiter desinens*, and appears in nine words with the ending -*oi* for the virtuous and an equal number for the non-virtuous.³⁵ This effect is achieved by the use of the same grammatical case, in this instance the nominative, a device called ὁμοιόπτωτον or *similiter cadens*. In addition, the effective *asyndeton* is used throughout, i.e., an enumeration without conjunction.³⁶ *Adoxoi*, "obscure", contrasts with *endoxoi*, "honored", representing an antithetical style element.³⁷

It is quite likely that also the targumic passage, in particular the characterization of the two brothers by their arguments, is somehow related to Greco-Roman anti-Epicurean rhetoric of this sort or, at least, to a Hellenistic-Jewish tradition, whether Alexandrinian or Palestinian, which suggested an anti-Epicurean rhetorical tirade at this juncture, i.e., at the incident in the field. This possibility becomes somewhat more plausible once it is recognized that the decisive targumic passage shows traces of a similar rhetorical structure apart from aiming at Epicureanism.³⁸

We find thus the *amplificatio*, dealing here, however, with the opinions and beliefs of the virtuous and the non-virtuous rather than with their social characterization as with Philo. The Targum uses brief phrases, many of them of the approximate length of Philo's *homoioteleuta*,³⁹ and a threefold *polysyndeton*, i.e., the conjunction ו, "and", between the parallel phrases, instead of the *asyndeton*, the rhetorician having a choice to do one or the other and even to mix them in order to achieve desired effects.⁴⁰ The quantitative balance (*parisōsis*) in the descriptions of the two brothers in the Targum parallels that of Philo.

The targumic text, however, goes beyond Philo's devices. It has two occurrences of word-initial *parechesis*: ⁴¹ דיין/דין and מתן אגר/מתגרעה/אגר. The former counts actually as a case of word-play (*paronomasia*) in ancient criticism and is achieved by employing two forms of the same root (*schēma etymologikon*).⁴² The "figure" of the identical grammatical case (*homoioptōton*) —the Hebrew and Aramaic equivalent being here the absence of a preposition— leads again to *homoioteleuta* which in this case include a phenomenon that became increasingly frequent in Roman Imperial times: the near-rhyme or actual rhyme.⁴³ Thus, lines 1-2 represent near-rhyme: חורן/דין;⁴⁴ lines 3-4, actual rhyme: רשיעיא/צדיקיא. We have seen that one of Acher's coinages also included near-rhyme.⁴⁵ Finally, the Targum as well as Acher use *epanaphora*,⁴⁶ i.e., the repetition of the initial element (word) אית (לית) in Abel's rebuttal) and זו, איכן, and אין respectively.

One of Acher's exclamations, איכן...זה, זה׳...איכן could possibly be the device called συμπλοκή (or *complexio*), to wit, the composite of *epanaphora* (repetition of the initial word) and *epiphora* (or *antistrophē*, the repetition of the last word), quite popular in the *peroratio*, the final summary in a rhetorical unit.

The structures of Acher's formulae (exclamations), however, and of our לית דין ולית דיין are so dense (terse, concentrated) that they must have been fixed coinages, i.e., *sententiae*.[47] The use of effective *sententiae* was one of the most important prescriptions of ancient rhetoric [48] and a favorite subject of analysis by the ancient critics.[49] These midrashic examples are such *sententiae* but not folk proverbs, being too reflective-intellectual and also too school-bound as their appearance in didactic-polemical texts indicates. This would thus exclude polygenesis, i.e., independent, spontaneous folk creations at different places, regarding the parallelism between לית דין and the Hellenistic examples to be introduced below.

Although our targumic item shows the earmarks of rhetorical structure,[50] it is, of course, simpler, rawer, but more symmetrical and clearer in its cadences, thus apparently already anticipating or showing the influence of the mishnaic style. It is not necessarily directly dependent on Philo (or vice versa): both may use a common pattern. Interestingly enough Philo has here fewer rather than more rhetorical devices, perhaps because in his extended homilies he grew frequently quite independent and dispensed with *sententiae*. The Targum, however, seems here to be still quite close to a rhetorical tradition which must have led it to apply here a common *sententia* that was a permanent fixture in Greco-Roman anti-Epicurean tradition, i.e., our לית דין. What this *sententia* may have been in its Greco-Roman garb will be shown once the afterlife of our לית דין in subsequent Midrash has been more fully explored.

1. Thus, in an often repeated item,[51] the claim is made that "the Sages wished to commit the Book of Ecclesiastes to a genizah", that is, not to canonize it, "because they found in it items that came (dangerously) close to heresy".[52] The obstacle was Eccl. 11.9a-c, "enjoy, O young man, thy youthfulness, and let thy heart indulge in the days of thy strength, and follow the ways of thy heart and the sight of thine eyes".[53] The "suspect" is here Solomon himself, who seems to recommend hedonism, and the Sages take him to task for his statement [54] which elicits the further midrashic comment: "(for), once the strap is relaxed, (the adage) 'there is no justice and there is no Judge' (will

prevail)". In consonance with the conclusion of this Midrash and the thrust of the item that precedes it, this rendering is perhaps more appropriate: "Should we then say that the strap (of divine reward and punishment) is relaxed (in view of this recommendation of hedonism) and that 'there is no judgment and no Judge?'" [55]

Solomon acquitted himself, however, and was praised by the Sages [56] when he concluded Eccl. 11:9 with the warning "but know that for all these (things) God will bring you into judgment" (11:9d). In the view of the Midrash, Solomon appeared to have recommended in his wording of Eccl. 11:9a-c hedonism as well as, implicitly, its usual concomitant, to wit, the denial of the existence of divine providence.[57]

In Greco-Roman culture, hedonism and the denial of divine providence (divine justice, reward and punishment) are, of course, two standard reproaches made against Epicureanism by hostile philosophical schools as well as popular rhetoric and must have been known even by the proverbial "man in the street". These reproaches frequently deal objectively with the intricacies of the Epicurean doctrine of pleasure and the problems of a non-directed cosmos. More often, they are caricatures, ascribing a gross hedonism and actual atheism to Epicurus and his followers and expressing shock at their dangerous impiety. Most valuable, however, would be a witness from rhetorical usage which would tie together these two accusations in one rhetorical period or phrase. An example of this sort is, indeed, available in the Twelfth or Olympic Oration of Dio Chrysostom (of Prusa, c. 40 - after 112) in whic he assails "certain men who have been wiser than all wisdom (36)", an ironical reference to the Epicureans who have set up the depraved and lewd goddess Pleasure ('$H\delta ον \grave{η} ν$) while at the same time "taking our gods from us" (37).[58]

Patristic literature developed along similar lines.[59] In Hippolytus' brief critical summary of Epicurus' doctrines, non-providence and hedonism are thus similarly combined in a coherent statement.[60] The acquaintance with Epicurean situations and criticisms that prevails also otherwise in earlier talmudic literature makes it highly probable that in this Midrash, too, talmudic criticism has the two principal dangers of Epicureanism in mind that appear also in Greco-Roman and patristic models.

2. Gen. R. LXIII. 11 on 25:29,[61] anonymous and lamentably brief, introduces Esau as an arch-sinner and denier of recompense and resurrection. Thus, at the death of Abraham (*sic*!) Esau exclaims: "harsh justice has hit this patriarch! Here is 'no deeding of recompense and

no resurrection of the dead' ".⁶² It is not impossible that this Midrash is a descendant of the targumic item: (a) Esau is as much an arch-sinner as Cain; (b) the mention of the "field" follows in most parallels; (c) the אין מתן (לית מתן) version of our *sententia* is used in both; (d) the difficult and abrupt מדת הדין could easily be a descendant of the Cain/Abel debate. It may still be ironical: "Fine justice has caught up with this hoary one. (This goes to show that) 'there is no...' " ⁶³

3. In *PdRK* ⁶⁴ Manasseh uses the positive version of our *sententia*, ... אית דין, "there is (after all) justice ...," in a moment of gratitude, when he was restored to Jerusalem. Even if this passage should presuppose that Manasseh used the opposite and original version of our *sententia* before,⁶⁵ his midrashic portrayal has accumulated so many fantastic features —from incest to mass-slaughter— that without a special effort individual components can no longer be isolated. Our *sententia* must have been used here, implicitly, for a number of heresies and transgressions and does no longer indicate Epicurean-related deviationism.

It is interesting to note, however, that extreme Greco-Roman anti-Epicureanism in the Roman Imperial period also occasionally mentions monster kings in one breath with Epicureans and marks them as total voluptuaries, especially Sardanapalus.⁶⁶ This habit, however, may be a Near Eastern or Judaic contribution to Greco-Roman culture. In a later phase it seems to characterize Roman emperors under the guise of foreign kings and thus belong to what is frequently called "resistance literature" against Rome, as represented, e.g., in apocalypses, the Sibylline Oracles, and others, even including Roman works.⁶⁷

4. Occasionally the Midrash portrays a whole generation of Israel as using our *sententia*, apparently in order to mark them as Epicureans. The Tannaim Akiba (who uses also Ps. 10:13a herein) and R. Meir comment thus on Gen. 6:3, לא ידון, "will not dwell", and interpret it as words of the wicked Generation of the Flood who say, according to R. Meir: "The Lord will not judge (לא ידין), " (for) "there is no Judge (אין דיין) in the world; the Lord (המקום) has abandoned (נטש) his world".⁶⁸ In a similar anonymous Midrash, Ps. 10:13a, "the despisers of God", refers to all the wicked and this is illustrated (or defined) by our coinage ⁶⁹ and elaborated upon: "The Holy One, Blessed-Be-He, abandoned his world and went away and sat himself in Heaven".⁷⁰ These items are quite close to a parody of the Epicurean teachings on the gods who sat impassionately in their intermundane spaces (often

called Heaven by the anti-Epicureans but also by Lucretius) and had no active relations to the world. This particular Epicurean teaching had always evoked much hilarity as well as sarcastic criticism, from the academy to the forum, in the Greco-Roman world as well as in patristics.[71]

5. Other later occurrences of our *sententia*, either in its original aramaizing form or a Hebrew version —some in a positive formulation (יש דין, אית דין)— do no longer indicate an acquaintance with Epicureanism or situations which involved actual Epicureans.

The original function of לית דין and its equivalents seems thus to have been to indicate that an Epicurean is speaking or acting. Beyond this, however, our *sententia* seems to have been actually patterned after a Greco-Roman slogan which, not unlike our saying, occurred in several variants and was a target of criticism in Greco-Roman anti-Epicureanism. In the following, a number of passages are listed, some Epicurean, some anti-Epicurean, some Greco-Roman, some patristic, representing a variety of literary genres, but all contributing to the establishment of the original pattern and its contextual tradition.

1. Thus Hippolytus, continuing his summary of Epicurus' philosophy,[72] mentions Epicurus' teaching that in death both body and soul dissolve and that consequently

μήτε κρίσεις εἶναι ἐν Ἅιδου
μήτε δικαστήρια,

No trials are there in Hades,
No tribunals of justice.

Hippolytus may quote here Epicurus' opinion correctly. The literary form, however, resembles suspiciously rhetorical coinage, employing, as it does, *parechesis* (repetition of the negative), extreme brevity (four words), and a near alliteration (as marked, above).[73] The intercalation "are there in Hades" is caused by the descriptive prose of Hippolytus and, as we shall see, by the raw material of a traditional contextual syndrome.[74]

2. Lucretius, the great Roman poet and interpreter of Epicureanism (c. 94-55 B.C.) was very fond of *parechesis*, alliteration, and other rhetorical-poetical devices which are abundant in his poem *de rerum natura*. Nevertheless, traces of a *sententia* (independent of his own alliterations) seem to be in evidence in his text.[75]

With the wide-flung sweep of his lines, such a coinage would not be used by him intact but would be distributed over several stichs or periods. His famous Epicurean-informed passage on the futility of the fear of death, afterlife, and punishment is found in the third book of his poem, lines 978-1023. The nucleus of such a coinage seems to be represented in the *parechesis* and alliteration

nec... (980) ... Tantalus... (981) nec Tityon... (984),
There is no... Tantalus..., there is no Tityus...[76]

Other important key words and thoughts which, as we shall see, mark this as a traditional Epicurean stereotype, are "as the story goes" (*ut famast*); the rock (of Tantalus or Ixion); Acheron (replacing Hades);[77] and the briefly sketched irony, immediately preceding the central core of the passage, that belief in them or fear thereof makes these false imaginings real and potent but in this very life.[78] The subsequent elaboration includes, among others, Sisyphus, Cerberus (the "Hell Hound"), a regrettable lacuna (1012), and a concluding repetition of the theme "Hell on Earth" for believing fools (1023).

3. Either this passage or a similar one from the Epicurean stock-in-trade underlies the lengthy prose debate between two discussants called A. and M., the latter representing, at this juncture, Epicureanism, in Cicero's *Tusculan Disputations*.[79] Step by step, M. tries to convince A. of Epicurus' famous "death does not concern us"; he demonstrates the irony of fearing in life non-existent punishment after death and thus becoming wretched in this life, I. v-viii (see Lucretius' "Hell on Earth"). Several ironical questions, I. v. 10, and several denunciations that stories of punishment in an afterlife are *portenta*, I. vi. 11, that is, extravagant stories (fables, myths, falsehoods) of poets and painters, follow (cf. Lucretius' *ut famast*). Furthermore, the key words Cerberus, Acheron, Tantalus and Sisyphus (I. v. 10) combined with the mention of the "inexorable" *judges* Minos and Rhadamanthus and an imaginary *trial* before them,[80] occur in rapid succession, their existence, of course, being questioned. Apart from the Epicurus quotation, however, no other *sententiae* or traces thereof emerge, probably because the structure of the debate, a rapid succession of logical arguments, precluded further pre-formulated items.

4. A semblance of our coinage, however, emerges in a passage of Seneca's *Epistles*, XXIV. 18.[81]

Non sum tam ineptus ut Epicuream cantilenam hoc loco persequor et dicam vanos esse inferorum metus

nec Ixionem rota volvi
nec saxum umeris Sisyphi trudi in adversum

I am not so foolish as to expound here again the old Epicurean tune and say that the terrors of the Netherworld are empty, that Ixion does not revolve on the wheel, that the rock is not shoved around by the shoulders of Sisyphus.

For full measure, he adds what is apparently a coinage of his own:

nec ullius vi̲s̲c̲eri et rena̲s̲c̲i posse c̲otidie et c̲arpi. that someone's entrails cannot be daily reborn and devoured.[82]

In conclusion he mentions Cerberus, the childishness of all this, [83] and the idea that death is nothing.[84] The presence of a literary tradition at the core of which is a coinage is thus evident in the key words, the beliefs, and the literary form, the latter manifest in *parechesis* (thrice "nec") and in initial (— —) and internal (= =) alliteration, centering around the consonents s — x — c.[85]

5. To return to the Greek and confirm that the preceding is hardly coincidental, the famous stone inscription of Diogenes of Oenoanda is here being reintroduced. Diogenes, c. 150 or 200 A.D., an ardent admirer of Epicurus, adorned the forum of his Asia Minor home town with a lengthy description of Epicureanism.[86] Having learned to laugh down death Diogenes can say

φοβοῦμαι γὰρ οὐδὲν διὰ τοὺς Τιτυοὺς καὶ τοὺς Ταντάλους
οὓς ἀναγράφουσιν ἐν ῞Αιδου τινές...

We fear in no wise on account of the T̲ityuses and T̲antaluses whom some have depicted in Hades.[87]

The denial, the alliteration,[88] the key words, and the intimation of fable, form again a familiar syndrome.

6. Quite illuminating is another exemple in a bilingual epitaph[89]

οὐκ ἔστι ἐν ῞Αιδου πλοῖον
οὐ πορθμεὺς Χάρων
οὐκ Αἰακὸς [90] κλειδοῦχος
οὐχὶ Κέρβελος [91] κύων.

No b̲oat is there in Hades,
No b̲oatman Charon,
No c̲ustodian Aeacus
No dog C̲erberus.

The repeated negative, the alliterations, the mention of Hades, and the terse formulation speak for themselves. The introduction of Aeacus who is also a judge of the dead, is important as a continuation of and mental association with the Minos-Rhadamanthus syndrome in which he is frequently included.[92]

7. Also Dio of Prusa in the Olympic Oration (37), after the mention of Epicurus and the latter's banishment of the gods, continues with what is apparently another version of this coinage, a fourfold polysyndetic alliteration plus *paronomasia* (ἐχ- / ἀρχ-) describing the state of the universe (τὰ ξύμπαντα) which is

    ἀγνώμονα καὶ ἄφρονα καὶ ἀδέσποντα
    καὶ μηδένα ἔχοντα ἄρχοντα...

freely:
"aimless and senseless and masterless and less a leader."

The four items form two semantic groups which could be rendered as "no sense, no steward." They are thus reasonably close to the Greco-Roman and Aramaic-Hebrew coinage, allowing for the usual genre-determined and individually colored variation.

8. The most intriguing passage, however, is found in Seneca's prose letter *Ad Marciam de consolatione* XIX. 4. After assuring Marica that the terrors of the Netherworld are fables (*fabulas esse*), and no darkness is imminent for the dead, he continues with pathos:

    nec carcerem [93]
    nec flumina igne flagrantia...
freely: no incarceration,
    no flows of conflagration.

Almost immediately thereafter:
    nec tribunalia et reos
    et in illa libertate tam laxa ullos iterum tyrannos,
    no tribunal seats and (no) defendants,
    (nor) in that lax liberty again those tyrants,

concluding with the thought that all these are vain terrors of the poets. The (separated) alliterative pair *tribunalia* and *tyrannos*, "tribunal seats", and "tyrannical (judges)," is reasonably close to דין and דיין, since the Latin is undoubtedly a metaphor for "trials" and "judges" or "court of justice" and "judges".[94]

The basic pattern of this Epicurean coinage is thus:

    Neither A_1 nor A_2

or extended

Neither A_1 nor A_2; neither B_1 nor B_2, etc.,

i.e., quite similar to the extended forms of the Targum and the Acher reports. In this formula, A represents the basic consonant of an alliterative pair of words. A_1 may be a thing or abstract or person, likewise A_2. Of course, the talmudic coinages offer no parallel to the pair of tortured sinners, having no mythology of this sort. They prefer abstracts, since the *sententiae* were used for dogmatic polemics, but not to refute myth. Nevertheless, the profile that emerges from the group Hippolytus (no. 1) and Seneca (no. 7), to a lesser degree the epitaph (no. 6, with its judge) and Cicero (no. 3, with the judges in the context), is thus:

neither an act (or procedure) *nor a judge*, or the reverse sequence.

The entire syndrome of motifs, i.e., the wider context in which our coinages most frequently appear, may ultimately go back to seminal words of Epicurus himself, such as the passage in his *Letter to Herodotus* 81, in which he speaks of false assumptions regarding the divine,

so that in consequence one expects or imagines eternal horror in accordance with the myths.[95]

Here is already *in nucleo* the danger of myth ("fable") and unnecessary or foolish fear of punishment.[96]

Some echo of this basic formula the profile of which the preceding analysis attempted to delineate, is discernible in the effective condemnation of Epicurean doctrine by the Stoic Hierocles (active during Hadrian's reign). The item is quoted in Greek by Aulus Gellius (*c.* 123-*c.* 165) in the name of his teacher Taurus in his Latin *Noctes Atticae* IX. v. 8 (P.K. Marshall, Oxford 1968, p. 284):

'Ἡδονὴ τέλος, πόρνης δόγμα·
οὐκ ἔστιν πρόνοια, οὐδὲ πόρνης δόγμα.

freely: 1 Pleasure an end: a prostitute's creed;
2 No Providence: beneath a prostitute's creed (... not even a ...).

The two abstract nouns, the double negative, and the alliterative wordplay *pron- / porn-* make it quite probable that this is a free, witty variation of our thematic structure (line 2: not A_1, not A_2) with a preceding introductory positive statement (line 1).

Apart from supplying one of the constituent elements of the *parano-*

masia, the use of *pornē* may have been in retaliation for similar Epicurean epithets for the Stoic doctrine of Providence.

The mood prevailing in the Greco-Roman passages varies from item to item, depending, as it does, on the context, the purpose, and the literary form (genre), and on the attitude of the author toward Epicureanism.[97] Nevertheless, if a generalization is admissible at all, it could be said that in varying degrees the items openly express, or still reflect (in the polemic of the anti-Epicureans), a certain strength of conviction which, with Lucretius and Seneca's consolation (no. 7), wax into a pathos with triumphal overtones: the fear of death, of myth, of arbitrary fate, has been banished.

In most of the Hebrew sources, the "Epicurean" speaker, likewise, speaks with great conviction but he speaks apparently in shock and despair, after a decisive event that seems to prove the non-existence of justice. This is true for Cain, Esau, Acher, and even the Sages who question Solomon.[98]

Even in Epicureanism, however, the disbelief in an afterlife was not always the result of an attempt to ban fear but of other philosophical and moral considerations and, last but not least, of the discovery of the injustices of life. This is obvious not only in the Danaë story but also in actual Epicurean teachings. In a famous sequence of his Fifth Book, 195-234, Lucretius demonstrates that the gods are not responsible for the world order (... *naturam rerum*..., 199) and introduces in support of this claim a catalogue of faults, shortcomings, and senseless catastrophes (summarized as *culpa*, defect) in nature as well as human life. Among the latter are ferocious animals hostile to man (218ff., see Acher's snake) and untimely death (221). Lactantius whose knowledge of Epicurus and Lucretius was most impressive —having once been a professional rhetor and possibly an Epicurean himself—[99] describes in a detailed passage the suffering of the righteous and the prospering of the impious as Epicurus supposedly observed it. According to Lactantius it led Epicurus to this denial of providence, especially when he saw that even the very temples of the gods were destroyed by lightning.[100] The latter is, indeed, an Epicurean motif,[101] and Lactantius may here be correct in his analysis and not have recast Epicurus in a Judeo-Christian mold.[102] The Epicureans did have several other motivations and philosophical bases for their denial of providence apart from their fight against fear.

Thus, since much of the Epicurean impetus was stimulated by and aimed at the Stoics, the Epicureans were pratically obliged to denounce "that old hag Providence (*pronoia*)" of the Stoics on these grounds alone. There was, furthermore, the well-attested Epicurean argument that divine providence would imply the ire of the deity, an affect unworthy of the gods.[103] Important also was an ethical consideration connected with the concept of the ideal *Sophos*. The Epicurean in Cicero's *de natura deorum* I. ix. 23 asserts that "there are so many great inconveniences in life that, although sages can alleviate them through the compensation of the conveniences, fools can neither shun the future ones nor bear the ones that are present".[104] This reflects Epicurus' teaching that the Sage does not expect any recompense; his reward is his insight, his truer way of life, and his peace of mind. The Sage "deems it better to experience misfortune with rational insight than fortune without it."[105] Epicurean preoccupation with the blows of fortune is also indicated in the famous reasoning on the relation of the divine to the evils, which in form and content seems to be by Epicurus himself[106]: "The Deity either wants to remove the evils and cannot, or can and does not want to, or does not want to nor can, or can and wants to",[107] which would make the Deity variously feeble (*imbecillis*), envious (*invidus*), envious as well as feeble, and, in the last instance, evoke the question "wherefrom do then the evils come and why does he not remove them?"[108]

That it was known that the Epicureans fought the idea of Providence not only in order to ban fear but also as a consequence of their observations of human fate, i.e., perceiving the lack of a compensatory justice, is also attested by one of Plutarch's most famous treatises: *de sera numinis vindicta* (*On the Delay of Divine Vengeance*, Mor. 548 B - 568). As the title indicates, the theme of this treatise is one of the specific objections of the Epicureans: the delay of punishment, considered beneficial and purposeful by the defenders of Providence but useless, harmful, or even non-existent by the Epicureans.

The discussion of Plutarch, his brother, his son-in-law and one Olympichus is triggered off by an attack against the doctrine of Providence on the part of an Epicurean who had left the gathering abruptly.[109] Some of the interlocutors add to the argument against Providence. Whether these arguments are made on the spur of the moment or whether they represent stereotyped Epicurean criticism or, perhaps, skeptical-academic propositions (of the New Academy) is difficult to determine.[110] Plutarch solves the dilemma by his belief in the immortality of the soul and punishment after death (560 A ff.), a solution preferred, independently, also in the talmudic world.

The Epicurean was thus a formidable opponent who had given much thought to a general problem of humanity, and the Greco-Roman Epicurean model of our *sententia* was an effective formulation of the position of the Epicurean School. That the *sententia* (γνώμη) in general had become increasingly academized and "lionized" in the time of the early Empire is clear from its intensive and clever use in the "declamation", especially the advanced *controversia*, as the collection of Seneca the Elder, and his own criticism of the over-use of *sententiae*, demonstrate (*c.* 55 B.C. - 37/41 A.D.).[111] The *progymnasmata* and related works, widely used as guides and patterns for the rhetoricians, were at the height of their importance in this period. Popular examples are the works of Lupus Rutilius (1st ct. A.D.), Theon, (Ps.- ?) Hermogenes (both 2nd ct.), and Aphthonius (*fl. c.* 400). The latter three treated the use and importance of the *sententia* in detail.

Epicurus' denial of Providence and the impiety accusation are the themes of declamations of the *suasoria* type in the rhetorical exercises of the time, as they are reflected in the later collection of Himerius.[112]

Such a coinage as ours, epitomizing Epicureanism in the literary form of the *sententia*, was thus useful to the proponents of talmudic culture as a clear target in their own dogmatic struggles against indigenous Epicureanism, just as it was for patristic culture. In this struggle the Talmudists chose to deal only with those aspects of Epicureanism that were well-known and represented a particular threat to their way of life, making this selection perhaps without knowing (or evaluating) the entire system. This is true, however, also of the Greco-Roman anti-Epicurean rhetoricians.[113]

It is intriguing to speculate why so little biblical material was used to formulate this polemical struggle. From the period of the Sumerian Job to that of his latterday Hebrew embodiment, and beyond, canonical books of wisdom had complained about the injustice of fortune and had frequently found a solution to this dilemma; and hedonism, in one form or another, was known not only in the West. We must thus assume that the Greco-Roman pattern of polemic was felt to have been at least equally adequate. Epicureanism was, furthermore, the slogan of a contemporary way of life and had to be fought as such by attacking its original formulation in its very impressiveness. Here, as so often elsewhere [114] the talmudic sages seem to have had an opportunity for applying their technical-rhetorical equipment which they shared with their Greco-Roman colleagues as representatives of a similarly structured scholar-bureaucracy and for which there was apparently a ready and understanding audience.

PART THREE

THE MIDRASH OF BEN ZOMA AND BEN ZOMA IN THE MIDRASH

1. An Heurematological Oration

Ben Zoma (*fl. c.* 110 A.D.) is the reported author of a midrashic item in which Greco-Roman rhetorical material and formal treatment are strongly in evidence. This item is represented in only slightly differing versions in Tos. *Ber.*,[1] BT *Ber.* 58a, and JT *Ber.* 13c, IX. 2.[2] The version of BT *Ber.* reads as follows:[3]

1 ת״ר הרואה אוכלוסי ישראל אומר
2 ברוך חכם הרזים
3 שאין דעתם דומה זה לזה
4 ואין פרצופיהן דומים זה לזה
5 בן זומא ראה אוכלוסא
6 על גב מעלה בהר הבית
7 אמר ברוך חכם הרזים
8 וברוך שברא כל אלה לשמשני
9 הוא היה אומר
10 כמה יגיעות יגע אדם הראשון
11 עד שמצא פת לאכול
12 חרש וזרע וקצר ועמר ודש וזרה
13 וברר וטחן והרקיד ולש ואפה
14 ואחר כך אכל
15 ואני משכים ומוצא כל אלו מתוקנין לפני
16 וכמה יגיעות יגע אדם הראשון
17 עד שמצא בגד ללבוש
18 גזז ולבן ונפץ וטוח וארג
19 ואחר כך מצא בגד ללבוש
20 ואני משכים ומוצא כל אלו מתוקנין לפני
21 כל אומניות שוקדות ובאות לפתח ביתי
22 ואני משכים ומוצא כל אלו לפני

1 Our Rabbis taught:[4] He who sees crowds of Israel(ites)[5] says
2 "Blessed be the Discerner of Secrets",

3   for the mind of each is unlike the other
4   and their features (or personalities) are unlike one another.
5   Ben Zoma saw (once)[6] a crowd
6   on a terrace of the Temple Mount.[7]
7   Said he: "Blessed be the Discerner of Secrets,[8]
8   Blessed be Who created all these to serve me".
9   (for ?) he used to say (for he once had said) :[9]
10 "How many labors labored Adam (or early Man)
11 until he found his bread to eat:
12 he ploughed and sowed and harvested and sheaved and threshed and winnowed
13 and assorted (the ears) and ground and sifted (the flour) and kneaded and baked [10]
14 and (only) after (all) this he ate.
15 But I rise [11] and find all these prepared before me.
16 And how many labors labored Adam (or early Man)
17 until he found a garment to put on:
18 he sheared and cleaned (the wool) and combed and spun and wove [12]
19 and (only) after (all) this he found a garment to put on.
20 But I rise and find all these prepared before me.
21 Many crafts(men) [13] rise early and come to the door of my house,
22 and I rise and find all these (things) before me.[11]

It is evident that b. Zoma's composition is designed to express gratitude for the progress of civilization within and through a multi-talented society and the ensuing division of labor which brings benefits to the individual, especially the Sage.

The history and evaluation of civilization is, of course, one of the great continuous themes of Greco-Roman literature, and of its myth, philosophy, historiography, and scientific inquiry alike. It comprises a great many, often contradictory, approaches and views, and found its expression in a number of literary genres. Those who made important contributions to this theme, or preserved significant material for posterity, are among the decisive names of the ancient world: Hesiod (*c.* 700 B.C., but not Homer); Xenophanes (*c.* 580 - *c.* 478); Anaxagoras (*c.* 500 - *c.* 428) and his pupil Archelaus; Aeschylus (525/24-456); Sophocles (*c.* 496-406); Euripides (485 ?-406 ?; Empedocles (*c.* 493 - *c.* 433); possibly Leucippus (*fl. c.* 440); Democritus (*c.* 460-370); Diogenes of Apollonia (*fl. c.* 435); the Sophists Protagoras (after 485 - *c.*

415), Gorgias (483-376), Hippias (*c.* 481-411), Antiphon (*c.* 480-411), Critias (*c.* 460-403), and Prodicus (*fl. c.* 435); Herodotus (*c.* 485-425); Thucydides (*c.* 460/55 - *c.* 400); Isocrates (436-338); Plato (*c.* 429-347); Xenophon (*c.* 430-354); Aristotle (384-322); Moschion (4th ct.); Theophrastus (372/69-288/285); Dicaearchus (contemporary of the former, influenced Josephus); Euhemerus (*fl. c.* 300); Epicurus (342/41-271-70) and his disciple Hermarchus (*c.* 325 - *c.* 250); Hecataeus of Abdera (*c.* 300); Zeno the Stoic (335-262); Hermippus (*fl.* 3rd ct.); Aratus (271-213); Polybius (*c.* 203 ?-120); Posidonius (after 135 - *c.* 50); Varro (116-27); Lucretius (*c.* 94-55); Cicero (106-43); Diodorus (Siculus, *fl. c.* 60 - *c.* 20 B.C.); Vergil (70-19 B.C.); Vitruvius (architect, under Augustus who reigned 27 B.C. - 14 A.D.); Philo Judaeus (of Alexandria, *c.* 30 B.C. - *c.* 45 A.D.); Manilius (*fl. c.* 10 B.C. - 10 A.D.); Seneca (*c.* 5 B.C. - 65 A.D., many of his letters epicureanize); Pliny the Elder (23/24-79 A.D.); Musonius Rufus (before 30 - *c.* 101/02); Dio of Prusa (Chrysostom, *c.* 40 - after 112); Plutarch (*c.* 46-120); Philo of Byblos (64-161); Diogenes of Oenoanda (*fl. c.* 150 or 200, Epicurean); Athenaeus (*fl. c.* 200); Aelianus (*c.* 170-235); Diogenes Laertitus (*fl. c.* 250); and Porphyry (232/3 - *c.* 305).[14]

The Old Comedy (5th-4th cts., so Pherecrates and Aristophanes) had already poked fun at anthropological theories and the New Comedy (4th ct., so Philemon the Elder) and later specimen (Athenion) followed suit.[15] Athenaeus, in his *Deipnosophistae*,[16] felt urged to offer a parody of the catalogues of inventors which had multiplied with the increasing interest in heurematology, i.e., the inquiry into the inventors of the basics of civilization.[17]

This formidable galaxy is continued by the Church Fathers, among them Lactantius (*c.* 300), Eusebius (*c.*300), and Augustine (354-430), and by medieval antiquarians who still preserved important ancient materials, as, e.g., Tzetzes (12th ct.).[18]

In welcoming the progress of civilization, the b. Zoma passage parallels that trend of Greco-Roman tradition which likewise endorses the achievements of man and/or expresses gratitude for the civilizing gifts (or stolen properties) of the gods. This feeling of achievement and the confident mood, however, quite prevalent among the educated of the Hellenistic-Roman Age,[19] was counterbalanced by a nostalgia for less complex times and a lost Golden Age, a mood which in its extreme expression was tantamount to the proposition that civlization had steadily declined and degenerated, or was an evil to begin with.[20]

Finally, systems, or *ad hoc* formulations, which combined both evaluations emerged, the most influential being that of the Stoic Posidonius, which asserted man's technical ascent but moral decline. The notes of triumph of the Epicurean Lucretius are tinged with spells of cynicizing pessimism and Seneca makes a somewhat artificial attempt in his 90th Epistle to praise his privileged status but condemn the complexities of culture which made his leisure possible.

A survey of some Greco-Roman treatments of the history of civilization, especially —but not exclusively— those which endorse progress, reveals remarkable parallels to b. Zoma's composition. Such a related treatment —a syndrome of philosophumena, moods, literary motifs, and motemes (i.e., the smallest meaningful units, such as keywords, symbols, and similes)— is, e.g., found in Plato's *Republic*, especially in 369c ff.[21]

1. In this work necessity as the creator of a division of labor and the need to *serve* and *benefit* one another are stressed throughout [22] (cf. b. Zoma's "to serve me"). In 372a the ideal social order is visualized and summarized: the craftsmen will make *bread and wine* (cf.b.Zoma's symbol for all food: bread) and *garments and shoes* (cf. b. Zoma's "garment"). A further amplification of the theme introduces "they will provide *meal and flour*", and "*kneading and cooking* these..." will finally produce "cakes and loaves" (cf. b. Zoma's specifications).

In 374d-e it becomes clear that this division of labor requires more leisure for the task of the "guardians" (Sage-philosopher-statesmen) than for all other crafts and endeavors.[23] This seems to be the meaning also of b. Zoma's proud deliberations: the various craftsmen "serve me".[24] The division of labor must create the necessary condition for the free exercise of the highest "craft" of the Sage.[25] The talmudic passage does thus not imply a preoccupation with one's self and an egocentric utilitarianism, as b. Zoma's utterance has been misread by critics of the Talmud [26] but an alignment with this Sage-ideology eminent in both cultures. To be sure, this division of labor has an enlightened self-interest at its base but the existence of the Sage, and of all other crafts and professions, makes possible an interchange of "give... and take",[27] and thus guarantees the ideal order of the state.

Both the *Republic* and b. Zoma's oration require the differences of human dispositions, according to Nature [28] and according to Creation, resp., as a basis for their demonstrations of a just practical order.

In b. Zoma's passage the impression of a somewhat foreign element in the strong stress on the full division of labor is inescapable, since it is a teaching that did not become generally accepted in talmudic culture.

Rather, the talmudic Sage was supposed (or forced by circumstances) to acquire an actual handicraft himself beside the "craft" of the Sage, a situation which approximates the Greco-Roman cynicizing ideal of the Sage who does manual (if not menial) labor or possesses a handicraft.[29]

The anonymous halakhic preamble which makes a blessing of crowds obligatory (lines 1-2) includes b. Zoma's formulation "Blessed be the Discerner of Secrets" as well as reminiscences of another source —see note 32— and is thus later than b. Zoma's oration, and perhaps created in the wake of Meir's effort (a generation later) to increase blessings even to one hundred a day.[30] In this undertaking, incidents and coinages of tannaitic Sage stories may have become the bases of permanent benedictions.[31] The blessing in b. Zoma's oration (lines 7-8), however, is original and, as we shall see, part of the total profile of the Greco-Roman pattern.[32]

Plato designed similar sketches of the ideal human society in two other dialogues: the *Gorgias* and the *Protagoras*.

2. In the *Gorgias* Socrates thus briefly distinguishes a class of crafts which is menial and provides

> "*Food*..., drink, ... *clothing*, bedding, shoes, or anything else which our bodies require..." (517d).

Among the purveyors of these things are

> "... *baker* or cook or *weaver* or cobbler or tanner... who are *servants* to the body",[33]

and, being "servile and menial and non-liberal in their care of the body" (518), have to be governed by the (higher) arts of gymnastics and medicine which will employ their products (517e). Obviously, keywords similar to b. Zoma's prevail throughout : *food, clothing, baker, weaver, to serve*; and a syndetic enumeration, in this instance of crafts, is found in the middle of the harangue.[34]

3. The use of the Prometheus-Epimetheus myth makes Plato's *Protagoras* [35] somewhat different from the two previous dialogues. Still, the keywords and the division of labor remain. Prometheus endowed the first men with the skills of the arts (and the use of fire, 321d, thus creating the division of labor, 322c-d), and they, in turn, soon invented houses,

> and *clothes* and shoes and bedding, and obtained *food* from the soil (322a).

Yet it was the deity, Zeus, who had to interfere and create society through the appointment of Hermes who thus saved a scattered mankind. Thus both, society and division of labor, are ultimately of divine origin, as in b. Zoma's Midrash.

4. Another such influential treatment of our theme is found in Lucretius' fifth book of *de rerum natura*, a syncrisis of the primitive and the advanced ages in human civilization. Of particular interest here are the concluding passages 1350-1457. The section on the gradual improvement of the textile and *garment* production, 1350-1360, is followed by that on *cultivation*, 1361-1378, yet when Lucretius has to summarize these developments [36] the order is reversed and resembles b. Zoma's:

Man grew tired of primitive *food* (acorns), rejected a bedding of herbage and leaves, and came to despise his aboriginal *dress* of pelts (1416-1418). The section on the individual stages of the preparation of garments (1350-1360) mentions in rapid enumeration

> treadles, spindles. shuttles, and beams:
> insilia ac fusi radii scapique... (1353).

Apparently, an enumeration of this sort has now become a requirement in such items. Early man is also with Lucretius the weaver (cf. Adam's activities), the division of labor in weaving involving woman, having occurred only subsequently (1355f.).

A similar enumeration, yet alleviated by a continuous alternation of active and passive verbs and grammatical subject, mainly for the sake of poetical form, is discernible in the section on cultivation. Still, a rapid sequence of themes emerges:

sowing, grafting, planting, cultivating, improving, tilling, and, as nouns (and results):

> tilled lowlands, meadows, pools, streams, crops, vineyards, olive trees, orchards, ornamentals (1361-1378).

The book concludes with yet another enumeration of cultural achievements, this time quite simple:

1448 Navigia atque agri culturas	Seafaring vessels and agriculture,
moenia leges arma vias vestes (*asyndeton*)	ramparts, laws, arms, roads, clothing,
et cetera de genere horum,	and all the rest of this sort.

The acme of achievement is here also the present (or a level continued in the present), a view not unexpected with one of the foremost representatives of Epicureanism:

> ... ad summum donec venere cacumen,
> ... until they reached their loftiest height (1457).[37]

This positive if not triumphant note is also palpable (perhaps less boastful) in b. Zoma's concluding lines.

5. Plato's endorsement of a structured society had to be reversed by Seneca once he assumed the pose of rejecting progress in a cynicizing fashion in his famous 90th *Epistle*.[38] It represents an attempt to disprove Posidonius' contention that the Sage (or philosophy) created the inventions and crafts of man.[39] To Seneca society is merely and unnecessarily kept busy —and noisy— "through all these crafts,,"[40] In attacking Posidonius Seneca mentions that the former gave a detailed description of weaving (90.20), and in Seneca's report this represents again such an enumeration (catalogue, list) of activities (which may have appeared in this form already in Posidonius' work):

... first, threads are twisted..., etc.,
next, the threads are stretched..., etc.,
then, thread is ... united with warp.[41]

Apparently Posidonius then proceeded to design a similar but much longer list on the farmer-miller-baker (cf. b. Zoma). Seneca merely mentions

ploughing, sowing, weeding (19.21)

and immediately proceeds to the milling (22) which involves

rubbing and crushing, followed by
sprinkling, kneading, molding, baking.[42]

According to Seneca, Posidonius further claimed [43] that the *sapiens* was responsible for all inventions (31).[44] Seneca, however, indignantly rejects this claim. It is not the task of wisdom and philosophy to bother with petty and ridiculous luxuries and contraptions (7-10, a famous cynicizing passage). A lower form of intelligence is reponsible for the inventions. Even if the Sage (not qua Sage but as an artisan) invented some of these things, he handed them soon enough over to more menial ministrants (*sordidioribus ministris*, 25, recalling b. Zoma's "to serve me"). This then is the division of labor which works for the *otium* (leisure) of the Sage, enabling him to deal with his own task (Nature, Truth, Virtue) to which all other tasks are merely ancillary. With this very last point b. Zoma would agree, but his initial blessings show him to be more positively inclined toward the tasks of the artisans.

6. The enumeration is found also with an earlier all important representative of rhetorical literature, i.e., Cicero, in his passage on human helpfulness in *de officiis*, II. iii. 11ff., where we hear that without

manus et ars, i.e., the use of the human hand and technology, there would be

> no health care, no navigation, no agriculture, no harvesting, no storage of fruits and produce, etc.

As protection from the rigors of the cold Cicero mentions housing rather than clothes (13). This list is finally concluded by the introduction of the *vita communis* (iv. 13f.).

Significantly, a summary of the contribution of the arts (*technology*) to the worthwhileness of life (iv. 15) uses successive rhetorical exclamations: "what pleasures... what comforts...," etc., and must be compared with b. Zoma's similar device: "how many labors......," lines 10 and 16, *supra*.

Cicero's discourse culminates in a statement on the division of labor: in giving and receiving, *dando et accipiendo*, through mutual exchange of commodities and conveniences [45] we lack nothing, anticipated in the famous formulation *homines hominibus maxime utiles esse possunt*, "men, to men, can be most useful" (ii. 11), and followed by the demand that man should gain the other's favor and attach him to his *service(s)*, *ad usus suos adiungere* (v. 17).[46] In others words, the לשמשני-motif of b. Zoma seems to be a reflection of sketches of this type. True, in Cicero's discourse there is no express mention of primitive man, but the achievements of civilization are projected against a virtual primeval starting point. Finally, the existence of individual gifts and talents in people for the performing of the different tasks of society had been mentioned earlier in Cicero's work: I. 98, 107f., 113.[47]

7. In *de esu carmium* I. ii (*Moralia* 993A f.), an effective pro-vegetarian tract, Plutarch makes an imaginary chorus of early men address his own carniverous contemporaries:[48]

> *O blessed ones* and *god-beloved*, you who are living now, upon *what* eon of life have you chanced, you who reap and enjoy a bounteous heritage of *good things*! (Cf. b. Zoma's lines 15 and 22.) *What* abundant vegetation (is there) for you; *what* vintage you reap; *what* wealth from (the) fields; *what* pleasures may you gather from (the) trees! [49]

Here we have not only some of the ingredients of our syndrome but parallels of literary devices to boot: the macarismus, i.e., the encomiastic benediction-like exclamation, the *Seligpreisung* (beginning with μακάριοι), extended by a synonymous parallel (*theophileis*, "god-beloved", cf. the twofold "blessed" of b. Zoma),[49] and five rhetorical exclamations (οἷον, ὅσα [twice] ὅσον, ὅσας). B. Zoma uses two such exclamations, lines 10 and 16 (כמה, וכמה) but in the second part of his oration, on the grateful and the ungrateful guest, he uses four (to be discussed, *infra*).

The catalogue-enumeration is not too well represented in Plutarch's item. The mention of the diet of primitive man is closest: mud, bark, grass, root(s), acorns (993E), but this enumeration is attenuated by the use of several connecting verbs.

8. Plutarch's macarismus suggests that this rhetorical-emotive device may be an older optional component of the syndrome. Indeed, in the *Plutus* (383 B.C.) of Aristophanes, 160ff., Chremylus praises *Plutos* (Wealth) in a left-handed, witty encomiastic formula:

... and all arts (τέχναι) because of thee [50] and (all wise) crafts (σοφίσματα) among men were invented.[51]

This is followed by an enumeration which lists various occupations (the "division of labor" theme):

This one (ὁ μὲν) sits and cobbles (162), another works in bronze (163),

to be followed, in turn, by nine asyndetic ὁ δὲ, "that one" (works in wood, in gold, waylays, burgles, fulls <cloth>, washes skins, tans, sells onions, commits adultery !).

Later on, in a syncrisis, *Penia* (-Poverty) demonstrates that without her no one would work, since *technē* and *sophia* would depart: "Who would work in bronze", etc., and, inevitably, eight other occupations follow, all introduced by ἤ, "or" (506ff.). In another such catalogue, 535ff., in which products are listed, the *garment* is mentioned among many others (ἱματίου... 540), products of the *baker* and tools for *kneading* (543f.). The *ploughman* had been mentioned earlier in 514.[52]

In 517ff. the thought is expressed that all these strenuous (and often smelly) taks could be performed by servants (θεράποντες) but Poverty has to remind Chremylus that without her there would be no such thing. Although quite different in detail, the Greek equivalent of the Hebrew moteme לשמשני, "to serve me", is here apparent.

This lavish syncrisis which implicitly projects primitive life against civilization is, apart from social satire, apparently also a parody on such philosophical reflections on civilization and on the related heurematology.[53]

9. Another fairly complete syndrome includes a startling detail

that also occurs with b. Zoma. Cicero's *Tusculan Disputations*, I. xxv. 61f., represents another sketch of the achievements of civilization, in which a discussant called M by Cicero explores the properties of memory.[54] He begins:

> What then is that power which *investigates* (traces, tracks out) *secrets* (illa vis... quae investigat occulta) which is (also) called invention (or inventiveness) and (creative ?) thinking (quae inventio atque cogitatio dicitur) ?

The formula "investigates secrets" is reasonably close to b. Zoma's חכם הרזים "Discerner of Secrets", especially in view of the fact that חכם frequently means "to be skilful, expert". In either oration the topics of early man, inventions, and areas of human enterprise follow, and in either case they are declared to be the creations of the Deity (63 end).[55] The macarismus as well as the rhetorical question may introduce a subject that is to be praised.

M. continues to speak of earth-derived man who achieved the naming of things (61/62),[56] gathered the scattered to institute society,[57] invented writing, and discovered astronomy (62). Great were also those who had *still earlier* discovered

> *fruits, raiment*, dwellings, and ordered life,[58] strongholds against the beasts (*qui* fruges, *qui* vestitum, *qui* tecta, *qui* cultum vitae, *qui* praesidia contra feras invenerunt, 62).

He thus distinguishes two levels of achievement, and mankind passed *a necessariis artificiis ad elegantiora*, from the indispensable crafts to the higher arts (*ibid.*). B. Zoma's composition likewise distinguishes similar levels, and similarly uses the asyndetic enumeration to dramatize the second level. Cicero's sequence closes with the brief encomium of Archimedes and his divine genius (63).[59]

If, indeed, b. Zoma's חכם הרזים, "Discerner of Secrets", is connected with Cicero's thought (or a later form of it), the Hebrew formula may have originally meant (rendered paraphrastically) "Blessed (Who creates) the investigator of the secrets (of Creation; i.e., the inventor)". It would thus be a benediction on the usefulness of inventions rather than a benediction on the variety of human disposition, but both would lead to the division of labor.

It thus seems that the over-all scheme that underlies b. Zoma's composition had been well established in Greco-Roman rhetoric for at least 150 years (Cicero) before the *floruit* of b. Zoma, but was still fully active and ever enriched from that time on to his own days (Plutarch).

The major contributors to this *topos*, however, did not limit themselves to complete sketches. In addition, they frequently alluded to the *topos* in their works. Other writers and orators, too, referred to it or used it briefly without contributing a full version of their own. From these partial and fragmentary treatments some further comparative detail can be gained for the understanding of b. Zoma's item.

1. The view that primitive man possessed already all crafts [60] is opposed by another conception of classical tradition, i.e., that he was originally devoid of all skill and experience and in a state of misery,[61] or, owing to a Golden Age, was amply supplied with everything, or, although primitive, was entirely without want.[62] B. Zoma must thus have met that tradition according to which early man possessed the knowledge of the basic crafts but without the division of labor. How Adam acquired these skills —"little by little", through experience, as with Diodorus, I. viii. 7, or through need and necessity as with the Epicureans— is not mentioned and also of no import in understanding the item.[63] B. Zoma, however, may have believed with the Stoics in the inventiveness of the Sage, Adam himself having been a "Sage", since we do have midrashic materials for this possibility.[64]

2. Other such briefer Greco-Roman items illuminate the theme לשמשני "to serve me", i.e., the idea that the craftsmen, the *fabri*, through the division of labor, make the highest "craft", that of the Sage, possible. The Sage, in turn, can and must utilize this division of labor.

As we have seen the idea of service was ubiquitous in the Hellenistic-Roman Age. Thus Seneca, *de otio* III, writes:

> It is, of course, required of man that he should further (be useful to, benefit) (other) men; if it can be done, many; if not, few. (*Hoc nempe ab homine exigitur ut prosit hominibus, si fieri potest, multis, si minus, paucis.*)

Quite famous is Pliny's formulation, possibly from a Stoic source, *nat. hist.* II. v. 18f.:

> deus est mortali invare mortalem,
> god(like) is for man to serve man.[65]

Diodorus, in introducing his sketch of social evolution, I. 1, appeals to mankind to be grateful to the "universal" historians, "for by their individual labors (efforts) they endeavored to help 'universal' life."[66] We cannot be overly astonished to find in the final stages of this development almost the words of b. Zoma, uttered by Seneca in one of his *Epistles*, LXIV. 7 :

> veneror itaque inventa sapientiae inventoresque, adire tamquam multorum hereditatem iuvat. *Mihi ista adquisita, mihi laborata sunt*: I *venerate* therefore the inventions of wisdom and the inventors; it is *gratifying* to take possession of the heritage *of many*, so to speak. (All) *this (pl.) is increased (procured) for me*, (all) this (pl.) is *labored for me*.

This must be compared with b. Zoma's line 8 : "Blessed be Who created all these to serve me".[67] Both are grateful and appropriate the achievements of former generations that had created the condition for the situation of the contemporary Sage.[68] Nevertheless, there is a cleavage between the non-liberal occupations and that of the Sage, the distinction being quite pronounced with Seneca. In *Ep.* 88.21ff., quoting an uncertain work of Posidonius, he specifies the four classes of skills (*genera artium*):

1. *volgares, sordidae*,[69] referring to the workmen who maintain life;
2. *ludicrae*,[69] referring to the entertainers who cater to the "voluptuousness"[69] of eyes and ears;[70]
3. *pueriles*: referring to the educators of boys who transmit the ἐγκυκλίους (*sic*) or liberal arts;
4. *liberales*, referring to the truly liberal, *liberae* (free), who are concerned with virtue.[71]

With b. Zoma there is merely the mention of the division of labor which he gratefully endorses but no other express value judgment. Nevertheless, this fact should not be overstated, and the keyword "serve me" may quite well indicate the central position of the Sage in society rather than the satisfaction of a private individual who enjoys advanced technical comforts.

3. As shown previously, the mention of the farmer-miller-baker and weaver-fuller-tailor as demonstration models of the progress of civilization is well established as a permanent feature for this literary

topos. A few shorter Greco-Roman items shed some further light on this stereotype.

The author of the (ps.-Platonic) *Epinomis*, 974d ff., mentions the *preparation of flour* (and all of agriculture) and also, among other things, *weaving*, as the foremost necessities of life. To Diodorus, I. viii., the first men lacked, among other things, *clothing* and *food*.[72]

Our two crafts are connected also in a long and steady tradition which describes their possible decadence through their misuse for debilitating pleasure and senseless artificiality. Plato already referred in a whimsical way to cookery that makes excessive claims (*Gorgias* 464d, cf. 462d-e) and to Thearion the Baker and Mithaecus who wrote a Sicilian cookbook and provided dainties (*ibid.*, 518b). Poverty's mention of fancy *raiment* is, of course, incisively satirical in the *Plutus*, 530, but the reference to *ploughing*, 525, is merely sarcastic. Critical views of the excesses of both crafts appear with the near-contemporaries Philo and Seneca. The former speaks in one breath of the chefs-confectioners and the dye- and perfume makers [73] of his day who debilitate the mind with their modish novelties (*de plant.* 159); the latter of the superfluousness of silk *fabric* and the *cook* (and soldier, *Ep.* 90.15), and of materialism as the creator of the workshop of the *weavers* (and the carpenters), the savory smells of the professional *cooks* (and of elocution and entertainment, 90.19)

4. A further indication that the syndrome "individual natures/ division of labor/divine sponsorship/progress" was still active close to the tannaitic period is demonstrated by a twelve line passage in Grat(t)ius Faliscus, *Cynegeticon* 2-12.[74] After the mention of primitive man, we find

> *ex artibus artis proserere* (8/9), from arts to plant the seed for (further) arts,
> *primum auspicium deus artibus... dedit* (10/11), Deity gave the first sponsorship to the arts,
> *tum partis quisque secutus exegere suas tetigitque industria finem* (11/12), then every man sought and adopted his (own proper) parts (tasks) and Industry reached its goal.

A profile of this *topos* drawn from its major literary formulations with its syndrome of motifs (themes), literary forms, and keywords (omitting shades of opinion and detail) would have to show these ingredients:

I Motifs (Themes) :[75]

1. The predicament of early man.
2. Endorsement of civilizationary progress.
3. Individual talents created by higher power.
4. Individual talents the basis of division of labor.
5. Division of labor the basis of functioning society.
6. Division of labor the basis of Sage's leisure.
7. Sage's craft the highest.
8. The Sage's gratitude.

II Literary Forms and Devices :

1. Introductory laudatory formula.
2. Enumerations of technical processes or crafts.
3. Syncrisis (of two stages of civilization).
4. Concluding laudatory formula.

III Keywords :

1. Praised..., how great..., how many...
2. Early Man.
3. Natures, minds, many.
4. Farmer-miller-baker / weaver-fuller-clothier.
5. To serve, service, benefit.
6. For me (or "leisure").

The ubiquity of the *topos* in philosophy and the literary sources must have been paralleled in oral popular rhetoric.[76] Being thus represented with the professional-administrational classes, in formal education, and with the wandering popularizers, it must have easily reached the Near East, the latter having been a political dependency of the West for four centuries at the time of b. Zoma. The connection of the *topos* with the *sophos*-ideology was probably an effective catalyst for its adoption in the Judaic culture.

Ben Zoma's speculation on Adam and the history of civilization is not an isolated case. To be sure the view of Rab (Abba Areka, 160/175-247),[77] that Adam taught the crafts to all mankind, may be somehow connected with b. Zoma's passage,[78] but his view in BT *Sanhedrin* 59b that Adam was a vegetarian, may possibly reflect Greco-Roman traditions regarding the vegetarianism of the first men.[79]

In another well-known passage [80] Adam's horror at the first experience of the shortening days before the solstice resembles a Greco-Roman motif on early man which is alluded to in Lucretius' work, V. 975f.; Manilius, *Astronomicon* I. 66; Statius, *Thebais*, IV. 282; and Dio, *Orat.* XII (Olympic), 28ff., esp. 32.[81] A generation after b. Zoma, Jose b. Ḥalafta expresses the idea that Adam possessed דעה, intelligence in "the pattern of the Deity", דוגמה של מעלה and thus discovered the fire and introduced the mule into human civilization.[82] Adam is here again a Sage in the midrashic tradition but apparently not unaffected by the Posidonian Sage who is also equipped with special *sophia*-sapientia [83] and thus responsible for the basic inventions of mankind. As pointed out before, an adaptation of Greco-Roman heurematology to Hebraic settings was probably facilitated by the precedent of Adam's naming of the animals in Genesis.[84]

To be sure, the possibility exists that this theme of Adam the Inventor is older than b. Zoma.[85] This, however, would not affect the contention that b. Zoma's is basically a Greco-Roman oration, both in sentiment and technical detail. A development parallel to this combination of biblical beliefs and Greco-Roman ideas of early civilization took place also in patristic thought, thus further illuminating the midrashic phenomenon.[86]

2. An Oration on Table Manners and Gratitude

In all sources b. Zoma's composition on the progress of civilization is immediately followed by another item of his which appears to be similarly related to Greco-Roman rhetoric. In this case much less ground has to be covered in order to demonstrate this relationship.

The text reproduced here is composite in that JT is reproduced because it reflects more closely the order and form of the presumed Greco-Roman pattern, but some lines of the Tos. are chosen (A-C) because they preserve richer detail, likewise closer to the pattern. In any case, the differences between the three versions are quite minimal.

1 וכן היה בן זומא אומר
2 אורח רע מהו אומר
3 וכי מה אכלתי משל בעל הבית
4 וכי מה שתיתי משל בעל הבית
5 חתיחה אחת אכלתי לו
6 כוס יין שתיתי לו

7 וכל טורח שטרח
8 לא טרח אלא בשביל אשתו ובניו
9 אבל אורח טוב אומר
10 ברוך בעל הבית
11 זכור בעל הבית לטובה
A כמה מיני יינות הביא לפני
B כמה מיני חתיחות הביא לפני
C כמה מיני גלוסקאות הביא לפני
12 כמה טורח טרה לפני
13 כל מה שטרח
14 לא טרח אלא בשבילי
16 זכור כי תשגיא פעלו
17 אשר שוררו אנשים

1 And b. Zoma had also once said:[87]
2 "What does a bad guest say?
3 'What then have I (really) eaten of the host's?'
4 'What then have I (really) drunk of the host's?'
5 'One slice (of meat) I ate of his!'
6 'A cup of wine I drank of his!'
7 'And all the trouble he inflicted (on himself)
8 he only inflicted for his wife's and his children's sake!'
9 But the good guest says:
10 'Praised be the host!'
11 'Remembered be the host for good!'
A 'How many kinds of wine did he bring before me!'
B 'How many kinds of cut (meat) did he bring before me!
C 'How many kinds of fine bread did he bring before me!'
12 'How much trouble did he take before me!'
13 'Whatever trouble he took,
14 he took only for my sake!' "
15 And Scripture thus says:
16 "Remember that you extol his deed
17 of which men (will) sing" (Job 36:24).[88]

The passages which directly or indirectly seem to have been the pattern for this item are found in Seneca's famous treatise on the spirit of giving and of beneficial deeds, *de beneficiis*, which includes a treatment of the subject of gratitude as incumbent upon and characteristic of the Sage (cf. *Ep.* 81.13ff.). The subjects of beneficial deeds and gratitude loom large in Greco-Roman culture, especially with Stoics and Epicureans, and are reinforced by the great role of friendship in Greco-Roman mores and thought. This entire area of inquiry partially reflects the all-important economic relationship of client and patron of late Republican and early Imperial Roman times. The significance of these themes in the Augustan period and beyond[89] is underlined by the prominence of the parasite and the glutton as well as the vulgar "maecenas" in satire, comedy, and mime.

The special attraction of such themes to talmudic culture with its strong interest in "manners" and considerate behavior (*derekh 'ereṣ*) must have been in part their connection with the Sage who in Seneca's curiously "paradoxical"[90] formulation is the only one "who knows how to repay gratitude (or return a favor)".[91]

Among the pattern passages for b. Zoma's item seems to have been *de beneficiis* I. xiv. 1. Here Seneca complains that "whoever gives a benefit (in this case a dinner invitation to his friends) is thanked by no one".[92] If this be at a public occasion, e.g., a convivium, the guest may well say

1. What favor then has he bestowed upon me?
2. One he bestowed also on that one hardly known to him over there!
   and on that one over there, a hostile and abominable one!
3. Did he at all consider me worthy of it?
4. In his sickness he was obsequious to his custom![93]

The bad guest, minimizing in detail the circumstances of the occasion, implies the host's motive to be selfishness (as also b. Zoma).

The reversal of the theme immediately follows, in xiv. 2. After a brief transition in which Seneca reminds the host to make such an occasion "personal", he makes the good guest say

1. I have received [94] the same as that one over there, but spontaneously!
2. I have received [94] what that one over there long deserved.
3. There are some who have the same thing but not given with the same words, not with the same graciousness of the giver.
4. That one received [94] as he asked; I did not ask.
5. That one received [94] being easily capable of repayment, even being promisingly old and wantonly childless; to me more was given, comparatively, because (it was given) without hope of reciprocity.

That this sequence is not a chance formulation but a rhetorical scheme which could be applied to other similar situations is shown by Seneca's employing it again in II. xxvi. 2ff., although in a somewhat wordier version. Here, Seneca is considering the causes of ingratitude (xxvi. 1). Among them is the exaggerated sense of one's own value (xxvi. 2). The recipient of a favor may easily say

1. This he has given me but how [95] late, but after how [95] many labors! [96]
2. How [95] much more could I have attained if I had chosen to cultivate X or Y, or myself! [97]
3. This [98] I did not expect. I have been thrown together with the multitude!
4. So little worthy he judged me?
5. (Concludingly) Better to have been passed up!

This item is not immediately reversed. After the intercalation of an historical example and further specifications of the causes of ingratitude (greed, ambition, jealousy) Seneca resorts briefly again to the same literary pattern (II. xxviii. 1):

This (*hoc*) he gave *to me* but to this fellow (*illi*) more, to that fellow (*illi*) earlier! [99]

The use of *hoc* and *ille* of the vocabulary of the earlier ungrateful recipient apparently serves here the function of evoking the earlier tirade and preparing the reversal,[100] after a brief appeal to leave jealousy alone.

II. xxviii. 2-4 represents the reversal:

1. *I should have received more* but *it was not easy for him to give more; his generosity* had to be divided among many.

Five other such "noble" sentiments follow, full of self-effacement, objectivity, and empathy with the host, some being exclamations, some rhetorical questions, some simple statement, all this resembling the form of b. Zoma's item.

The pattern which underlies both the Latin and the Hebrew versions is approximately the following:

The ungrateful guest-recipient
utters several complaints (use of *epanaphora*, of interrogatives and emphatics),

demeaning the banquet and intentions of the host-donor,
summarized in incisive negative value-judgments.

The contrasting *amplificatio*:

The good guest-recipient
utters the same number of (or slightly more) positive statements,
equally stereotyped,
(over-)evaluating and excusing the gift of the host-donor.

The stress on the personal ("me", "for me", etc.) is strong throughout as is, naturally, the use of the first person. The approximate quantitative balance between the positive and the negative statements, maintained by both Seneca and b. Zoma, follows a rhetorical rule of style (*parisōsis*).

The difference between the Greco-Roman and the Hebraic seems to be mainly one of atmosphere, i.e., of the cultural setting, rather than of ethics or metaphysics. The Greco-Roman mirrors clearly the patron/client relationship and public prestige factors as well as the strong competitiveness of upper Roman society whereas the Hebrew sources focus on the family and more modest circumstances. The victuals are simple and non-luxurious, representing the minimum of a festive meal (wine, fine breads, meat), but still generous.[101] Still, the difference of atmosphere should not conceal the fact that the principal social value and the literary form in both items are quite close to one another.

The question whether the unit on Adam and the item on the guest once formed one oration is no longer answerable. The presence of the theme of gratitude in both units is not decisive, since the redactory technique of the compilers of Mishnah, Tosephta, and the Talmudim consisted frequently in combining items on the grounds of keywords, preferably those occurring initially. In this case the pertinent keywords could have been טורח/יגיע ("trouble"), ברוך/ברוך ("blessed be", especially considering the subject of the tractate, i.e., *Berakhoth*, "Blessings"), possibly בשבילי/לשמשני ("me", "for me"). The sequence of the two items could therefore be the arrangement of the compiler. Yet, there is no clear criterion for a reliable decision.

The strong similarity between Seneca's twofold attempt and b. Zoma's item may indicate that the syncrisis of the good guest and his bad counterpart (or the parasite and the true client) was also a rhetorical school exercise for the practice of the rhetorician's eloquence and ingenuity. It surely must have been a popular *topos* for the statement of the practical ethics of the *sophos*-ideology, and probably a fairly standardized one as the comparatively close relationship of the talmudic item to the Greco-Roman pattern suggests.[102]

3. Stoic Paradoxa

Ben Zoma seems to have resorted to Greco-Roman rhetorical materials beyond the preceding two items. Thus, in *P.A.* 4.1 (4.1-4, Taylor) and its satellites *AdRN*, A, ch. 23 (p. 75f.), and B, ch. 33 (p. 72), b. Zoma seems to have used Stoic *paradoxa*:

1 איזהו חכם? הלומד מכל אדם ...
2 איזהו גבור? הכובש את יצרו ...
3 איזהו עשיר? השמח בחלקו ...
4 איזהו מכובד? המכבד את הבריות

1 Who is wise (or: a Sage)? Whoever learns from everyone.[103]
2 Who is strong (or: a hero)? Whoever conquers his impulse.[104]
3 Who is rich (or: a rich man)? Whoever rejoices (is satisfied) with his portion.
4 Who is honored (or: an honoree)? Whoever honors others (lit. "the creatures").[105]

The Stoic *paradoxa* (*mirabilia, admirabilia, inopinata*) belong to the most popular rhetorical formulas of antiquity, especially in the period from 100 B.C. to 200 A.D. They state in an extreme and abrupt form some of the major ethical premises of the Stoic concept of the Sage [106] but were frequently augmented by other *sophos* materials, especially of Epicurean and Cynical origin.[107] Cicero, in his treatise *Paradoxa Stoicorum*, discusses six in detail and likewise deals with them in *de finibus* IV. xxviif. 74-77 and *pro Murena* 60-66. The double headings of his chapters, in Greek and Latin, could be freely rendered, as to their essence, as follows:

1. Virtue is the only good.
2. Virtue alone is self-sufficient and alone achieves happiness.
3. All offenses are the same and all right deeds are the same (i.e., equally evil and equally meritorious. Most often fought or ridiculed by others; often omitted in catalogues of paradoxes).
4. Only the Sage is sane.
5. Only the Sage is free.
6. Only the Sage is rich.[108]

Catalogues and enumerations of *Paradoxa*, whether plain or lavishly expanded;[109] discussions of them, whether pro or con; and allusions to them, whether in poetry or prose, are extremely frequent in ancient literature, especially in the rhetorical genres.

The *paradoxon* is not paradoxical in the contemporary sense. It is, rather, according to the apt definition of Cleanthes, "against the opinion", *para - doxon*, generally held by the public, i.e., it is startling, contrary, non-conventional but not a-logical, contrary to reason. It occurs in a number of different literary formulations the most frequent being these:

1. A brief statement beginning with *sapiens* or *ho sophos*: The Sage is, ... does, ... will, etc. (Seneca *Ep*. 81.10). The statement may also begin with μόνος, "only the Sage", as in Lucian's *Piscator* 35, corresponding to the Latin solus sapiens amicus est, "only a Sage is a (true) friend" (Seneca, *Ep*. 81.11).

2. A propositional clause or sentence beginning with ὅτι, "that", e.g., "that only the Sage is rich", as in all six superscriptions of Cicero's work.

3. Stated negatively: None but the Sage..., nemo... nisi (praeter), Seneca, *Ep*. 8.11, 13, ; negamus quemquam... nisi, 81.10.

4. Reversed: speaking of the fool instead of the Sage, or, antithetically, of both: Only the Sage is free, only the fool a slave, etc. (Rich material with Arnim, *op. cit., loc. cit.*).

5. Introducing the ethical value as the grammatical subject; apud sapientem esse ipsa honesta, "(only) with the Sage is (found) actual honor (or 'virtue')", Seneca, *Ep*. 81.13.

6. Truly paradoxical and antithetical: Solos sapientes esse

    si distortissimi sint, formo(n)sos
    si mendicissimi, divites
    si servitutem serviant, reges,
Only the Sages are, (even) if most ugly, handsome;
        (even) if abjectly poor, opulent;
        (even) if serving servitude, kings,
as in Cicero's *pro Murena* 61.[110]

7. The rhetorical question and its answer as in *P.A.* 4.1 *et al.*:

"Who then is free?" "The Sage who masters himself".
Quisnam igitur liber? sapiens sibi (sibique, mss.) qui imperiosus.
                (Horace, *Satires* II. vii. 83) [111]

"Who then is sane?" "He who's no fool".
Quisnam igitur sanus? qui non stultus.

(Horace, *Sat.* II. iii. 158) [112]

The four choices of *P.A.* 4.1, i.e.,

1. Sagacious, 2. strong, 3. rich, 4. honored; or
1. Sage, 2. hero, 3. rich man, 4. honoree (honorability),

are approximated (with due allowance for minor variations) in Stobaeus *apud* Arnim (all four out of four); Horace, *Ep.* I. 1. 106ff. (three out of six); Lucian's *Hermotimus* 6 (three out of five); [113] *vitarum auctio* 20 (three out of seven); [113] *Nigrinus* 1 (possibly three out of three); Cicero, *de fin.* III. xxii. 75 (at least three out of eight); 2 Corinthians 6:8ff. (three out of seven).

The reasoning behind the *paradoxa* —why, e.g., the Sage is rich— is rarely incorporated in these lists of *paradoxa* but rather in the extensive essays in which they are found, and even in the context of the satires.[114] Quite often, the reasons given vary, or the same reasons are found with different *paradoxa*. Even the constitutive elements of the *paradoxa* themselves occasionally recombine.

That b. Zoma's details are characteristic of *paradoxa* is confirmed by a number of significant parallels. Thus, the claim that the Sage "learns from all men" is approximated in Stobaeus' Zeno quotation *apud* Arnim, ὅτι ἐστὶν μύξημένος πάντόθεν, "because he grows (is augmented) from all quarters."[115]

The mention of self-conquest is extremely frequently found in the *paradoxa*, although it is mostly freedom which is achieved by it, not strength, as in Horace *Ep.*, *supra*. Thus Cicero recommends *refrenet... libidines*, "let him curb his desires (cf. b. Zoma's "impulse") and repeats *cum cupiditatum dominatus excessit*, "once the domination of desires has passed" (*Par. Stoic.* 33 and 40) under the fifth paradox ("only the Sage is free") but then treats also mastership, commandership (*aliis imperare*, etc.) within the same section, 17. Perhaps גבור meant similarly "master", or "lordly" in *P.A.* In *de finibus* 75, however, this self-rule gives the Sage the title "king", a frequent paradoxic epithet. Yet even the vocable "strong", "manly", "brave", is found in the *paradoxa*, such as *fortis* (Varro), ἀνδρεῖος (Lucian, *vit. auct.*), and ἀνδρός and ἰσχυρός (Zeno-Stobaeus), combined with ever varying and yet similar teachings of self-rule. In other words, "free", "strong", "lordly", "royal" are semantically related in the *paradoxa* thus placing our Hebrew *gibbōr* squarely into this category.[116]

The third of b. Zoma's statements, on the truly rich one (*dives*, πλούσιος), represents Cicero's sixth paradox and is the most frequent of all the *paradoxa*.[117] The Hebrew uses practically the same vocabulary as the Greco-Roman sources, e.g., Cicero's *Par. Stoic.* 51 :

contentum... suis rebus esse... sunt... divitiae,
to be content with one's things are riches.[118]

The possible connotation of "joy" of the hebrew שמח is paralleled in the Epicurean-informed coinages of the *paradoxa*, such as Usener, fr. 602 (εὐδαιμονίας) and Seneca's *Epistle* II. 5,

honesta res est *laeta* paupertas (*Usener*, fr. 475),
a noble thing is joyful poverty.[119]

The fourth and last of b. Zoma's paradoxes —that the Sage is honored by honoring others— is represented with Horace's series in *Epistle* I. i. 107 (*honoratus*), and, perhaps, Seneca, *Ep.* 81 (*ipsa honesta*, "actual honor", see *supra*, Form #5).[120] Perhaps the full implication of this idea is expressed in an Epicurean "paradox" (*Gnomologium Vaticanum* 32) :

ὁ τοῦ σοφοῦ σεβασμὸς ἀγαθὸν μέγα
τῶν σεβομένων ἐστί,

Honoring the Sage is a great *bonum* to the honorers,

who are, of course, sagelike, too. Honor is thus self-generating in those who honor others, especially since the Sage's honor cannot come from any outside source nor as a reward for his virtues.[121] Seneca's "if you wish to be loved, love", seems to represent another variant.[122]

Whether or not the proof texts are b. Zoma's, the *paradoxa* occur anonymously without them even in talmudic literature,[123] in the meeting of the "Elders of the South" with Alexander the Great and are part of his ten questions.[124]

The wide diffusion of this literary and ethical pattern with rhetorical writers who just like b. Zoma were also civil servants of one type or another, strengthens the result of this literary analysis : that b. Zoma applies here a rhetorical commonplace, though an impressive and creative one, which was prominent in Greco-Roman culture.[125]

4. An Anti-Epicurean Sorites

In *Aboth de R. Nathan*, version B, chapter 33, Schechter, p. 72, b. Zoma is the author of a sorites:[126]

1	אל תציץ לכרמו של אדם
2	ואם הצצת אל תרד
3	ואם ירד[ת] אל תביט
4	ואם הבטת אל תיגע
5	ואם הגעת אל תאכל
6	ואם אכל (*sic*)
7	הרי אדם נמצא טורף נפשו
8	מחיי העולם הזה
9	ומחיי העולם הבא

1 Don't peek at a man's vineyard;
2 If you peeked, don't enter (lit., descend);
3 If you entered, don't look;
4 If you looked, don't touch;
5 If you touched, don't eat;
6 If you (lit., he) ate,[127]
7 You (lit., a man) will be found tearing your (his) soul (cf. Job 18:4)
8 Off the life of This World
9 And the World-To-Come.

Schechter, n. 9, suggests נמצא אדם זה, "it will be found: this man is tearing..." (9).

The understanding of this item offers considerable difficulties.
1. The author of a late variant of our item thus suggests an allegory of Israel. This variant sorites is found in the late Midrash collection *Seder Eliahu Rabba*... (*sic*; ed. M. Friedmann, Vienna-Warsaw, 1904, 1960, § 8 [§ 7], p. 43, preceding n. 31.).

Although the author given there is Eliʻezer the Great, i.e., b. Hyrcanus, (*fl.* 90 A.D.), this item is obviously dependent on b. Zoma's. Its author reinterprets the original sorites by a clear initial statement: "The vineyard of the Holy-One-Blessed-Be-He is the House of Israel".[128] Leaving the sorites form intact he ends with a summarization of four of the five acts involved which also here lead to "being cut off the World". Apparently he interprets the item as a warning to a potential exploiter or persecutor of Israel who is addressed in person. The original terse formulation of the acts in b. Zoma's sorites (without prepositions and direct objects), however, did not furnish adequate wording for such an undertaking and the interpreter was forced to modify them: the exploiter is warned not to "peek *at it*; enter *into it*; have enjoyment (or profit) *from it*; eat *its fruits*". This hardly relieves the forcedness of the interpretation. Perhaps this late interpreter wished to apply the item to some contemporary economic or political dilemma in Midrashic fashion rather than reconstruct the original meaning of the unit.

2. It has always been attractive to the conventional interpretation of b. Zoma's adventures and sayings to see in them warnings of Gnosticism or some sort of ecstatic speculation. Again, the symbolism does not fit. What, e.g., would "touch" be? Or "eating"?

3. The Stoic allegory of philosophy as an orchard (or rich, fenced-in field, *D.L.* VII. 40) is similarly ill-fitting. The Stoics, among others, did indeed make such a comparison, logic being the wall (or fence), physics the trees (or soil), and ethics the fruits (or crop) according to Sextus Empiricus, *Adv. Log.* I. 17 (*D.L.* interchanges the last two items). Our sorites could thus have been a warning not to deal with philosophy nor any of its traditional subdivisions. There is little likelihood, however, that b. Zoma would have condemned Greek philosophy indiscriminately. Furthermore, in order to be effective, b. Zoma's formulation would presuppose the general knowledge of this Greco-Roman simile (which is infrequently used even in Greco-Roman rhetoric) with all, scholars and public alike.

4. B. Zoma's warning cannot refer to standard ethic and its catalogue of transgressions, such as curiosity, trespass, greed, and theft, because the gravity of the punishment is out of proportion. Even as a homiletical exaggeration or metaphor of guilt it is too severe and explicit.[129]

5. One could see a connection of b. Zoma's thought to that of his colleague b. Azzai —a doubtful method in any case— i.e., that b. Azzai's "one misdeed (transgression) draws another in its wake" underlies our passage.[130] In this case one would have to assume further intermediate links in this chain of transgressions of b. Zoma's sorites to end up, finally, with eternal damnation. This procedure, however, would represent an *argumentum ex silentio* and fly in the face of b. Zoma's clear statement which connects damnation directly with these rather innocuous transgressions.

6. It is most unlikely that our item reflects the Stoic teaching that

all transgressions are equal in that they all fall short of an absolute, i.e., virtue (Cicero's third paradox). Although b. Zoma, as we have seen, knew Stoic paradoxes, the strong and ubiquitous stress of talmudic culture on distinctions and gradation in law and ethics would exclude any such consideration.

7. Bacher speaks of asceticism on the part of our Tanna and sees a connection between his "whoever conquers his impulse", *supra*, and our passage (*Tannaiten* I, p. 430). There is, however, no clear sign of a sustained and programmatic asceticism as ethical ideal and necessity for the attainment of salvation either with b. Zoma nor in tannaitic culture of the second century. Whatever asceticism there may have been in the first century was at best an elitist or optional or emergency effort but never an ethical imperative the neglect of which would entail eternal damnation. On the special asceticism (austerity) of the scholar according to b. Azzai, however, see Appendix I, No. 10. The asceticism described there is specific as to food, drink, clothing, and posture, and the acquisition of Torah and honor. B. Zoma's sorite speaks of a general total prohibition of some kind and a loss of eternity.

8. If b. Zoma's sorites is interpreted in the light of Greco-Roman rhetoric, however, it can be shown that in form and content it seems to reproduce a well-known and incisive Epicurean formulation of hedonism which is fought not only here but also in Greece and Rome.

Athenaeus, *Deipn*. VII. 280 a-b and XII. 546 e, *Usener*, fr. 67, preserves a passage from Epicurus' *Peri telous* :

οὐ γὰρ ἔγωγε δύναμαι νοῆσαι τἀγαθὸν

1 ἀφαιρῶν μὲν τὰς διὰ χυλῶν ἡδονάς,
2 ἀφαιρῶν δὲ τὰς δι' ἀφροδισίων,
3 ἀφαιρῶν δὲ τὰς δι' ἀκροαμάτων,
4 ἀφαιρῶν δὲ τὰς διὰ μορφῆς κατ' ὄψιν ἡδείας κινήσεις.

D.L. X. 7 omits some words (which are marked by parentheses in the following translation of Athenaeus):

I myself, indeed, cannot conceptualize the Good
1 abstracting the pleasures of taste;
2 abstracting those of sex life;
3 (abstracting) those of hearing;
4 (abstracting) those of form (in motion, delightful to the sight.)

Cicero, *Tusc. Disp.* III. xviii. 41, explicitly announcing his role as a translator of the original passage, offers a Latin version which is reasonably literal, the repetitive keywords being *detrahens eas quae* (abstracting those which...) but preferring the order (1)-(3)-(4) and concluding with a different item which, however, may be a euphemism for (2):

sive quae aliae voluptates in toto homine gignuntur quolibet sensu,
or other pleasures produced by whatever sense in the whole man.[131]

In xx. 46, *Usener*, fr. 63, he prefers a shorter version. Epicurus is quoted as being more explicit as to what pleasure is:

Taste, he says,
and the embrace of bodies,
and "shows" and song,
and forms by which the eyes are pleasantly moved.

This passage thus has the same order as Athenaeus' excerpts. In xix. 46 the sequence is satirized: ... featherbed; ... harpist; ... platter of balsam; ... sweet potion and food. It appears, still more sarcastic and imaginative, in xviii. 43.[132]

Cicero's quotation in III. xviii. 41, *supra*, ended with the (circular) syllogism that what remains after the abstractions of the senses is the pleasure of mind which, however, cannot be true pleasure without the hope of sensual (sense-bound) pleasures, experienced in freedom, according to nature, and without pain. Q.e.d.[133] The Ciceronian text mentions explicitly that all these are the original words of Epicurus including this final reformulation of the *summum bonum* which goes beyond Athenaeus' quotation. In other words, according to Cicero Epicurus' formula —or a variant of it— once existed with the climactic utterance at the end.

It thus seems that the statement of Epicurus and the sorites of b. Zoma are reasonably close to one another. Both describe the possible loss of man's highest goal with the aid of chainlike or enumerative syllogisms. The climactic statements are last.[134] B. Zoma's last three links, "seeing, touching, tasting", correspond to three of four items in Epicurus' definition. The initial "peeking" and "entering" in the Hebrew item may be introductory, a *mise en scène*, to put the would-be hedonist into the "vineyard". There is no mention of hearing, perhaps owing to the comparative lack of dangerous pleasures of hearing (entertainment) in Judaic culture.[135] The versions of Athenaeus and Cicero in their brevity and fourfold *epanaphora* resemble that of b. Zoma in its brevity and fivefold (or threefold) *epanaphora* (*aphairōn - detrahens* / ואם).

The only remaining difficulty is the metaphor of the vineyard. Its precise meaning and genesis can no longer be established with certainty. It may simply stand for the "Garden" of the Epicureans, vineyards being not unknown as the meeting places of the Sages or as metaphors thereof in tannaitic culture.[136] The identity of this particular vineyard would gradually unfold itself to the listener (or reader) from the context. On the other hand, "vineyard" could be a direct metaphor for pleasure because of the pleasantness of its grapes, just as it is in the fable of the lean fox in the vineyard of Eccl. Rabba on 5:14. "A man's" vineyard must have been a later elaboration when perhaps the item was understood ethically. It is missing in *Seder Eliyahu Rabba*. B. Zoma's sorites is thus throughout a polemic against Epicureanism using the very elements of its most forceful formulation.

5. A Chria on Absent-mindedness

Ben Zoma's possible leanings toward Greco-Roman rhetoric may perhaps help to explain the obscure and difficult story of Genesis Rabba II. 4 on Gen. 1:7, Theodor-Albeck p. 17, and its less complete parallels Tosephta *Ḥagigah* 2.6, ed. Lieberman, pp. 381ff.; JT *Ḥagigah* II. 1, 77a (9a, New York); and BT *Ḥagigah* 15a.[137]

The text of Genesis Rabba will follow here. Only essential variants are indicated.[138] Brackets enclose detail which may be of a later date, as discussed throughout this section. Parentheses indicate additions in English made for a better translation.

1 כבר היה שמעון בן זומא
2 עומד ותוהא·
3 עבר ר׳ יהושע· שאל בשלומו
4 פעם ופעמים ולא השיבו·
5 בשלישית השיבו בבהילות·
6 אמר לו ״מה זו בן זומא ,מאין הרגלים?״
7 אמר לו ״לא מאין ר׳·״
8 אמר לו ״מעיד אני עלי שמים וארץ
9 שאיני זז מיכאן
10 עד שתודיעני מאין הרגלים!״
11 אמר לו [״מסתכל הייתי במעשה בראשית
12 ו]אין בין מים העליונים

13 לתחתונים כב' וג' אצבעות!
14 [ורוח אלהים מנשבת אין כתוב כאן
15 אלא מרחפת׳ כעוף שפורח ומרפרף
16 בכנפיו [על קנו] וכנפיו נוגעות ואין נוגעות]."
17 הפך ר' יהושע ואמר לתלמידים
18 "הלך לו בן זומא!"
19 [ולא שהו (var. היו) ימים קלים
20 ובן זומא בעולם].

1   Once [139] b. Zoma had been
2   standing,[140] deep in thought.
3   R. Joshua passed by (and) greeted him
4   once and twice, and he did not answer him.[141]
5   The third time he answered him confusedly (or hurriedly),
6   (i.e.,) when he said "What's this, b. Zoma, whence (*mē'ayin*) do the feet (carry you)?"[142]
7   he said: "From Nothing (*mē'ayin*) Nothing (is born)" (Epicurus).[143]
8   He said to him: "I adjure you by Heaven and Earth[144]
9   I shall not stir from here
10 until you let me know whence the feet (carry you)".[145]
11 Said he to him: ["I contemplated Creation
12 and] there is between the Upper Waters
13 and the Lower (Waters) only two to three fingers' (breadth)."[146]
14 ["and 'God's Spirit blew' is not written here
15 but 'hovered', i.e., like a bird[147] who flies and flaps
16 with his wings over his nest
    and his wings do and don't touch."]
17 R. Joshua turned and said to the students:
18 "B. Zoma is (or has) gone".
19 [And hardly had a few days passed
20 and b. Zoma (was) in the (Other) World].

This story seems to derive from a Greco-Roman literary genre —a brief anecdote or *chria* (χρεία)— which ridicules the Sage as absent-minded, impractical, or other-worldly, and demonstrates that he contradicts his own principles in word or deed. This genre may have had its origin in an early reaction against the Milesian school of philosophy or in the opposition to a later "modernism", as, e.g., during the Peloponnesian War, when the seer Diopeithes was able to pass a law that forbade the discussion of astronomy and meteorology (directed against Anaxagoras). It may have, indeed, embodied the natural reaction of the unlearned against the philosopher (or expert), as Plato interpreted it. However this may be, it became finally part and parcel of academic lore in Greco-Roman *sophos* literature and was preserved and utilized by the very class that was the target of the wit of this genre. It cannot be denied, however, that the Greco-Roman philosopher had established similar self-critical genres himself and the possibility exists that the story of the absent-minded Sage was assimilated so easily because of the existence of similar literary genres. The latter, of course, are the final product of centuries of clashes between the different philosophical schools which sharpened the wit, the aggressiveness, and the attempt to catch the opponents at self-contradiction.

It is thus Thales, one of the early Seven Sages, who according to *D.L.* I. 34, fell into a ditch [148] when being led out of his house by an old woman so that he might observe the stars. Promptly he incurred his companion's sarcasm: "You, O Thales, not being able to see the (things) at *the feet*, the (things) in the sky you fancy to know?" [149]

This *chria* is already referred to in Plato's *Theaetetus* 174a where it is a Thracian (maidservant) before whom Thales, "astronomizing", falls into a well, only to be scoffed at for his anxiousness to know "the things in heaven (in the sky)", but "the things in front of him and at *the feet* would escape him".[150] To Plato, Thales is here the prototype and leader (*koryphaios*, 173c) of the great philosophers (cf. 174a, end) and not merely an astronomer. Of this task of the philosopher, however, the search of "the earth beneath" and the "sky above" (Plato quoting Pindar, *ibid.*) are part and parcel.[151]

Still wittier —using a *double entendre*— is a gnomic version in the name of the Cynic Bion, one of the supposed creators of the diatribe, *c.* 325 - *c.* 255, quoted by Stobaeus:[152]

> Most ridiculous are the astronomers (stargazers) who do not see the fishes at *the feet* [153] by the sea-shores but profess to see those in the sky (i.e., the stellar constellation).[154]

It is apparent from this item that the basic story generated further attempts at such witty contrasts and word plays. Indeed, Plato himself tried his hand at it. When commenting on our story he added the thought that the philosopher —spending all his efforts on the question *what man is*— hardly knows whether his next-door neighbor *is a man* (or some other creature).[155]

An anecdotal version, likewise with Stobaeus, ≠ 22, p. 8, *ibid.*, seems to represent a collation of the Platonic and Laertian versions closer to the former, in the name of Serenus.[156] Here Thales "rightly suffers", for, while "ignorant of the (things) at *the feet*", he watches "the things in the sky". (Ps.-)Maximus Confessor, 580-662, and Antonius Monachus "Melissa", 11th-12th cts., under whose names much classical *sophos* material has been collected, carry the last item almost *verbatim*.[157]

That this *topos* existed also in a variant in which it is applied to all philosopher-astronomers is evident from Cicero's quotation of what he identifies as Ennius' *Iphigenia* in *Republic* I. xviii. 30. This warning or complaint concludes:

> quod est *ante pedes* nemo spectat, scaeli
> scrutantur plagas
> what is *before the feet* no one observes,
> they search the zones (*double entendre*
> "snares" intended?) of heaven

Similarly, *D.L.* VI. 28 applies our topic to the "mathematicians", who gaze at sun and moon but overlook the things close by ("at the feet", ἐν ποσί...).

Closer to the midrashic item in time or place are Lucian's novel application of the *topos* to a figure of his plot in his *bis accusatus* 34, Eusebius' use of Plato's Thales, *Praep. evang.* XII. 29. 4 (vol. 2, p. 120, Mras; on Iamblichus see our n. 150), and Hippolytus' mention of Thales in *ref. omn. haer.* I. i. 4 (p. 4, Wendland). All three continue clearly the antithesis sky/feet:

Eusebius:	... ἐν οὐρανῷ...	/	... παρὰ πόδας...
Lucian:	... ἄνω...	/	... πρὸ τοῖν ποδοῖν...
Hippolytus:	... ἐν οὐρανῷ...	/	... ἐν ποσίν...

At an earlier date Antipater of Sidon, *fl.* 130 B.C., had used it in an epigram on a professional bird-chaser who gazes at what is in the "ether" but does not notice a biting viper "at his feet" (*Anth. Pal.*. VII. 172).

All these examples of our topic do not account for numerous other instances of its use without the catchword "feet"; or mere allusions; novel and derivative uses; and still more general applications to various other groups of people. There are, finally, occurrences of the theme in other literary media, especially the comedy. A farcical variant is introduced in Aristophanes' *Clouds* 225-233, where Socrates, "walking on air" contemplates the sun, readily admitting that involvement with the earth prevents the search for things above. Remote derivative uses are found with Menander and Dionysius the Elder (the Syracusan tyrant).[158] It is unlikely that any of these marginal uses could have been the precise model for the talmudic passage. Yet the wide distribution of the topic, even in fables, e.g., Aesopus No. 40, Perry (Halm No. 78), in gnomologies, florilegia, and additional patristic sources, makes the conclusion, presently to be made, more plausible.[159]

The total profile of the Thales (or philosopher-astronomer) anecdote includes then these motemes:

Philosopher-Astronomer-Sage,
preoccupied with celestial (-philosophical) matters,
not watching his feet ("the feet"),
suffers embarrassment,
is rebuked by someone (lowly person)
in form of witty antithetical (contrastive) statement (or question).
Occasionally : *double entendre* (Plato, Bion).

It is highly probable that a version of this literary syndrome was the pattern for b. Zoma's encounter with R. Joshua.[160]. It seems thus to be Zoma's preoccupation with celestial matters which prevents him from recognizing or greeting his superior. Still in a trance he hears the word *mē'ayin*, "whence",[161] which in Hebrew is homonymous with "from nothing", and promptly, in a *double entendre*, quotes Epicurus' "Nothing (לא) from Nothing (מאין)..."[162] R. Joshua's renewed entreaty, repeating (or introducing for the first time according to Tos.) conspicuously the word "feet", triggers off b. Zoma's mysterious "reply" that "between the Upper and the Lower Waters (between Heaven and Earth) there is only two to three fingers' (breadth)."

In our texts the second answer is preceded by the apologetic-sounding words of b. Zoma "I was envisioning the Work of Creation, מסתכל הייתי במעשה בראשית (lines 11-12). The fact, however, that he was engaged in cosmic speculation is obvious from the Epicurean quotation which is quasi-cosmological and almost always connected with other Epicurean beliefs of this sort in rhetoric,[163] and will become still clearer from b. Zoma's second answer. This brief sentence on "the Work of Creation" may then quite well be a later addition, especially since b. Zoma is still not quite awake (in contact with reality) and unable to reply coherently. This impression is confirmed by R. Joshua's concluding words "he is (still, עדיין, BT) gone". The apology and the keyword "Work of Creation" may therefore be an addition, probably made in order to give the story a more indigenous flavor (cf. the Temple Mount as location in BT), unless it is already the work of those who considered the item mystic-theosophic speculation of the kind collected in Ḥagigah.

The literary form of this genre requires that Joshua has the last word, and a word of ridicule or condemnation at that. As we have seen this final word or phrase is quite frequently a *double entendre* in Greco-Roman literature. It is not utterly impossible that this is true, too, in the case of our tannaitic anecdote. Joshua's "Ben Zoma is gone" may thus not only refer to his absent-mindedness but also indicate that he is insane. The same is true for the variant found in the Tosephta, מבחוץ, "he is *out*".[164]

That the occupation with celestial things by the astronomer and physicist —perhaps also by the cosmologist-metaphysician... is useless and even apt to cause insanity is acknowledged by Xenophon's Socrates, *Memorabilia* IV. vii. 6, in reference to Anaxagoras, who occasionally seems to have played the role of the unwordly Sage, cf. *D.L.* II. 7 (neglect of patrimony and public affairs) and (Ps.-)Plato, *Hippias Maior* 283a and 281c. Similar things were told of Democritus.[165].

However this may be, what then is the full meaning of b. Zoma's reply regarding the small distance between the Upper and Lower Waters (triggered off by the keyword "the feet") ?

One of Epicurus' main thrusts was directed against fear —fear of myth, of irrational gods, even fear of an irrevocable fate such as directed by the stars. He not only rejected astrology (together with the Providence of the Stoics) but even astronomy, fearing that heavenly bodies, obeying "perfect" eternal laws, could become again divine agents, thereby threatening man's freedom and peace of mind.[166] In one well-known passage he totally contradicted the prevailing opinion of antiquity by claiming that "the size of sun (and moon) and the heavenly bodies is for us precisely what it appears to be (i.e., to the human eye)."[167]

Epicurus' extravagant teaching was used forcefully and at length by Lucretius, v. 564-591; Philodemus, c. 110-40/35, readied it for the rhetoricians.[168] It must have become one of the popular targets of ancient anti-Epicurean ridicule [169] as is evident from Cicero who used it at least three times in his works.[170] He added an important element: "to him (Epicurus) it (the sun) is perhaps *a foot* long",[171] and, again, "Small, indeed, it appears to us! To me, as for one, about a foot long".[172] The first *Academica* passage, apart from ironical questions directed to Epicurus on his little sun, includes the express mention of philosophical ridicule directed at Epicurus.

It thus seems that Epicurus' foot-sized sun is represented in our talmudic story. The mention of "feet" by Joshua may have triggered off b. Zoma's recollection of the Epicurean motif the keyword of which was "foot" (or afforded to the author of the *chria* another opportunity to make b. Zoma utter Epicurean stances).[173] Understandably, b. Zoma's mention of the small size of heavenly dimensions had to be in Hebrew terms [174] which excluded the use of the Greco-Roman "foot" and necessitated its replacement by "fingers" [175] or equivalents.[176] If this be so, b. Zoma's *foot*-sized sun "above" is the counterpart of the *feet* "below", in accordance with the requirement of the genre and parallel to the fishes of the sea-shore and the fishes as a constellation.[177] B. Zoma thus knows about the foot-sized sun above but does not know whence his foot (feet) had led him here below. Our story differs from the pattern in that b. Zoma is shamed before a superior. Yet, the students of R. Joshua before whom he castigates b. Zoma, may be a vestige of the subaltern of the pattern story.

A striking proof for the correctness of the main lines of the analysis ventured *supra* is offered by a passage in dialogue form in Lucian's *Icaromenippus* 6-7. Lucian ridicules philosopher-scientists —some of them short-sighted (weak-sighted; *double entendre*: obtuse? ἀμβλυώττοντες)— who, nevertheless, measure the sun, etc. They know how many *ells* (! πηχῶν) lie between the sun and the moon but are ignorant of how many *stadia* there are between Megara and Athens. Here are all the ingredients of our syndrome: impractical celestial expert; ridicule; contrastive statements on the above and the below; the minimal measurements, adapted to the requirements of the new context. Of course, neither Lucian nor the tannaitic author of our story are necessarily responsible for combining the Thales motif with the Epicurean measurement: both may have heard a current pattern story, or Lucian may follow here as so often in the footsteps of the great wit Menippus of Gadara. Furthermore, the Lucian parallel makes it likely that b. Zoma is not portrayed as a gnostic in our story but as a mere "astronomer-Sage", perhaps with Epicurean leanings.

It does not amount to an additional proof but is comforting to know that the small measurement of the sun is also known in contemporaneous as well as later patristic sources. In his *Apology*, Aristides, a contemporary of Hadrian, states that the sun is much smaller than the heaven, IV. 2, cf. VI. 1-3; and Theophilus, in the same second century, in his letter to Autolycus, likewise declares the sun to be "a very small heavenly body". Curiously, both writers do not fight this teaching but accept it.[178]. Tertullian, however, c. 150 - c. 230 disapprovingly reports that Epicurus conceived of the sun as foot-sized (*pedalem*); and Arnobius, around 300, has God denounce gainless and useless investigations, such as, "whether the sun is larger than the earth or measures only *a foot across*...[179]

The meaning of the testimonial and brief exegesis of Gen. 1:2, "the Spirit of God hovered...", should not be blown out of proportion and used to prove mystical inclinations on the part of b. Zoma, if the passage is his at all. Its main burden seems to be the exegesis of the verb רחף as "hover", i.e., the demonstration that this hovering which usually describes a certain reduced flight of birds that requires little space, serves also in the biblical text as an indication of a narrow space.[180] This exegesis does not necessarily include an express speculative belief of b. Zoma that the "Spirit of God was birdlike.[181] It is not utterly impossible that this exegesis is rather playful, i.e., added in support of a portrayal of b. Zoma as a pedantic as well as absent-minded scholar.

The epilogue of b. Zoma's sudden death is not a part of the literary pattern. Moreover, it does not fit an originally mild disapproval of scholarly absurdity and the playfulness of the genre. It may represent already the later mystical understanding of the story which transformed it into a warning not to engage in dangerous speculation which can threaten a man's life,[182] or a somewhat earlier stage at which b. Zoma seems to have been considered an actual Epicurean on the grounds of the quotations, in the story, cf. the similar episode of the "Four Who Entered Paradise" in BT *Ḥagigah* 14 b *et al*. (in which b. Zoma likewise becomes insane and/or dies early, apparently also there considered to be an Epicurean).[183]

It is, of course, impossible to determine with any degree of certainty whether or not this strange meeting between Joshua and b. Zoma is historical, since the use of a particular literary form, even a sterotype such as a Sage anecdote, does not yet by itself indicate fiction. A true event can easily be described by means of a literary convention. On the other hand, it can be argued that no author would wish to invite disbelief in a true story by writing it in a literary genre that serves to transmit didactic-legendary material and is known as such. Neither can the authenticity of b. Zoma's Epicurean-colored utterances be confirmed or denied. Still, it is likely that they have been supplied by some of his detractors in order to make him look somewhat more ridiculous, hardly for any true Epicureanism on his part but perhaps for some other reason.[184].

The use of the *sophos* as a model in a story with a moral is a technique which gained momentum in post-Socratic philosophy with the decline of the Greek *polis* which had served as such a model of demonstration before, as, e.g., in Plato's *Protagoras, Gorgias,* and the *Republic.* In Judea the same phenomenon arises after the gradual erosion of political sovereignty.[185] Quite frequently this *sophos*-centered teaching introduced the anti-Sage, i.e., the tyrant, the boor, or the fool, in order to put its lesson across. Yet the *sophos* class in either culture must have finally acquired enough self-criticism and humor to prefer, occasionally, to portray the Sage (or all the learned) in a negative light —regardless of ths ultimate origin of this criticism.[188] A principal motif of such self-criticism was the absent-minded Sage.[187] Yet even this frequent use of the Sage figure as a demonstration model of ethical values does not totally exclude the possiblity of a historical basis for a few such stories in the Greco-Roman and the Judaic cultures.

It is evident that b. Zoma is here the subject of such a "critical" *chria* just because he belonged to this class of חכמים -*sophoi*.[188] On the other hand, it is equally obvious that our story goes further than the Greco-Roman pattern in that it makes the Sage utter two Epicurean statements that "incriminate" him to a certain degree. This deviation from the expected pattern, however, may be in line with another group of talmudic sources in which b. Zoma, and frequently together with him b. Azzai (and once Elisha b. Abuyah), are given a lesser and ambiguous status, that of תלמידי חכמים, "Disciples of the Sages,"[189] or merely "Disciples",[190] a fact which Talmud and Midrash have tried to harmonize.[191] Yet it is factual that b. Zoma and his companion were never ordained, although their opinions were highly esteemed and the Halakhah of the "twin" scholars is found in the Mishnah as well as the Gemara.[192]

In view of this situation and the foregoing analysis of b. Zoma's total Midrash,[193] a possible reason for his ambiguous position suggests itself. He may quite well have resembled the Greco-Roman rhetor (in behavior and/or method) to a certain extent and as such appeared somewhat alien or odd (or even dangerous) to his more conservative peers and other contemporaries. His haggadic teachings are Greco-Roman inspired to a considerable degree which makes his literary items longer and more structured than that of other Tannaim.[194] Moreover, much of the Haggadah of b. Azzai, his frequent co-author and colleague in a number of statements, is distinguished by strongly Epicurean-colored items [195] and by similar (yet fewer) rhetorical characteristics. In an often quoted passage [196] b. Zoma is "the last (i.e., probably, among the greatest) of the *Darshanim*",[197] and in some sources he is so classified together with b. Azzai.[198] This little understood term, given only to an extremely limited number of authorities, could, in this early period, quite possibly have reference to his Greco-Roman -influenced skill, extended to him by admirers and preserved in the later tradition. Although his Halakhah is not essentially different from that of other Tannaim, items of his, introduced by the phrase "they asked b. Zoma", and vaguely chriic in character,[199] are comparatively numerous and distinguished by great exegetical acumen.

One interpretation of his which made the recitation of the "Exodus from Egypt" a requirement also "by night",[200] found the enthusiastic approval of Ele'azar b. Azariah, and the latter's endorsement became part of the liturgy of the Eve of Passover ritual.[201] Yet it is not impossible that even this popular item is not entirely free of Greco-Roman influence.[202]

It is not necessary to see in the statement "this is one of the biblical passages (by or on) which b. Zoma shook the world" (referring to a difficulty in the text of Gen. 1.7) [203] an indication of Greco-Roman speculations on water as the primeval matter and ancient myth related thereto,[204] or unknown esoteric Rabbinic lore,[205] since the phrase "shook the world" may merely emphasize his boldness and acumen in pointing out difficulties in the basic biblical text —cf. the variant reading of the Septuagint *ad loc*.— or his ability to posit *aporiae*, a must for the Sage in both cultures.[206] Even if the root רעש may here not yet have the additional acoustic connotation which it possesses in medieval and later Hebrew, it still seems to refer to his rhetorical eloquence and forcefulness if not shrillness.[207] Such epithets based on the technical and intellectual proficiency of Greco-Roman philosophers and rhetoricians are quite frequent in rhetorical literature. They are found, e.g., in most of the biographical sketches that accompany the doxographic sections of Laertius' *Lives*, coined by the compiler himself or representing, occassionally, traditional by-names. We find thus a Stoic by-named "Siren" —*D.L.* VII. 160— and the Epicureans are cited for their "Siren-like" power of persuasion.[208] Because of his eristic aggressiveness Alexinus was nicknamed Elenxinus (*D.L.* II. 109).

It is then possible that b. Zoma's very persuasiveness and Greco-roman manners are criticized in our story by putting Epicurean slogans in his mouth, and disavowed and "ridiculous" ones at that. These slogans, of course, deal with "physics" not because b. Zoma was a dangerous heretical speculator but because the structure of the literary genre in question required an astronomer-cosmologist.[209] B. Zoma's main interest, on the contrary, seems to have been centered around ethics, manners, and social culture like so much of Greco-Roman rhetoric. The Story of the Four, BT Ḥag., et al., however, may have taken some (meta-)physical utterances of b. Zoma as a sign of truly heretical Epicurean speculation and added him as the speculating type to the other three types of Epicureans. In fact, our very Thales-b. Zoma *chria* may have been the catalyst. Such cases of mistaken identification of playful, parodistic, or satirical items and their use as factual events are extremely frequent in the Greco-Roman culture.[210] The existence of this phenomenon in a highly humor-conscious as well as scholarly culture, such as the Greco-Roman one, makes such a parallel in the tannaitic-Judean one more plausible, especially since there seem to be other cases of this sort in the cynicizing talmudic material.[211] The final interpretation of the Thales-b. Zoma *chria* by which it became didactic teaching which warns of the dangers of indigenous mystical-theosophic speculation must have taken place prior to the codification of this material in the Tosephta section of *Ḥagigah* in amoraic times.[212].

It must remain a matter of speculation whether b. Zoma's lack of ordination was somehow connected with this rhetorical make-up of his, i.e., whether he preferred the rhetorical aspects of the Sage's activity by choice and did not strive to obtain ordination or whether the Sages hesitated to endorse him fully because of his ways. Perhaps the tradition of his early death is not entirely inauthentic: he may have died too early to obtain ordination and thus traditions on the *reason* of his premature death came into being.[213]

In his teachings b. Zoma was, of course, quite "orthodox". Even in his preference for Greco-Roman styles and techniques he (and his associate b. Azzai) must have differed from the other scholars of his time only by degree, since much of the academic and literary procedure in Judea was also reasonably close to Greco-Roman culture. In any society, however, slight esthetic and technical differences between individuals or groups loom frequently larger than essential ones.

B. Zoma's rhetoric, finally, reflects (indirectly) the contribution of a number of Greek philosophical schools and movements. This mixture was, of course, already found with Greco-Roman rhetoric and, although differing from writer to writer, and probably from rhetor to rhetor, had a certain stability produced not only by the technical aspect of this discipline but also by the common ideal of the *sophos*. Among the ingredients of this mixture were Platonic, Cynical and Stoic elements combined with various amounts of pro- or anti-Epicureanism,[214] and some Pythagorean, Skeptic, and minor other materials.[215] If this be called eclecticism, it was developed in Greco-Roman rhetoric prior to its use in Judaic culture, but it was a serviceable and communicable mixture on a high ethical level. B. Zoma, and like him others who were rhetorically inclined, made selections from this material on the grounds of an indigenous monotheistic-transcendental tradition [216] and an ample indigenous regulatory law, and could thus afford the adoption of an attractive, semi-technical system in support of probably unshaken basic beliefs.

PART IV. APPENDIX

EPICUREA ET RHETORICA OF BEN AZZAI?
A SURVEY [1]

1. *The Meaning of Sacrifice*

The sacrificial cult is for the benefit of man ("for your own sake") not for the benefit of the Godhead who needs no food and cannot be bribed by it.[2] BT *Menaḥoth* 110 a; *Sifre* Nu. 28:8, #143.

Compare with Philodemus, *de musica*, *Usener*, fr. 386: "The Divine is not in need of veneration but it is *natural for us* to honor it, above all with pious thoughts, but also according to various traditional customs".

Sallustius, 4th ct. A.D., ed. Nock, ch. XV ("for our good", etc.), cf ch. XIV ("for our needs", etc.). These two chapters Epicureanize.

Cicero, *de nat. deor.* I. xvii. 45 (Velleius, the Epicurean, declares that the urge for piety is basic to worship).

Lucretius, V. 165-169 (no bribe).

This specific argumentation combined with the express endorsement of sacrifice as *beneficial to man* is only found with the Epicureans. [3]

2. *Laughter at Death*

Gen. R. LXII. 2 on 25:8: To the Saints (supplied by Ps. 116:15; cf., however, 3., *infra*, which suggests the Sage), death is cause for laughter (via Prov. 31:25), confidence, non-concern (Judaic modification: because of future reward).

Cf. variously Epicurus, *Letter to Menoeceus* 124f. (*apolauston*); *Kyriai doxai* II (Death is of no concern, nothing); Seneca, *Ep.* LXVI. 18f., *Usener*, fr. 60 (*gaudio... dulce*), and many others.[4]

3. *The Sage's Death (including "laughter").*

AdRN A, ch. 25, p. 79f.:/his mind is clear/he converses on Torah/ possibly still carries out religious duties/amidst laughter/(Judaic adaptation: on the Sabbath, etc.).[5]

Cf. *D.L.* X. 22 (*Letter to Idomeneus*); Cicero, *de fin.* II. xxf. 97-99.
Is Petronius' death as, e.g., in Tacitus, patterned after Epicurus' death?
Although the death of the Sage is an extremely common theme in Greco-Roman literature (Palamedes, Anaxagoras, Antiphon of Rhamnus, Socrates) and although all these display a similar syndrome of motemes (see A.-H. Chroust, *Socrates, Man and Myth*, Notre Dame, 1957, 216-222) the combination of this syndrome and the next item, 4., *infra*, both with Seneca and b. Azzai, speaks for an Epicurean rhetorical source. Moreover, both the midrashic and Epicurean-colored Greco-Roman occurrences speak of a natural death (including illness) and not of an unjust execution.

4. *Two bona and Two mala*.

"A *positive* (good) characteristic (*sign*) it is,[6]
  if one's mind is *perturbed* by one's wisdom;
A *negative* (bad) characteristic (*sign*) it is,
  if one's wisdom is perturbed by one's mind.
A *positive* (good) characteristic (*sign*) it is,
  if one's body *suffers* through scholarship;
A *negative* (bad) characteristic (*sign*) it is,
  if one's scholarship *suffers* through the body (i.e., pain)."

This passage from Tos. *Ber.* 3.4 (Lieberman, p. 12)[7] reflects Epicurus' view as formulated in Seneca's *Ep.* LXVI. 45: apud Epicurum *dua bona* sunt ex quibus summum illud beatumque conponitur, ut
  corpus *sine* dolore sit
  animus *sine* perturbatione
"With Epicurus there are two goods of which that highest bliss (Supreme Good) consists, that"
  the body be *without* pain,
  the mind without perturbation.
(*Usener*, fr. 434, cf. fr. 74). Likewise Cicero, *de fin.* I. xviii. 59, as deduction *a minore ad maius*:[8]
  Quod si corporis gravioribus *morbis* vitae iucunditas *impeditur, quanto* magis animi *morbis impediri* necesse est.
  If life's agreeableness is impeded by the body's diseases, how much more is it necessarily impeded by the mind's diseases.
These formulations are repetitive-antithetical-reversible. The Hebrew lists the item on mind first. The statements of Seneca (47) as well as of the fuller *AdRN* version (ch. 25) are followed by the description of the Sage's death!

5. *Celibacy.* ⁹)

6. *Education of Women.*

Education of girls is enjoined upon any man, Mi.*Soṭah* 3.4.¹⁰

The inclusion of women in Epicurean learning and Epicurean *contubernia*, unique in antiquity, was well-known (and a target of malicious gossip). The very few quasi-legendary women-Cynics are represented as exceptional in the Greco-Roman *chriae*. With the Epicureans the education of women was closer to a stable situation, at least in the beginning.

7. *Endorsement of Controversial Books.*

In the face of opposition b. Azzai maintained his firm opinion that Ecclesiastes and Canticles had been canonized in the past without debate: Mi. *Yadayim* 3.5. Apparently some scholars had considered Ecclesiastes secular, i.e., non-inspired (*ibid.* and Tos. *Yad.* 2.14). According to Lev. R. XXVIII. 1 on 23:10 (see n. 68, *supra*, Part II) some considered most of Ecclesiastes outright heretical and Epicurean because of its hedonism (and lack of belief in Providence). The same may have been true of Canticles.¹¹

B. Azzai's emphatic defense may perhaps presuppose his attraction to these books. Since his views are often non-conventional, this possible attraction may not have been some minor detail but the general spirit of the books which, indeed, is quite different from that of the remaining canon and may have been, in the eyes of the opposition, "hedonist". It is very unlikely that his reasoning was that of Akiba, who evaluated Canticles most highly on the grounds of a quasi-mystical and/or symbolic interpretation, since b. Azzai's supposed addiction to mysticism represents only the view of later generations.¹²

Nevertheless, in view of the scarcity of sources the proposition made here must remain tentative.

8. *Man in God's Image and imitatio dei.*

Man in the image of God is stated as a "great principle", כלל גדול, in *Sifra* on Lev. 19:18, 89 b, *Ḳedoshim*.¹³

Although biblical in origin, the elevation of this verse to a "great principle" implies a fresh impetus. The formulation of such *kephalaia* —basic ethical principles— is established in rhetoric at least since

Demosthenes, especially in connection with the Hellenistic versions of the Golden Rule, and subsequently reached the world of the Talmud.[14]

Epicurus' stress on man's approximation to the gods includes the doctrines that (a) the gods are models of all virtues, especially *ataraxia*. Man must achieve this by *imitatio dei* (ὁμοίωσις θεοῦ). The gods and the Sage achieve the same perfection; (b) man is physically similar to the gods, the human form, as most perfect, being best for both.[15]

B. Azzai seems to teach a variant of the former: God modestly states his work first ("... created God", Gen 1:1, cf. the position of the Hebrew words) and only thereafter His name, unlike earthly rulers who state their names first and then their status or achievements.[16]

These are, of course, widely held Greek beliefs, although not all Greek views make the gods perfect nor do all agree on the physical resemblance between the gods and man. One Diogenes item declares "good men to be the images (*eikōnas*) of the gods, *D.L.* VI. 51, but the present writer believes that this item is suspect of later origin and Epicureanizing (see *Cynicism*). Of course, b. Azzai would not relinquish the biblical belief in creation, nor would he claim that man is physically similar to the Godhead, nor is his *imitatio dei* unique in talmudic sources. Rather, since owing to an Epicurean stimulus in Greco-Roman rhetoric these themes became prominent again and even combined as with Epicurus, b. Azzai's teaching may well be a distant reflection of this phenomenon.

9. *Avoidance of Sin.*

On the avoidance of sin to escape further sins and its possible relation to Epicurus' avoidance of trouble to avoid further troubles, see n. 130, *supra*. *Ibid.*: on the formula "run to... avoid" (whether Stoic or Epicurean).

10. *The Sage's Asceticism.*

In *AdRN* A, ch. 11, p. 46, b. Azzai states that:
   If a man makes himself lowly for the sake of Torah
   and eats dates (and) dried fruits [17]
   and puts on soiled clothes (rags)
   and sits in wait at the door of the Sages,
   every passer-by says: "maybe this one is a fool".
   In the end you find the entire Torah with him".

Cf. Seneca, *Ep.* XVIII. 10:

    water, meal, and bread crusts;

ibid., 7:

    pallet (*grabatus*), coarse cloak (*sagum*), bread, hard and 'sordid'.

D.L. X. 11: half-pint of wine... or water;

ibid.:   plain bread and water, cf. fr. 181, *Usener*.

ibid.:   a little pot of cheese is indulgence.

Seneca, *Ep.* XX. 8f.:

    reduce yourself to lowly conditions (*redige ad parva...*).[18]

ibid. (fr. 206, *Usener*):

    on a pallet, in rags (*in panno*)...

    for these will not be only spoken words but tested (by deeds).[19]

    non enim dicentur tamtum ille, sed probabuntur.

Although austerity and asceticism are the practice and goal of the Sage also in Cynicism (mostly as a struggle against luxury and "vanity") and even in Stoicism (as practice toward virtue and self-conquest) as well as with Pythagoreanism (often in the form of tabus but also as moderation), b. Azzai seems to echo an Epicurean item on austerity which became a rhetorical cliché, as the parallel Epicurean-colored keywords, especially in Roman rhetoric, suggest.[20] That b. Azzai's item is, indeed, thus related to the Epicurean passage in Seneca (probably through rhetorical descendants) becomes still more likely in view of this parallel:

    Reduce yourself to lowly conditions from which you cannot fall (ex quibus cadere non possis), as *supra*;

B. Azzai, *AdRN* A, ch. 25, p. 81:

    Descend from your place two or three steps and stay (there).[21] Better that they say to you "move up" than they should say to you "get down". Testimonial: Prov. 28:7 (similar wording).

Although the second half of b. Azzai's apophthegm resembles the testimonial, being a paraphrase of it (probably in order to enhance its verity), the item is clearly parallel to Seneca's "from which you cannot fall" [22] and approximates a particular feature of Epicurean asceticism: the avoidance of the good life and of social status as a measure of caution thus eliminating possible trouble and pain.[23] Epicurus, of course, went still further by asserting (according to Seneca) that austerity (just as simplicity) can be enjoyable as a welcome change from luxury, or as an exercise which proves that evil is easy to endure, or as a means to bestow a sense of freedom on the Sage.[24]

11. *Memento mori*.

Versions of an utterance of an older contemporary, Aḳabiah b. Mahalal'el, appear also in the name of other authors,[25] among them b. Azzai, so in *Derekh Ereṣ Rabba* I (originally III).

The profile of these texts approximates this scheme:
1. An admonition to consider always man's origin and destiny;
2. Verbs in the imperative: consider! know! etc. (in the original wordings);
3. Man's origin: a drop (of semen);[26] demeaning adjective added (fetid, etc.).
4. Man's destiny: dust and worms;[27]
5. Preamble: consciousness of these prevents sin (in view of Final Judgment).

This must be compared with Marcus Aurelius, *Medit.* IV. 48. 2 (cf. also VI. 13).

> ... consider [28] how ephemeral and mean all mortal things are: yesterday a little slime,[29] to-morrow a mummy and ashes. Epilogue: ethical admonition (without "Judgment").

Much of Marcus Aurelius' work stoicizes, but Epicurean passages are quite numerous (see n. 162). Yet this sentiment of Marcus Aurelius is so much a part of general ancient thought that Epicurean elements are not easy to detect. Epicurus, however, stressed more than others this *memento mori* and made it a permanent exercise:

> *Gnom. Vat.* 10 ("remember", "mortal", "past, present, future");
> Seneca, *Ep.* XXVI. 8 (fr. 205, *Usener*): *meditare mortem*, cf.10, and *transire ad deos* (var. *divos*);
> *ibid.*, 9: "It is an excellent thing to learn death",
> egregia res est mortem condiscere.
> (Epilogue on achievement of freedom).[30]

The midrashic item is thus rhetorically affected but only vaguely Epicurean-colored. The disgust the Gnostics felt for the manifestations of life is probably not yet active in this instance, since their influence is felt only at a somewhat later period and, in any case, our passage can be sufficiently illuminated by rhetorical patterns.[31]

12. *Inclination and Fate.*

B. Azzai is among those who speak of human inclination (or will or freedom of choice, טובה) and its interaction with divine guidance, *Mekhilta* on Ex. 15:26 :[32]

> Once a man desires in his will to obey
> he is (thereafter) led to obey (by Heaven) whether in his will or not;
> when (he desires) in his will to disobey,
> he is led to disobey (thereafter) even against his will.[33]

This is vaguely reminiscent of Epicurus' *Gnom. Vat.* 16 :

> No one looks at evil and chooses it but he is baited by it as being (comparatively) good vis-a-vis the (still) greater evil, and (thus) is caught.[34]

In spite of all dissimilarities in both form and content, there is a vague resemblance between the two utterances. They are equally terse; speak of man generally; use two passives (or grammatical substitutes thereof); and do not explicitly name any higher power. Nevertheless, the impetus leading to a discussion of this sort may not have come from Epicureanism : theological-philosophical treatments of such problems were quite common in Alexandrian Judaism.[35] Moreover, Epicurus is here mainly interested in the cause of the failing of man, whereas b. Azzai asks and answers the question how divine guidance combines with man's initiative; and this, in turn, he is able to combine with reward and punishment for obedience and non-obedience. Yet both Epicurus and b. Azzai consider the small measure of momentum supplied from somewhere (Epicurus' "entrapment" and b. Azzai's "grace" and "condemnation"), and both assume an initial freedom of choice on the part of man. This entire cluster of problems, however, is also quite frequently discussed by Philo.[36] Yet Philo himself is similarly sensitive to the philosophical problems of his environment and affected by rhetoric.

Whatever the precise stimuli may have been, the item, at least in its formal structure, seems to have the earmarks of some rhetorical contact.

13. *Man and the Cosmos.*

A Midrash ascribed to b. Zoma or b. Azzai (BT *Ber.* 6 b ; BT *Shabbath*

30 b), being somewhat ambiguous, resembles a number of different Greco-Romans items.

Of Eccl. 12:13, "... God fear and keep His commandments, for this is the whole man", כי זה כל־האדם, b. Zoma or b. Azzai said: "The entire world was created only to be associated (לצוות) with this man".

The exegetical basis for this statement is the fact that the two Sages (as well as other authorities, *ibid*.) were struck by the rare phrase כל־האדם, "the whole man" ("all the man"). B. Azzai or b. Zoma thus interpreted כ[ו]ל as a noun, "the All", i.e., the world, and "man", as being syntactically joined to it in the construct case.

This thought resembles vaguely Aristotle's: "... man, perfected, is the best of creatures, but without law and justice, he is the worst of all", *Polit*. 1253a, #15, end.

Although the exegesis of the two Sages is clear to a certain degree, it may leave room for the possibility that they wanted also to say that righteous man (the Sage) is an equal companion to this cosmos.

The idea of a companionship of God, man, and universe, all being governed by law and reason, is a commonplace with the Stoics that was adopted by rhetoric. Cicero, e.g., *de legibus* I. viii. 22f., closes a sorites-like cadence with the inference that "the entire world must be adjudged to be one common society of gods, and men",[37] the preceding keywords being: wisdom (22), reason, law, justice, obedience to heavenly order, divine mind, and all-powerful God (23).

EPILOGUE

The Midrash of b. Azzai which has been briefly outlined *supra*, represents only a part of his midrashic creation —although the greater part of it. This is unlike b. Zoma's Midrash, which was treated *in toto* and found to be rhetorically affected *in toto*. The remainder of b. Azzai's Midrash, however, seems to be almost free of *rhetorica*,[1] although not devoid of much interesting detail. The latter must have further strengthened the impression he made on his contemporaries, perhaps as a somewhat erratic personality.[2]

A certain affinity to rhetorical *Epicurea* cannot be denied in his teachings, although he certainly was no Epicurean and perhaps not even aware of this preference. Nevertheless, his thought contributed to the enrichment of the talmudic doctrine of the *ḥakham-sophos* through this influx of Epicurean reminiscences.

NOTES TO PART ONE

¹ See Berthold Häsler's very recent *Bibliographie der Epikuräerforschung*, Veröffentlichungen des Instituts für hellenistisch-römische Philosophie der Deutschen Akademie der Wissenschaften zu Berlin, Heft 3 (not seen); P. H. DeLacy, "Some Recent Publications on Epicurus and Epicureanism (1937-1954)", *Classical Weekly (CW)*, *48* (1955), 169-177; W. Schmid in *Gnomon*, *27* (1955) 405-431. All histories of philosophy. Pauly-Wissowa, *et al.*, *Real-Encyclopädie der classischen Altertumswissenschaft (P.-W.)*, vol. II (Stuttgart, 1907) s.v. "Epikuros (4)", 133-155 (v. Arnim); Suppl. XI (1968) 579-652 (H. Steckel). *Oxford Classical Dictionary (OCD)*, (Oxford, 1949) 324f. (K. O. Brink). *Reallexikon für Antike und Christentum*, ed. T. Klauser, vol. V (*RAC V*) (Stuttgart, 1962) *s.v.* "Epikur", 681-819 (W. Schmid). R. Philippson, *Studien zu Epikur und den Epikuräern* (Hildesheim, announced for 1969, reprint of earlier essays). G. A. Panichas, *Epicurus* (New York, 1967). N. W. DeWitt, *Epicurus and His Philosophy* (Minneapolis, 1954) —to be used with caution, see among others Elder in *American Journal of Philology (AJP)*, *77* (1956) 75-84; *RAC*, *V*, *passim*; Merlan in *The Philosophical Review*, *64* (1955) 140-143. Cf. also *Actes du VIIIe Congrès, Paris, 1968*, Association Guillaume Budé (Paris, 1969), p. 98, n. 3. Additional literature and text editions throughout this essay.

² Close to such an assertion is F. Ueberweg (-K. Praechter), *Die Philosophie des Altertums (Ueberweg)*, 12th edition (Berlin, 1926) p. 578ff, but he speaks of a "Nachblüte". S. Dill, *Roman Society from Nero to Marcus Aurelius* (New York, 1956 [1904]) and DeWitt, *op. cit.*, stress the reaction of Epicureanism against the increasing "religionization" in late antiquity and the clash of Epicureanism with Stoicism, Platonism and Christianity.

³ On the Herculanean papyri found in Piso's villa, many of which probably represent the private library of Philodemus (n. 5, n. 7, below), Epicurean philosopher-in-residence of Piso, see W. Schmid, "Zur Geschichte der Herkulaneischen Studien". *Parola del Passato (PdP)*, *10* (1955) 478-500 and W. Crönert, *Kolotes und Menedemos* (Leipzig, 1906, recently reprinted). Further: A. Vogliano, *Epicuri et Epicureorum Scripta in Herculanensibus Papyris servata* (Berlin) 1928.

⁴ Among the vast literature: P. Boyancé, *Lucrèce et L'Épicurisme* (Paris, 1967); D. R. Dudley *et al.*, *Lucretius* (New York, 1965); L. Edelstein, *The Idea of Progress in Classical Antiquity* (Baltimore, 1967) ch. IV; C. Bailey (ed., tr.) *Lucretius, De Rerum Natura*, 3 vols. (Oxford, 1947); O. Regenbogen, *Kleine Schriften* (Munich, 1961) 296-386; P. DeLacy, "Lucretius and the History of Epicureanism", *Transactions...American Philological Association (TAPA)*, *79* (1948) 12-23. On some differences between Epicurus and Lucretius see W. Schmid, "Götter und Menschen in der Theologie Epikurs", *Rheinisches Museum (RM)*, *94* (1951) 97-156, end.

⁵ *P.-W* vol. 38 (1938), *s.v.* (5), 2444-2482 (R. Philippson); *OCD*; *RAC*, *V*; Crönert, *op. cit.*, P. and E. A. DeLacy, *Philodemus: On Methods of Inference* (Philadelphia, 1941). See n. 7, Horace, and n. 10, below.

⁶ Such judgments are based (1) on the evaluations of classical writers, (2) on modern evaluations which frequently consider the seriousness, coherence, originality and effectiveness of a thought system. The strongest factor in these judgments, however, is (3)

the chance survival of the works of a philosopher. For this reason, we are really unable to evaluate realistically Metrodorus, Hermarchus, or Colotes among the earliest Epicureans, or Demetrius Laco(n) who may, with more identifications of his work and, perhaps, more finds, take the place of Philodemus in the future, see Philippson, "Pap. Herc. 831", *AJP*, *64* (1943) 148-162; Crönert, *op. cit.*; W. Schmidt in *Epicurea in Memoriam Hectoris Bignone* (Genoa, 1959) 179-195 and "Die Netze des Seelenfängers", *PdP*, *10* (1955) 440-447. The change which Demetrius and Philodemus introduced was a re-evaluation of Epicurus' rejection of mathematics, poetry, rhetoric, music and other disciplines (more below).

[7] Lit.: Roman histories and works on Roman civilization, literature, religion, and thought. Briefest bibliographical survey: H. J. Rose, *A Handbook of Latin Literature* (New York, 1960) 534ff. M. Schanz - C. Hosius (- G. Krüger), *Geschichte der römischen Literatur*, I-IV, var. editions (Munich, variously 1920-1935). C. Bailey, *Phases in the Religion of Ancient Rome* (Berkeley, 1932); T. Frank, *Life and Literature in the Roman Republic* (Berkeley, 1930); *Vergil*, (New York, 1922); S. Dill, *op. cit.*; R. Syme, *The Roman Revolution* (Oxford, 1939); M. L. Clarke, *The Roman Mind* (New York, 1968 [1960]); C. Koch, *Religio* (Nürnberg, 1960); L. Friedlaender, ... *Sittengeschichte Roms*, 9th to 10th editions, 4 vols. (Leipzig, 1920-1923).

Specifically: CAESAR : DeWitt, *op. cit.*; M. Cary and T. J. Haarhoff, *Life and Thought in the Greek and Roman World* (London, 1940) p. 337. A. Momigliano, "Reviews and Discussions", *Journal of Roman Studies*, *31* (1941) 149-157 (Caesar's Epicureanism is still controverted). J. W. Duff., *A Literary History of Rome*... to... the Golden Age, third edition (New York, 1963 [1953]), p. 205 and ch. V.

PISO : Cicero, *In Pisonem*. W. Allen Jr., P. DeLacy, "The Patrons of Philodemus", *Classical Philology* (*CP*), *34* (1939) 59-65; Momigliano, *op. cit.*; *OCD* (5); P. DeLacy, "Cicero's Invective against Piso", *TAPA*, *72* (1941) 49-58.

CASSIUS : Plutarch, *Lives* : *Caesar* 66; *Brutus* 37, 39.

ATTICUS : R. J. Leslie, *The Epicureanism of Titus Pomponius Atticus* (Philadelphia, 1950).

HORACE: DeWitt, "Epicurean Doctrine in Horace", *CP*, *34* (1939) 127-134; "The Epicurean Doctrine of Gratitude", *AJP*, *58* (1937) 320-328. P. Green, *Essays in Antiquity* (Cleveland, 1960) 160ff.; J. I. M. Tait *Philodemus' Influence on the Latin Poets* (Bryn Mawr, 1941, Diss.); E. Fraenkel, *Horace* (Oxford, 1957 : "... full adherence to the Epicurean creed") p. 255 on *Epist*. i. 18; 96-103, see p. 254. Very perceptive, Schmid *RAC*, V, col. 766ff. —Epicurean "withdrawal" merely as a basis for a religiosity that evaluates fear positively is claimed for Horace by Koch, *op. cit.*, p. 120. R. C. Getty, "Recent Work on Horace", *CW*, *52* (1959) 167-188.

VERGIL : T. Frank, *op. cit.*, chs. VII-IX. He doubts, p. 109, whether Vergil ever left Epicureanism behind, sees restatements of it in the first book of the *Aeneid* and in the *Georgics*, 11 years before his death; see also p. 182ff. W. F. Jackson Knight, *Roman Vergil* (London, 1944, "Penguin" 1966), likewise, speaks of a permanent strong influence of Epicureanism , p. 80f. etc., but Rose, *Handbook*, claims that Vergil abandoned it in the *Aeneid* (p. 237).

SENECA : *OCD* (2); Edelstein, *op. cit.*, ch. IV; H. Mutschmann, "Seneca und Epikur", *Hermes*, *50* (1915) 321-356, triggered off a long controversy in the classical journals. K. Abel, Review of L. Campose's *Seneca e l'epicureismo* (Benevento, 1960) in *Gnomon*, *33* (1961) 793-796. H. Cancik, *Untersuchungen zu Senecas epistulae morales*, *Spudasmata*, *18* (Hildesheim, 1967).

PETRONIUS : *OCD*, *s.v.*, (2), "Arbiter" ; G. Highet, "Petronius, the Moralist", *TAPA*, 72 (1941) 176-194; *The Anatomy of Satire* (Princeton, 1962) : "an intelligent Epicurean observer", p. 115. More cautious : J. P. Sullivan, *The Satyricon of Petronius* (Bloomington, Ind., 1968). The reference to Epicurus as "pater veri", "father of truth", *Sat.* 132, end, who recommends the pleasures of love (he did not) is, of course, supposed to represent the vulgarized popular concept of Epicureanism. G. Bagnani, *Arbiter of Elegance, Phoenix Suppl.*, 2 (Toronto, 1954).

[8] OVID : *Tristia* III. iv. 25 quotes Epicurus' famous "live unobtrusively". More below.

MAECENAS : DeWitt, *Epicurus...*, 341f. *OCD*.

JUVENAL : P. Green, *op. cit.*, p. 179. G. Highet, "The Philosophy of Juvenal", *TAPA*, 70 (1939) 254-270; *Anatomy...*, p. 243 : his prescription of moderation (V) is Epicurean. See his satire on love , VI. 461-464, 471-473, Lucretius' similar attitude, IV. 1173-1184, and the warnings of Epicurus himself, below.

[9] *Ueberweg*, p. 445 and Index; H. Usener, *Epicurea* (Stuttgart, 1966 [1887]; Rome, 1963 [1887]) Index, p. 427 (*Usener*).

[10] Among his Epicurean friends were Suffeius, Marius, Matius, Marcius Fadus, etc., see *ad familiares*, *de finibus*, indexes. *OCD*, *P.-W.*, *RAC*, V, Some of his major works include substantial portrayals with subsequent refutations of Epicureanism, such as *de fin.*; *de natura deorum*; *Tusculan Disputations*; *de divinatione*; *de fato*; and *in Pisonem*. See also DeLacy, n. 7, above; on Atticus, n. 7, above. M. N. Packer, *Cicero's Presentation of Epicurean Ethics* (New York, 1938, Diss.). R. Heinze, *Vom Geist des Römertums*, third edition (Darmstadt, 1960, repr.). Philodemus as the source of his portrayal of Epicurean doctrine on the gods : R. Philippson, "Die Quelle der epikuräischen Götterlehre in Ciceros Erstem Buche De Natura Deorum", *Symbolae Osloenses* (*SO*), XIX (1939) 15-40. Cicero's anti-Epicurean essays and arguments were still a model for the Christian apologetes Lactantius and Arnobius, *c*. 300.

[11] Italiam totam occupaverunt, *Tusc.* IV. iii. 7 ; ... non solum Graecia et Italia sed etiam omnis barbaria..., *de fin*. II. xv. 49, see I. v. 13, I. vii. 25, I. viii. 27, etc. Praises : *de fin.* II. xxxv. 119, *Tusc.* V. xxxii. 89. Cicero once appealed to Memmius (to whom Lucretius had dedicated his poem) to preserve the original site of Epicurus' Athenian Garden which Memmius had purchased (*ad fam.* XIII. i.). Beside those listed, above, Cicero mentions the Roman Epicurean teachers Amafinius, Rabirius and Catius. His presumed edition of Lucretius is mentioned in the passage of Jerome discussed below, n. 152ff. (libros... quos portea Cicero emendavit), and he once praised highly Lucretius' poems (*sic*) to his brother Quintus, *ad. fam*. II. ix. 3, ... poemata ... multis luminibus ingeni... multae tamen artis...

[12] So. e.g., Friedlaender, *op. cit.*, III, p. 299. Pliny, whose scientific observations and death at the outbreak of Vesuvius have been famous acquired additional renown when his description of the Qumran (Dead Sea) community, *nat. hist.* V. xv. 73, became relevant again. Mommsen's claim that Pliny was in the employ of Titus at the siege of Jerusalem in 70 has not been generally accepted, see *OCD*, p. 704.

Caesar, Cassius, Petronius, and Pliny all spent some time in various military, political or administrational capacities in the Near East, and Zeno, Phaedrus, and Philodemus were natives of that region. — Additional detail on Epicureanism in Rome : Friedlaender, *op. cit.* III, p. 270, n. 1.

[13] The latter was very positively inclined toward Epicureanism as his own literary works clearly indicate, cf. C. R. Haines, ed., tr., *Marcus Aurelius Antoninus*, rev. (Cam-

bridge, Mass., London, 1930), via Index. — On the peace between Roman emperors and philosophical schools see M. Rostovtzeff, *The Social and Economic History of the Roman Empire*, 2nd edition, 2 vols. (Oxford, 1957) p. 591, n. 34, especially the letters of Plotina to the philosophers of the Epicurean school and to Hadrian. See also *RAC*, V, col. 769. On this and the endowment of philosophical schools by Marcus Aurelius see H. Diels, *Archive für Geschichte der Philosophie*, *4*, (1891) 486-491. The active support of the emperors and their final joining the ranks of philosophy was the more remarkable after their persecution of philosophers in some phases of the early Empire, especially under Domitian (81-96).

[14] R. D. Hicks, *Stoic and Epicurean* (New York, 1910) p. xix. Plutarch's lifetime : *c.* 46 - *c.* 120. More on him, below.

[15] His oral teachings (Greek) edited by his pupil Arrianus (*Discourses* and *Encheiridion*, 2nd Century) have much material in common with talmudic lore, including his cynicizing nostalgic description of the Sage, see H. A. Fischel, *Cynicism and the Ancient Near East* (*Cynicism*), forthcoming; "Studies in Cynicism and the ancient Near East : The Transformation of a *Chria*", in *Religions in Antiquity*, Essays in Memory of Erwin Ramsdell Goodenough, ed. J. Neusner, *Numen Suppl.*, XIV (Leiden, 1968) 372-411 (*Studies*); "Story and History : Observations on Greco-Roman Rhetoric and Pharisaism", in *American Oriental Society Middle West Branch Semi-Centennial Volume*, ed. D. Sinor (Bloomington, Ind., 1969) 59-88 (*Story*). So, e.g., *Disc.* II. xx. 34f.

[16] According to Josephus, *Ant.* X. xi. 7 (277ff.) Daniel refutes Epicureanism, i.e., proves the existence of divine providence in the universe. The argument is similar to Plutarch, *de Pythiae Orac.* 8, 398 B, cf. *Usener*, p. 355. In *Ant.* XIX. i. 5 (32) Josephus mentions a certain Pompedius (or Pomponius), an Epicurean, and his life of ease, suggesting inconsistency between his belief and his action, a frequent criticism. The passage *contra Apionem* ii. 19 (180f.) mentions generally philosophers of the nations who deny divine providence. Two famous passages —a frequently repeated ingenious interpretation notwithstanding— do not portray the Sadducees as Epicureans. Josephus' language is here quite non-philosophical (in contradistinction to the other passages) stating simply Jewish theologumena of the Sadducees, *Ant.* XVIII. i. 4 (16) and *Bell. Jud.* II. viii. 14 (164f.).

[17] *OCD*; *RAC*, V; Crönert, *op. cit.*, via Index. Other representatives of this early Epicurean school of the East are Nicasicrates and Timasagoras, see *P.-W.*, *s.v.*, "Philodemus;" Crönert, *op. cit.*, *Ueberweg*, pp. 436, 484, 134*. Philonides was apparently the editor of Epicurean anthologies which were widely used thereafter, see *Usener*, p. 148.

[18] See n. 69, below.

[19] Diogenes Laertius, *Lives of the Philosophers* (*Vitae philosophorum*), ed. H. S. Long, 2 vols. (Oxford, 1964), X. 4 (*D.L.*). B. Z. Wacholder, *Nicolaus of Damascus* (Berkeley, 1962). The activities of Philodemus, however, should be considered under Roman Epicureanism.

[20] Mentioned by name only twice, a fact caused by the hyperbole of Philo's style. See "Index of Names" and "Index of Notes", vol. X, *Philo*, ed., tr., F. H. Colson *et al.* (Cambridge, Mass., London, 1962).

[21] Increase of opposition by itself does not yet indicate an increase in the true strength of Epicureanism, since the former may be wholly rhetorical and literary but not directed against living representatives, Moreover, such opposition is frequently aimed at inner heterodox deviationism in the opponent's camp, the Epicureans merely being literary scapegoats. Anti-Epicureanism may also be a product of the urge for dialectic and con-

troversy, the latter being an important part of philosophical and theological training. Finally, opposition arose whenever the classical position of Epicureanism was believed to threaten the progress of a scholarly or scientific discipline, such as physics or medicine, a fact which provoked Galen's (129 - c. 199) opposition to Asclepiades (*Usener*, Index, p. 427).

22 *P.-W.*, *Suppl.* V (Stuttgart, 1931) 153-172, Philippson. Editions : C. W. Chilton (Leipzig, 1967), A. Grilli (Milan, 1960), I. William (Leipzig, 1907). According to Hicks, *op. cit.*, his *floruit* was closer to 200.

23 *OCD*; *P.-W.*

24 Chs. 38, 46, 53ff.

25 Especially Colossians and Ephesians. On Paul's encounters with Epicureans and on "Epicurean" features in his own make-up see the somewhat extreme claims of N. W. DeWitt, *St. Paul and Epicurus* (Minneapolis, 1954). Precise details on all patristic data in B. Altaner, *Patrologie*, 5th edition (Freiburg, 1958); on Justin : p. 175f., and J. Quasten, *Patrology*, 3 vols. (Utrecht, 1950-1960); on Justin : II, p. 38-40.

26 In the latter part of his book, however, he recognizes that Celsus was some sort of Platonist. Cf. H. Chadwick, *Origen, Contra Celsum* (Cambridge, 1965 [1953]) xxiv-xxix. — Origen's school was attended by Gregory Thaumaturgus, 233-238. The reading of classical literature, especially of philosophy, was encouraged. Others who were once connected with or attended the school include Pamphilus (founder of the library), Gregory of Nazianzus (c. 350), and, possibly, Eusebius (b. c. 264), cf. R. R.Ruether, *Gregory of Nazianzus*, Oxford, 1969. On Jewish Caesarea with its partly Hellenized population, its Talmudists, and, especially, the school of Abbahu (3rd ct.) see *Jewish Encyclopedia*, vol. 3, New York, 1906, *s.v.* (J.E.).

27 *OCD*, "Diogenianus (2)".

28 The tenth chapter, our most important source for the history of Epicureanism and the biography of its founder is, with its 154 text portions, second only to the treatment of Zeno the Stoic with its 159 units. Plato is third with only 109. The length of the Stoic report is apparently caused by the wider range of Stoic concerns , by the availability of anecdotes, *chriae*, and D.L.'s effort to make an impression with his knowledge. His sympathies, however, are revealed by his emotional and determined defense of Epicurus. U. von Wilamowitz-Moellendorff, on the grounds of a set of other indications, argues that D.L. was, indeed, an Epicurean. See his *Antigonos von Karystos*, 2nd ed. (1881, repr. Berlin 1965), p. 321.

29 Editions: *Usener* (see n. 9, above); texts of all major remains except *Sententiae Vaticanae* (*Gnomologium Vaticanum*) as well as mentions of Epicurus, fragments, *incerta*, discussions of problems (Latin), Indexes, all as of 1887. Few Herculanean items. Still indispensable. The latest and most complete edition including papyri (and Italian translation) is that of G. Arrighetti, *Epicuro, Opere* (Torino, 1960). On others (Diano, Bignone, etc.) see Häsler. Edition and English translation of the major items: C. Bailey, *Epicurus* (Oxford, 1926). On Aristotle and Epicurus: E. Bignone, *L'Aristotele perduto e la formazione filosofica di Epicuro*, 2 vols. (Florence, 1936 ; contended). More on Epicurus' style, below

30 The opinion of Mutschmann, *op. cit.*, that Seneca and his correspondent Lucilius used copies of the original letters has been rejected in classical scholarship. They used collections or epitomes. *D.L.* X. 35-138 preserves three fundamental letters, *To Herodotus, To Pythocles, To Menoeceus* (one of these possibly by Metrodorus). For fragments of many others see *Usener* and Arrighetti ,*op. cit.*, section "Epistulae".Edition of the

three letters also by P. von der Muehll, *Epicurus, Epistolae Tres et Ratae Sententiae* (Stuttgart, 1966 [1922]).

³¹ E.g., the *Sententiae Vaticanae* (see n. 29, above), c. 80 items, in all major editions except *Usener* (the item was discovered too late for inclusion).

³² Or *Ratae Sententiae*, variously rendered as "Catechism", "Doctrines", "Sovran Principals". See *D.L.* X. 138-154; edition by von der Muehll, see n. 30, above; see *RAC*, V, col. 758.

³³ Memorization was recommended and practiced in the Epicurean movement and is reflected as one of its peculiarities in the satires of the anti-Epicureans, see *D.L.* X. 12, 36, 83. Personal diaries, too, were kept being likewise a target of parody: see the example by Carneades (Plutarch, *Moralia* 1089 C), *Usener* fr. 536.

³⁴ The "greater" and the "lesser" epitome. Ambrosius still knew such a epitome, *Usener* fr. 358a. Cf. *D.L.* X. 118 for an ethical epitome of one Diognes. The *Letter to Herodotus* may be such an abridgement.

Lucretius' poetic recreation of Epicurus' system, although important for subsequent Roman literature and all of Western culture, was probably unknown in the Near East outside Latin speaking circles. It was mastered pratically by heart, however, by Lactantius in North Africa.

³⁵ Plutarch's bulky anti-Epicurean polemic occupies 1086 C - 1130 E of his *Moralia*, i.e., the essays *Non posse* ... ("That Epicurus Actually Makes a Pleasant Life Impossible"), *Adversus Colotem*... ("Reply to Colotes in Defence of the Other Philosophies"), and *An recte dictum*... ("Is 'Live Unknown' a Wise Precept ?"), in vol. XIV of the Loeb Classical Library edition of Plutarch's *Moralia*, by B. Einarson and P. H. DeLacy (Cambridge, Mass., London, 1965).

³⁶ On Greco-Roman rhetoric cf. *P.-W.*, "Rhetorik", *Suppl. VII* (1940) 1039-1138 and the standard histories of literature. Monographs that will open up the field are G. M. A. Grube, *The Greek and Roman Critics* (Toronto, 1965); M. L. Clarke, *Rhetoric at Rome* (London, 1953); E. Norden, *Die antike Kunstprosa*, 5th edition (repr. Darmstadt, 1958); George Kennedy, *The Art of Persuasion in Greece*, Princeton, 1963.

³⁷ Aelian(us) represents anti-Epicureanism in its increasingly popularized and somewhat gossipy form, especially in his fragments but also his *Variae historiae*, ed. R. Hercher (Paris, 1858, via Index). With his interest in miracle stories, anecdotes, curiosa, gnomic materials and moralizing he frequently got hold of Greco-Roman items that were used also in talmudic literature, see *Cynicism*.

With some of the Latin Church Fathers, especially Minucius Felix (c. 200), Arnobius, and Lactantius, his student, anti-Epicureanism became more systematic again, but the two latter were "students" of Cicero and former professional rhetoricians, possibly with early Epicurean leanings. According to K. Ziegler, "Der Tod des Lucretius", *Hermes*, 71 (1936) 421-440, p. 428, Lactantius was rather a Stoic before.

³⁸ Aëtius, c. 100 A.D.; used in Ps.-Plutarch's *Placita* and Joh. Stobaeus' *Eclogae*; Diocles of Magnesia, born c. 75 B.C., used by D.L., *et al*. The earliest pattern is Theophrastus' (372/69-288/85) *Physikōn doxai*, on the pre-Socratics. Similar sketches of beliefs and opinions existed on practically all other branches of knowledge.

³⁹ The succession of philosophers as the heads of schools, or as masters and disciples, in form of a literary genre was initiated by the Alexandrinian Sotion between 200 and 170 B.C. Others active in this genre were Sosicrates of Rhodes (*fl.* c. 140 B.C. ?) and Alexander Polyhistor (b. c. 105 B.C.).

⁴⁰ E.g., by Favorinus of the Hadrianic period and Flavius P. Philostratus (b. c. 170 A.D.). Earliest pattern was by Antigonus of Carystus, c. 290-239.

⁴¹ See n. 36, above, and H. I. Marrou, *A History of Education in Antiquity* (New York, 1956). — *D.L.* represents a mixture of all these literary forms. One of his models was a woman philosopher, Pamphila, of the Neronic age, another Hermippus of Smyrna, *fl.* 3rd ct. B.C. — The Mishnah tractate *Pirḳe Aboth* is partially a diadochic-doxographic work.

⁴² Most modern treatments of Epicureanism speak of its decline in Roman Imperial times (3rd-4th cts.) and quote Julian's famous (fragmentary) letter to a priest (301 C-D) of 367 A.D. and Augustine's letter 118 to Dioscorus (21 see 12, *Usener* fr. 317) of 410 A.D. as to the near-disappearance of Epicurean literature. The very same Julian, however, called on all other philosophies, Epicureanism included, for a united front against Christianity, cf. J. Geffcken, *Der Ausgang des griechisch-römischen Heidentums* (Darmstadt, 1963 [1929]), p. 133. Also Friedlaender, *op. cit.*, *loc. cit.*, took Julian's opinion (and that of Usener) as to the near-disappearance of Epicureanism with a grain of salt. Indeed, in the 5th ct. the epigrams of Pallades still show Epicurean coloration, *RAC*, *V*, col. 777. (On epitaphs, see n. 69). The Epicurean academy had vanished long ago as well as the groups of zealous Epicureans. But then Epicureanism and anti-Epicureanism had become part and parcel of the general rhetorical and philosophical lore and an epicureanizing tendency or a bookish Epicureanism was still possible.

⁴³ Technical term (pl.; sing.: Tanna) for the teachers of the rabbinic civilization whose work is reflected in Mishnah, Tosephta, early Midrash, and materials outside these collections, especially a large number of quotations (*baraithoth*, some collected by M. Higger) in the Jerusalem Talmud (JT, i.e., Talmud Yerushalmi or Palestinian Talmud, codified c. 400 A.D.) and the Babylonian Talmud (BT, i.e., Talmud Babli, codified c. 500) as well as some monographs (*Megillath Taʿanith*, etc.), c. 70-200.

LITERATURE : Major encyclopedias of Judaism, such as *Jewish Encyclopedia* (*JE*); *Universal Jewish Encyclopedia* (*UJE*); *Encyclopaedia Judaica* (*EJ*; to "Lyra"); *Jüdisches Lexicon* (*JL*); histories of the Jewish people of this period, e.g., S. W. Baron, *A Social and Religious History of the Jews*, 2nd edition, 14 vols. and Index vol. to date, esp. I and II (Philadelphia-New York, 1952-); S. Zeitlin, *The Rise and Fall of the Judaean State*, 2 vols. (Philadelphia, 1962, 1967); M. Avi-Yonah, *Bime Roma u-Bizantiyon* (Jerusalem, 1962; German : Berlin, 1962); and introductions to the earlier talmudic literature, among others, H. L. Strack, *Introduction to the Talmud and Midrash*, 5th edition (Philadelphia, 1931); C. Albeck, *Mavo' la-Mishnah* (Tel-Aviv, 1959); Y.(J.)N. Epstein, *Mevo'ot le-Siphrut ha-Tanna'im* (Tel-Aviv, 1957). Further : W. Bacher, *Die Agada der Tannaiten*, I, second edition, II (Strassburg, 1903, 1890 and recent reprints); A. Guttmann's new "Bibliography 1925-1967" in a reprint of M. Mielziner, *Introduction to the Talmud*, 3rd edition (New York, 1968 [1925]) and *Rabbinic Judaism in the Making* (Detroit 1970); *Entsiklopediyah talmudit*, ed. M. Berlin, *et al.*, 14 vols. to date (Jerusalem), 1953-).

⁴⁴ The teachers (pl.; sing. : Amora) who continued and further developed the talmudic tradition after 200, both in Palestine and Babylonia.

ADDITIONAL LITERATURE : W. Bacher, *Die Agada der palästinensischen Amoräer*, 3 vols. (Strassburg, 1892-1899 and recent repr.); *Die Agada der babylonischen Amoräer*, 2nd edition (Hildesheim, 1967 [1913]), *Tradition und Tradenten* (Berlin, 1966 [1914]); J. Neusner, *A History of the Jews in Babylonia*, 5 vols. (Leiden, 1965-70); Y.(J.)N. Epstein, *Mevo'ot le-Siphrut ha-Amora'im* (Tel-Aviv, 1962); C. Albeck, *Mavo' la-Talmudim* (Tel-Aviv, 1969). Texts : BT : any edition in conjunction with L. Goldschmidt, *Der babylonische Talmud...*, 9 vols. (Berlin 1897-1933, vol. 9 : Haag, 1935) and R. N. Rabinowitz

(Rabbinovicz), *Sepher Diḳduḳe Sophrim*, 16 vols. (Munich, vol. 16, Przemysl, ed. H. Ehrentreu, 1867-1897). JT : Krotoshin (1866); Vilno (Wilna), 8 vols. (Romm, 1922) and B. Ratner, *(Sepher) Ahabath Ṣiyyon Virushalayim*, 10 (12) vols. (Vilno, 1901-1913, repr. Jerusalem, 1966ff.). Additional text-critical aids in the respective notes, below.

[45] A related development, i.e., the silent and, perhaps, unconscious adoption and adaptation of popular rhetorical Cynicism, its values, anecdotes, and literary forms, and its simultaneous official rejection in rabbinic culture within the first two centuries A.D. is claimed in *Cynicism*.

[46] See Part III, *infra*.

[47] Apart from talmudic passages that include expressly the Hebrew equivalents for "Epicurean" (see n. 48) and "Epicureanism" the following items have been discovered previously :

1. "Live unobtrusively", in Bacher's *Amoraer*, II, p. 9, n. 6. (Details, below, n. 64).

2. References to an "automatic" world, as in Midrash Pss. 1. 22 and Josephus, *Ant*. X. xi. 7 (278), see S. Lieberman, "How Much Greek in Palestine ?" in *Biblical and Other Studies*, ed. A. Altmann (Cambridge, Mass., 1963) 123-141, p. 130, and E. (M). Stein, see n. 32, *ibid*.

3. An echo of the famous Epicurean "nothing from nothing", ingeniously reconstructed by S. Lieberman, "How Much Greek...", p. 138. The brief talmudic formula, however, is far removed from the explicit formulations of Epicurus and Lucretius but close to later popular abbreviations, such as found in Persius' caricature of Epicureanism in *Sat*. III. 83f., "de nihilo nihilum". On this see J. W. Spaeth Jr., "Epicurus in Perseus *Sat*. 3. 83f.," *TAPA*, 73 (1942) 119-122. Cf. Part III, n. 157.

4. S. Lieberman, "Some Aspects of After Life in Early Rabbinic Literature", in *Harry Austryn Wolfson Jubilee Volume*, 3 vols. (Jerusalem, 1965), vol. II, 495-532, p. 505, discusses the (Epicurean) metaphor of death as a ship reaching the harbor, in Eccl. R. on 7 :1 and *Gnom. Vat*. XVII, but cautiously declares it to be current among all intelligent people of the era.

[48] Most of the anti-Epicurean statements include the Hebrew term אפיקורוס and אפיקורסות and are listed in (C)H. J. Kas(s)owski, *Thesaurus Talmudis Concordantiae Verborum*, 21 vols. to date (Jerusalem, 1954-00); see "Epikuros", *EJ* and *JL*; "Epicurus", *UJE*; "Apikoros", *JE*; "Epicureans and Epicureanism", *EJ*, English (New York-Jerusalem, 1971). See also A. Marmorstein, "Les Épicuriens dans la littérature talmudique", *Revue des Études Juives (REJ)*, 53 (1907) 181-193, and S. M. Wagner, *Religious Nonconformity in Ancient Jewish Life* (Ann Arbor, 1965; D. H. L. Diss., Yeshiva University, 1964), ch. X.

[49] JT *Ḥagigah* 77b, II. 1 (Krotoshin and Vilno); Song of Songs (*Shir ha-Shirim*) Rabba (*SSR*) on 1. 4, #1; Tosephta (Tos.) *Ḥagigah* II. 3-4, ed. M. S. Zuckermandel, *Tosephta* (repr. Jerusalem, 1963) p. 234. On Lieberman's Tosephta edition see n. 52, below.

[50] In special midrashic-mystical works, such as *Alphabethoth de-Rabbi Akiba*, the Hekhaloth literature, and others, see G. G. Scholem, *Major Trends in Jewish Mysticism*, 2nd edition (New York, 1946).

[51] On the reasons for this statement see the discussion, below.

[52] S. Lieberman, in his *Tosephta ki-pheshuṭah*, pt. V (New York, 1962) p. 1289, treats manuscript variants and talmudic-midrashic parallels including later medieval occurences.

Another important critical treatment of text and context is that of E. E. Urbach, "*Ha-masorot 'al torat ha-sod bi-teḳuphat ha-Tanna'im*" in *Studies in Mysticism and Religion* presented on Gershom G. Scholem's 70th birthday (Jerusalem, 1967), 27 pages (no continuous pagination), pp. 12-17.

⁵³ הציץ, "he looked", is not repeated for Acher, line 24, and Akiba, line 25, although all other variants have it. Commentators, both medieval and modern, who see in this passage a mystical meaning, occasionally stress this fact: Akiba escaped, since he did not glance (at the Divine Presence). As we shall see, the original intention of the statement was quite different. Actually, repetition of הציץ is unnecessary: it is implied both in lines 24 and 25.

⁵⁴ JT adds: נכנס בשלום, "entered in peace (and left in peace)". The text of BT, however, is quite sufficient, since the episode of the entry has been mentioned initially.

⁵⁵ Minor textual variants which do not contribute to meaning are not listed here. Among the major differences in the parallel passages are:

1. All parallels lack Akiba's warning, lines 6-9.

2. Tos. and JT add two more *testimonia* characterizing Acher and Akiba: Eccl. 5: 5 and Cant. 1: 4, a or b. As will be shown, these are later additions.

3. In JT, b. Azzai is "stricken" and b. Zoma dies. More on this detail below.

4. In JT and Tos. ms. L the names of the sages are missing initially. They are, however, introduced in the progress of the narrative.

5. Tos., JT and *SSR* supply additional anecdotal material on some or all of the four, either within our item or preceding it. Detailed discussion of this will follow, below.

⁵⁶ In "Part III" the present writer will proffer the thesis that Epicurean shadings of talmudic teachings derive from encounters with the rhetoric of Greco-Roman administrations and public orators.

⁵⁷ (Mishnah) *Pirḳē Aboth* (*P.A.*) 2. 14 (2.18 Taylor) warns the believer to be prepared for such encounters. BT *Ḥagigah* 5b includes an obviously legendary contest and battle of wits (*altercatio*) between Joshua b. Hananiah and an Epicurean before Hadrian in which the Epicurean forfeits his life. The item represents a famous piece of folklore (silent answers on silent questions) that remained current in several attractive versions to the present day. (Modern commentators have overlooked the fact that this debate centers around a well-known Epicurean teaching: that the gods are not concerned with the fate of mankind).

Sifre XII, Friedmann 67b, introduces arrogant questions of the (Epicurean) Israelites; and they are hard on Moses, Targum Jonathan Deut. 1 :12.

Whereas the defense of the faith against Epicureans in these items was laudable and necessary although dangerous, voluntary entanglements with Epicureans must have aroused suspicion. See also the censoring of Acher for reading Greek books, *Ḥag.* 16b, JT *Megillah* I. 9, and other well-known talmudic items directed against the use of Greek or Greek wisdom, such as BT *Megillah* 9a; JT *Shabbat* 3c, I. 6; (Mishnah) *Soṭah* 9.14; BT *Soṭah* 49b; Tos. *Abodah Zarah* I.20; BT *Menaḥoth* 99b, etc. See "Greek and Latin, Rabbinic Knowledge of", English *EJ*. See n. 217, below.

⁵⁸ BT *Soṭah* 4b, top; BT *Kethuboth* 63a. This view became dominant in all later portrayals of b. Azzai in Jewish tradition, including most modern treatments, see Bacher, *Tannaiten* I, p. 407f. (emphatic print). L. Finkelstein in his charming popular book *Akiba* (New York, 1936) p. 162, claims that also b. Zoma was unmarried (because of his poverty)

but does not offer sources for this statement. However this may be, b. Zoma's celibacy never was a *cause célèbre*.

⁵⁹ The celibacy of b. Azzai is clearly established in talmudic tradition. Thus in a tannaitic passage, BT *Yebamoth* 63b, after a statement of his in which he glorifies the biblical commandment of פריה ורביה (propagation of the race), he is being challenged by his contemporaries for his inconsistency. His defense is the famous ומה אעשה שנפשי חשקה בתורה אפשר לעולם שיתקיים על ידי אחרים, "but what shall I do now that my soul is in love (cf. Gen. 34:8) with Torah; perhaps the world will propagate itself by others". Although this passage may refer only to his failure to raise children, his celibacy is expressly mentioned in BT *Soṭah*, top. Here Amoraic discussants are puzzled to hear opinions in matters of sex legislation from one "who never married", דלא נסיב (Aramaic). The ensuing discussion (*gemara*) then attempts to legitimize b. Azzai's opinion through legal fiction: "One could use the assumption (ואי בעית אימא, "if you wish I could say") he had married and separated (נסיב ופריש הוה) or that he had heard it from his teacher or that he had special insights by reason of his piety" (quoting Ps. 25:14).

A further difficulty is represented by this Amoraic formula פריש הוה. In all probability it indicates here continence, or non-consummation of marriage in accordance with similar uses of this root, cf. J. Levy, *Wörterbuch über die Talmudim und Midrashim*, reprint, 2nd edition (Darmstadt, 1963) vol. IV, p. 141b and M. Jastrow, *Dictionary of Talmud Babli...* (New York, 1943 [1903]) ,*s.v.* (Hebrew and "Chaldean") 1241f. This particular verb, his pre-occupation with Torah, and the motif of the sacrificial devotion of a sage's wife (Akiba's daughter) seem to be the threefold literary basis for a moving story in *Midrash Shir ha-Shirim*, ed. L. Grünhut (Jerusalem, 1897) 5b (to be distinguished from *SSR* and *SS Zuta*). According to this story (overlooked by Bacher and the encyclopedias) b. Azzai did not consummate his marriage when during the wedding night he recognized that his pre-occupation with Torah made him an unsuitable marriage partner and the devoted bride offered to be a servant for life in house and academy.

The medieval French and German commentators, however, whose work forms the Hebrew commentary Tosaphoth on the Babylonian Talmud, apparently felt uneasy about this tradition of continence and tried to suggest less likely but more conventional meanings for פריש. Tosaphot on *Soṭah* 4b, *s.v.*, ברתיה, thus thinks of a partially completed marriage ceremony (only the "engagement" part), Tosaphoth on *Yeb.* 63b., *s.v.* שיתקיים, of actual divorce (גירש). Apart from these precarious "witnesses" for b. Azzai's marriage the only source (equally shaky) which mentions a marriage of b. Azzai is BT *Kethuboth* 63a; but this mention is merely a brief note appended to the famous story, fully spelled out, of Akiba's bride who waited for him 24 years. This note claims that the same thing happened also to b. Azzai who married Akiba's daughter, and like mother like daughter. This note is apparently caused by the uncertainties and duplications in the traditions on Akiba and b. Azzai which overlap in many more instances (e.g., martyrdom in the Bar Kokheba upheaval; various sayings and opinions, etc., see Bacher *Tannaiten*. B. Azzai's martyrdom: Midr. Lam. on 2:2; Midr. Pss., ch. 9; *Yalḳut Shime'oni*, *ibid*.).

⁶⁰ Mainly *D.L.* X. 1-28, usually quoted as *Vita Epicuri*.

⁶¹ It is, of course, irrelevant that among others, Diogenes the Cynic —some of whose exploits and sayings were also known to the Talmud and became attached to Hillel the Elder, see *Cynicism*— did not marry either. In the case of Diogenes this fact is never stressed —although his women-hating *sententiae* became well-known— and the later

Cynical tradition did not follow his example; on the contrary, his principal disciple Crates did marry the Cynical philosopher Hipparchia and this peculiar Cynical-philosophical marriage became exemplary (*D.L.* VI. 96-98, ch. 7). The Hipparchia tradition with additions of the story of Arete (daughter or sister of Aristippus the Cyrenaic, *D.L.* II. 72, 86, see *Cynicism*) and the legend of "Secundus the Silent Philosopher", see B. E. Perry, *Secundus the Silent Philosopher* (Ithaca, 1964) became the basis of the Judaic portrayal of Beruriah, the scholar-wife of R. Meir (see *Cynicism*).

⁶² *D.L.* X. 119, Long; Arrighetti p. 27; Bailey, *Epicurus*, p. 167; *Usener* fr. 94, p. 130; fr. 19, p. 97f: καὶ μὴν καὶ γαμήσειν... The text used by R. D. Hicks in his edition of Diogenes Laertius (Cambridge, Mass., London) 2 vols., 1950, 1958, has καὶ μηδὲ, "the Sage will *not* marry...", a less well attested and ecclectic text (see Hicks himself, p. xxxvii) but perhaps not entirely without psychological value, since copyists and editors throughout all ages must have been influenced by the later caricature of Epicurus' opinion.

⁶³ *Usener*, p. 98 (read "*Disc*. I, 23, 3") and p. 525, 1.18.

⁶⁴ *Stromata* II. 23, *Usener* fr. 526. See E. A. Sophocles, *Greek Lexicon of the Roman and Byzantine Periods* (Boston, 1879) *s.v. aphalkē* (distraction). According to Clement Epicurus follows here, too, Democritus. One does not have to assume that the original meaning of one of Epicurus' most famous sayings, λάθε βιώσας, "live unobtrusively" (or "withdrawn", "inconspicuously", "unknown", "im Verborgenen") refers to this rejection of marriage, as R. Vischer, *Das einfache Leben* (Göttingen, 1965) p. 74, suggests. This coinage refers rather to the Epicurean ideal of withdrawal (*ataraxia*, somewhat different from the Stoic *apatheia*) from public life and from any pain and turmoil of this sort. Sources: *Usener* fr. 551, Bailey fr. 86. See Plutarch's essay, *Moralia* 1128ff., which includes this saying in its title: *ΕΙ ΚΑΛΩΣ ΕΙΡΗΤΑΙ ΤΟ ΛΑΘΕ ΒΙΩΣΑΣ* or An recte dictum sit *latenter esse vivendum*, "Is 'live unknown' a wise precept?" (so Einarson - DeLacy, *op. cit.*). This *sententia* appears in BT *Sanhedrin* 14a and 92a as R. Eleʻazar's (ben Pedat, died c. 280): לעולם הוי קבל וקיים, see Levy, *op. cit.*, *s.v.* קבל. Ovid's formulation, *Tristia* III. iv. 25, is similar: Crede mihi, bene qui latuit, bene vivit, "believe me, who hides well lives well".

⁶⁵ In the anecdote (*chria*) concerning Arcesilaus and a certain Hemon, *D.L.* IV. 34, who said that to him it was "not right that the sage fall in love", the young dandy is, of course, supposed to be an Epicurean. See also the *chria* of Chrysippus, quoted below. See *Anthol. Palat.*, X. 93, an epigram by Lucilius. Quite contrary to another vulgarized view of Epicureanism is also *D.L.* X. 118, *Usener* fr. 62: "Intercourse (*synousiē*; many variants of this basic root occur in the mss.; Bailey fr. LI lists, in addition, *aphrodisia*, "pleasures of love"), they say, has never done any good; one can be glad if it has done no harm".

⁶⁶ *Ep. ad Att.* VII. ii. 4. *Adv. Col.* (*Moralia*) 1123 A, see 100 D.

⁶⁷ *Disc.* III. vii. 19.

⁶⁸ Of the Platonic school (Academy), c. 318-242, see *D.L.* IV. 28-45. The anecdote: IV. 43.

⁶⁹ In epitaphs sentimental or witty coinages in the Epicurean mood were very popular, see R. Lattimore, *Themes in Greek and Latin Epitaphs* (Urbana, 1962) § 74, 260-265. Some of these formulations, quite un-Christian, were still used on Christian tombs (§ 4, p. 320, top, and p. 330, middle, have an Epicurean flavor, not commented upon by the author). For the present theme a Tarsian epitaph is of interest. Tarsus, in the late 2nd ct. B.C., went through an episode of tyranny under Lysias, an Epicurean,

mentioned, e.g., by Athenaeus (early 3rd ct. A.D. Athenaeus is usually positive on Epicureanism), *Deipnosophists* V. 215 B-C. From Tarsus we have the epitaph of one Dionysus : "I never married and I wish my father never had", S. K. Eddy, *The King is Dead* (Lincoln, Neb., 1961) p. 155. — More on the Epicurean epitaph with Friendlaender, *op. cit.*, III, p. 299ff; *RAC*, V, col. 773 f. W. Peek, *Griechische Grabgedichte* (Berlin, 1960), lists an Epicurean item on a Sidonian, No. 201, and an anti-Epicurean one, No. 470, from Miletus.

[70] See Arcesilaus' witticism about eunuchs and men, above. B. Azzai extends the semantic power of Gen. 9:7 back to verse 6a and 6b, combining the opinions of R. Eliʿezer and R. Jacob. A paraphrase of his exegesis would run as follows : "he who does not multiply and is not fruitful spills man's blood and is worthy of death, diminishing the image of God in which He made man". The entire section is introduced by R. Eleʿazar's famous "A man who has no wife is no man", *Yeb.* 63a ! (Amoraic).

[71] If, indeed, *niphgaʿ* was intended to indicate insanity. In detail, below.

[72] Especially Plutarch but likewise all anti-Epicurean sources. Actually, Epicurus has an aesthetic-ethical theory of worship and ὁμοίωσις θεοῦ, i.e., gradual approximation of the divine. Other accusations are of a technical-philosophical nature and thus did not enter popular rhetoric.

[73] The reproach of inconsistency is strongly explicit with b. Azzai : "They said : 'There are some who preach well and act well, others act well but do not preach well; you, however, preach well but do not act well.' " (*Yeb.* 63b end).

[74] Both traditions according to Hermippus, a generous dispenser of chriic and legendary biographic materials. A. dies insane after drinking; similarly Lucretius after imbibing a love potion. Details below. Apparently owing to the lack of an authentic biography Arcesilaus' *bios* had to be created from popular items, among them *chriae*, describing the *sophos* in general or other Sages who were likewise founders of philosophical schools. Items used in his "biography" appear also in that of Hillel the Elder, see *Studies*, p. 379.

[75] *Sifra* on Lev. 1.1, נדבה 2.12, 4a Weiss, and *Sifre* Nu. בההעלתך, 103 Horovitz (read Shimeʿon b. Azzai for Shimeʿon ha-Temani).

[76] Gen. Rabba V. 4 on 1:9, Theodor-Albeck p. 34. Read מיטטור, the Roman *metator*, i.e., surveyor (Jastrow). Levy, III, 87b, prefers, less likely, מטרטר, "to gather with noise", after the text of Midr. Pss. 93. In any case, there is no hint of a Metatron speculation in this as 19th century scholars were inclined to claim, e.g., M. Friedländer, *Die religiösen Bewegungen innerhalb des Judentums im Zeitalter Jesu* (Berlin, 1905), p. 186.

[77] The fire ensued because the Torah was given in fire at Sinai according to b. Azzai, which is not a mystical interpretation. Similarly JT *Ḥagigah* II. 1. In Ruth Rabba VI. 4 on 3 :13 and Eccl. R. on 7 :6 the same is said on R. Eliʿezer and R. Joshua, quite unmystically. It seems that actually in all these cases the fire had the function of indicating the acuteness of rational thinking applied by these sages (so also for Jonathan b. Uzziel and others), or/and that angels assembled at such an amazing feat (cp. Bornstein in *EJ*, s.v., "Elisha b. Abujah"). The connection with the Sinaitic revelation is, of course, b. Azzai's personal *ad hoc* interpretation. In the larger episode regarding Yohanan b. Zakkai and his disciples engaged in *Merkabah* speculation, *Ḥagigah* 14b, the fire is likewise not necessarily a concomitant of mystical insight but another case of incisive interpretation, see Eleʿazar b. Arak who "gave his interpretation and fire came down from heaven and encompassed all the trees..." Even in *Ḥagigah* 13a where a child is consumed

by fire when interpreting Ezekiel, the episode may not allude merely to a fire of danger (or blasphemy) but imply that the child understood (so I. Abrahams in the Soncino translation of BT) and is a sage (so expressly Hananiah b. Hezekiah, BT *ad loc.*). In the court inquiry of Acher's daughter before Yehudah ha-Nasi (more below) the fire seems to indicate Acher's former meritorious study of Torah and precedes such an incisive decision. The mystics, to be sure, had their own function of fire but all the preceding passages are apparently non-mystical.

[78] Including a variant of the Epicurean "nothing from nothing", mentioned above, n. 47. The remaining Epicurean-like bits will be discussed in Part III.

[79] Treated in detail in Part III.

[80] Tos. *Ḥag.* II. 5, p. 234 Z.; JT, *Ḥag.*, 77a, II. 1; BT *Ḥag.* 15a; Genesis Rabba II. 4 on 1.2.

[81] Treated in detail in Part III, Section V.

[82] Contemporary scholars, too, maintain this view. Lieberman, "How much Greek...", p. 139, speaks of a Sethian type of Gnosticism, I. I. Efros, *Ancient Jewish Philosophy* (Detroit, 1964), 56-59, of a Simonian one (of Simon Magus).

[83] *RAC*, V, col. 800, where Schmid also offers one case of actual gnostic borrowing from Epicureanism.

[84] For the metaphysical and theological implications of Epicureanism see especially A. J. Festugière, *Epicurus and His Gods* (Cambridge, Mass., 1956); O. Gigon, *Epikur* (Zurich, 1968 [1949]); G. Freymuth, "Zur Lehre von den Götterbildern in der epikuräischen Philosophie", *Deutsche Akademie der Wissenschaften zu Berlin* (Institut für hellenistisch-römische Philosophie, Veröffentlichung 2, Berlin, 1953) 5-43 and "Methodisches zur epikuräischen Götterlehre", *Philologus, 99* (1955) 234-244; P. Merlan, *Studies in Epicurus and Aristotle* (Wiesbaden, 1960); F. Solmsen, "Epicurus and Cosmological Heresies", *AJP, 72* (1951) 1-23. Schmid in *RM, loc. cit.*; recent essays of Kleve in *SO*.

[85] N. W. DeWitt, "Organization and Procedure in Epicurean Groups", *CP, 31* (1936) 205-211; "Epicurean *Contubernium*", *TAPA, 67* (1936) 55-63.

[86] II. ix. 15, in a passage which is quite similar to an item in Jerome, *In Is.*VII. xviii. 1. Schmid, *RAC*, V, col. 801, suggests that this stereotype may go back to Ammonias Saccas.

[87] *Adv. Marc.* V. xix. 7 and I. xxv. 3.

[88] *De recta in Deum fide* II. 19 (GOS IV. 100) : *RAC*, V, col. 799. Cf. n. 47, No. 2, *supra*.

[89] *Adv. haer.* III. xviii. 1, cf. III. xxiv. 2.

[90] II. xxxii. 2.

[91] *RAC*, V, 801f.; now also R. Jungkuntz, "Fathers, Heretics and Epicureans", *Ecclesiastical Journal, 17* (1966) 3-10; H. Hagendahl, *Latin Fathers and the Classics* (Göteborg, 1958) via Index. Less informative : A. Simpson, "Epicureans, Christians, Atheists in the Second Century", *TAPA, 72* (1941) 372-381. For the Talmud see the encyclopedias, *s.v.* "Epicurus", etc., and especially Marmorstein, *op. cit.*, and Wagner, *op. cit.*, ch. X.

[92] Of course, his frequent mention together with b. Azzai may also have been operative in finding, somehow, an Epicurean aspect in his teaching. See also the possibly conscious effort to find four sages for the sake of literary form, to be discussed, below. On Gnosticism and the Talmud see A. (I.) Altmann, "Gnostische Motive im rabbinischen Schrifttum", *Monatsschrift für Geschichte und Wissenschaft des Judentums (MGWJ, 83* (1963 [1939]) 369-389; G. G. Scholem, *Jewish Gnosticism, Merkabah Mysticism, and Talmudic Tradition* (New York 1960).

⁹³ A survey in Bacher, *Tannaim* I, pp. 430ff.; see also A. Büchler, "Die Erlösung Elisa b. Abujahs...", *MGWJ*, *76* (1932) 412-456. L. Ginzberg in *JE*, V, 138f. is quite uncritical.

⁹⁴ Some are listed in *JE*, see n. 93. A survey of many medieval and modern opinions in T. Wechsler, *Ṣephunot be-masoret Yisra'el* (Jerusalem, 1968) ch. II, p. 18ff.

⁹⁵ JT *Ḥagigah* 77b, II. 1 (original version), Ruth R. VI. 4 on 3:13 and Eccl. R. on 7:8. The report of the latter two sources that the first part of the story happened on a Sabbath, probably introduced to make the breach of the law still more glaring, or to add traditional atmosphere, is of a later date and a common feature also of other later versions of adaptations of *chriae* in Talmud and Midrash; see *Cynicism*.

⁹⁶ *D.L.* X. 25 and 5; see *Usener*, Index p. 411. Metrodorus' (*D.L.* X *passim* and *Usener*, via Index) and Epicurus' memories were celebrated on the 20th of every month, a custom well-known in antiquity and ridiculed by Menippus of Gadara in a special satire (*D.L.* VI. 101). Philodemus, in one of his epigrams, once invited Piso to such an occasion (*Anth. Palat.* IX. 44). Epicureans were nicknamed *eikadistae*, "celebrators of the 20th", because of this custom.

⁹⁷ καταγρονοῦσι τοῦ θείον, "look down upon", make light of.

⁹⁸ Literally: "in as far as", or "seeing that I..." (ὅτε).

⁹⁹ The Greek context mentions that Danaë did not deem her persecutors worthy of an answer.

¹⁰⁰ In the parallel BT *Ḳiddushin* 39b it is Huṣpith the Interpreter whose tongue is dragged by a pig. Acher's exclamation is: "The mouth that uttered pearls licks the dust", perhaps evoking the additional ironic association "pearls before swine". In BT *Ḥullin* 142a the exclamation is provoked by seeing Huṣpith's tongue on a dunghill. For still further details see Part II, *infra*.

¹⁰¹ See the poetic cycle of Machon in Athenaeus' work, XIII. 578 B - 583 D, also ed. A. S. F. Gow, *Machon, The Fragments* (Cambridge, 1965). Others are found throughout *Deipn.* XIII and in the Diogenes material, *D.L.* VI. See also Lucian's *Dialogues of Courtesans*.

¹⁰² One of the earliest calumnies of this sort is refuted by Seneca in his *de vita beata* XII. 4. Anti-Epicurean gossip on Leontion in Athenaeus' *Deipn.* XIII. 588 B.

¹⁰³ *D.L.* and *Usener*, via Indexes, e.g., *D.L.* X. 5, 6, 7, and Festugière, *op. cit.*, p. 29.

¹⁰⁴ BT *Ḥagigah* 15a, continuing the discussion of the Four, anonymous.

It must be kept in mind that the major themes as well as minor thematic detail heard by the listener are often rearranged or redistributed over several stories when renarrated by the listener. See *Cynicism*, "Displacement of Motemes".

¹⁰⁵ Later amplification? See n. 95, above. The radish may have been the payment.

¹⁰⁶ See Ginzberg, *JE*, V, 138f., who pleads for this "shocking" or "detestable".

¹⁰⁷ Leontion calling a competitor and latecomer (*hystera*) to a party "uterus" (*hystera*), *Deipn.* XIII. 585 D; Metaneira remarking on a parasite that he always gets involved with pebbles, falling into pebbled plaster or being condemned by the pebbles of the judges, 584 F; Gnathaena giving witty *ad hoc* nicknames to two lovers, 585 A. Three successive *double entendres* of hers in one allusion: 582 A. Witty reference to "Silencetown" before a babbler: 584 Df. The "Tank" (a nickname) who falls into a jar: 584 B. Thais using a pun on Aegeus (her lover) and "goat" (dative, *Aigei/aigi*): 585 E, etc. The Greek examples are precisely as brief as the Hebrew item.

¹⁰⁸ Judah the Prince, also called simply "Rabbi", editor of the Mishnah, *fl. c.* 200. JT *Ḥag.* 77c., less reliably, has "daughters".

¹⁰⁹ The incident, if at all historical, continues with a legend : "Fire descended from Heaven and enveloped his seat whereupon he wept : 'If this be so an account of those who dishonor Torah, how much more so on account of those who honor it.' "

¹¹⁰ Of the sacrifice (so Rashi) or, perhaps, of incense ?

¹¹¹ Plutarch, *Non posse*... (*Moralia*) 1100 A-B. This theme of Epicurus' low origin was thus quite alive in the second century A.D.

¹¹² אמר מיליא על, "said words on", see Jastrow, *s.v.*, מילא II and מילתא. The passage is *SSR* 1. 4, § 1. It may be more than a mere summary of the similar story in JT 77a, II. 1, and may not merely refer to his persuasiveness but to actual incantations, an echo of the anti-Epicurean Epicurus "biography".

The apparent affinity of much of the Acher "biography" to that of Epicurus may have been more extensive than the parallels reported *supra* indicate. Owing to a lack of sources, however, additional parallels must be suggested with less confidence. Nevertheless, two more suspect parallels may be briefly discussed here in order to complete this survey.

1. In the biographic material on Acher in JT *Ḥagigah* II. 1, 9a (New York-Vilno; Aramaic), we find another significant anecdote. During a vaguely described anonymous persecution the persecutors attempted to compel the Jews to break their strict Sabbath laws by forcing them to carry burdens on that day. The victims, however, decided that two men carry each burden, a procedure which did not represent a legal infraction of the Sabbath law. Acher revealed this subterfuge to the persecutors who promptly forced the Jews to use single carriers. The latter thereupon used a legally "neutral" area —neither in the private nor in the public domain— to set down their burdens, thus circumventing the prohibition of carrying directly from one type of domain to the other. Again, Acher revealed his strategem to the persecutors and on his advice the victims were forced to carry glassware which they could not easily set down.

This story, a *hapax legomenon*, has strong legendary features : the anonymity of the event, the ingenious evasions and betrayals, the artificiality of the plot. Its thrust is evidently to mark Acher as an informer, traitor, and collaborator with the enemy.

It so happens that an attempt to denounce Epicurus as a traitor and collaborator with the enemy, has also been made in the anti-Epicurean biography. Reference is to Epicurus' well-known client relationship to Mithres (Mithras), a "barbarian" of Syrian origin and an important official of the Thracian ruler Lysimachus to whom Epicurus was somehow indebted. DeWitt, *Epicurus*, p. 54, assumes that Lysimachus afforded Epicurus protection in Lampsacus after a flight from Mytilene and sees in the assertion of Epicurus' loyalty to Athens in *D.L.* X. 9f., where his faithfulness to the gods, his native city, and Hellas is strongly emphasized, a proof for the existence of such an accusation of disloyalty. Furthermore, according to DeWitt, *Kyriai Doxai* 6 is defensive and refers to this incident. Indeed, there was a tradition according to which Epicurus was accused of addressing this self-same Mithras as Παιᾶνα καὶ ἄνακτα (*Paian Anax*, "Healer and Lord"), probably an exaggerated apostrophe in line with Epicurus' usual style, but maliciously interpreted as an act of deification (*D.L.* X. 4, end, cf. Plutarch, *Moralia* 1097 B and 1126 F. Discussion of Epicurus' possible relation to Ptolemy I of Egypt can here be omitted).

The question whether this is historical or originated with the renegades from Epicurus' school, Timocrates and Herodotus, or through the jealousy of his antagonist Theodorus the "Atheist", is not essential for our investigation. The mere suspicion of disloyalty to the gods and the factual denial of providence by Epicurus could have easily evoked the further allegation of political and cultural disloyalty in all anti-Epicurean quarters.

However this may have been, this aspect of anti-Epicureanism was alive in Plutarch's and Laertius' times, i.e., the Tannaitic Period. And although it is conceivable that in Judea, too, religious non-conformism could by itself lead to the accusation of political disloyalty, in view of the other leanings on the rhetorical anti-Epicurean biography we must assume that it is not impossible that in this instance, too, the Judaic teachers used a Greco-Roman anti-Epicurean pattern against Acher, employing, of course, literary detail of their own which suited their cultural environment (oicotypification).

2. Another *hapax legomenon* which follows the preceding item in JT may similarly contain a vague allusion to anti-Epicurean biography. According to this story Acher's father, Abuyah, once gave a circumcision party for his son Elisha. The guests enjoyed themselves in secular fashion but R. Eli'ezer and R. Joshua entertained themselves by combining words of Torah, Prophets, and Hagiographa and were suddenly enveloped by the usual fire. Abuyah, alarmed, was reassured that this was the fire of joy, similar to that at Sinai (Dt. 4.11), whereupon, seeing that the study of Torah had such reward, he vowed to consecrate his son to it. Since Abuyah's intention however, was thus not for the "sake of Heaven" (pure, for its own sake, non-materialistic), it did not fulfill itself in his son (so Acher's own words). Although Acher's father is described in the story as one of the "great of Jerusalem", he was apparently not learned and looked up to the Sages in the fashion of the layman.

In the anti-Epicurean biography, likewise, Epicurus' father was an uneducated man, i.e., an elementary schoolteacher, a fact strongly stressed as demeaning (Cf. *D.L.* X. 3 after Timon, *fr.* 51 D. Cf. the description of the lowly task of the schoolmaster in Demosthenes' *de corona*, § 258). Furthermore, wherever the pro-Epicurean biography suggests a respectable background for the founder of the School (cf. the title of Metrodorus' work *On the Nobility of Birth* and *D.L.* X. 1), it may do so in reaction to this anti-Epicurean denunciation. Epicurus' parents, too, supported their son's aspiration. Diogenes of Oinoanda, almost five centuries after the event, quotes Epicurus as stating that his mother sent him provisions (which he declined) and his father money (fr. 64, W.; 53, Ch.; 63, G., col. II-III). Plutarch, *Moralia* 1100 A-B. mentions the opinion of Neocles, Epicurus' brother, that nobody was ever from childhood on wiser than Epicurus. Even if this is not an error on Plutarch's part for Neocles, Epicurus' father, this detail could be compared with Abuyah's over-ambitious aspiration for his son. Just as the anti-Epicureans, however, must have insinuated that once a schoolmaster's son, always a schoolmaster's son, so the talmudic source seems to suggest a similar situation regarding the progeny of an ambitious and materialistic ignoramus.

The total "biography" of Acher is, of course, composite, and not wholly negative. His skillful and positive exegesis, usually in dialogue with his prominent student R. Meir (on Acher's teachings as authoritative see n. 224 ,*infra*), his own conviction that he was lost beyond redemption, and the famous legend of R. Meir's attempt to find final peace for him after the death of both (motif "smoke from the tomb", JT, *ibid.*) are quite moving and somewhat in contrast with the report of his crimes. Such contradictory tendencies, however, are characteristic of the Midrashic Sage biography as well as of the Greco-Roman rhetorical counterpart. Both reflect the tendencies of opposed schools of thought and both work with isolated anecdotal materials. (The often-found modern tendency to harmonize and assume different phases in the life of a particular sage or a moral lesson in this contrast, is quite inappropriate in view of the nature of the sources.)

113 The origin of the Hebrew noun אפיקורוס for an Epicurean or sympathizer with Epicureanism is as much a mystery today as it was a century ago. The Hebrew seems to

be a precise transcription of the personal name of the philosopher Epicurus. The problem is thus the transition from the Greek name Epicurus to a common noun in Hebrew (pronounced variously Apikouros, Apikoros, Apikoires, etc., in later Jewish tradition). It is not intended to sketch here the lengthy and complex scholarly controversy. Suffice to say that the derivation from the Greek ʼΕπικούρειος, "Epicurean" (Jacob Levy), offers difficulties regarding the phonetics of transcribing Greek into Hebrew (i.e., the pronounciation of Greek loanwords in Hebrew), and the claim of a relationship of the term to an extended Hebrew root פקר, "abandon" (made variously by amoraic tradition, Maimonides, Kaempf, Jastrow) is somewhat contrived and fits only the later talmudic use of the term for irreverent and deviationist enemies of the Sages (admitted by Wagner).

We suggest that the transition from the Greek name to the appellative (common noun) took place outside Hebrew, i.e., in Greco-Roman rhetorical usage (in its widest sense) and is also vaguely traceable in patristic literature. The tannaitic usage would thus be a reflection of the Greco-Roman environment.

In Plutarch's *de sera numinis...*, *Mor.* 548 B ff. (cf. Part II, *infra*, text between notes 108 and 109) the Epicurean participant in a discussion in which also Plutarch and his brother are involved, is called ὁ ʼΕπίκουρος, i.e., "Epicurus", This parallels Plutarch's nomenclature for an Aristotelian whom he calls "Aristotle" in *de facie...*, 928 E ff. (Fabricius unnecessarily suggested to emend the text and read *Epikoureios*).

Previously Cicero, *in Pisonem* XVI. 37, had called Piso sarcastically "Epicurus": ... Epicurus noster, ex hara producte non ex schola..., "... our Epicurus, product of the sty rather than the school...", which still reverberates in Horace's self-classification, *Epist.* I. iv. 16, Epicuri de grege porcum, "a hog from Epicurus' herd". Cicero, *op. cit.*, XXV. 59, contributes further *hic homullus ex argilla et luto factus Epicurus* for Piso, "this little man, (this) Epicurus of mud and clay". Seneca once addressed playfully his friend Lucilius nec ego, Epicure..., "nor do I, O Epicurus" (*Ep.* XX. 11).

In patristic literature Jerome, *Epistola*, XXIII, end (Migne, *PL* 22, 447, § 154) suggests to the recipient of the letter in a postscript... *potestis intelligere, si Epicuros et Aristippos cogitetis*, "you will understand if you think of the Epicureans and Aristippians" (actually, "the Epicuruses and Aristippuses;" equivalents of the former plural are also attested in Hebrew). He refers to his Christian antagonist Rufinus as *Aristippus nostris temporis*, "the Aristippus of our time" (*adv. Ruf.* III. 30, *PL* 23, 502 A, § 559) and demonstrates in theological detail why Jovinianus is "the Epicurus of the Christians" (Epicurus Christianorum, *adv. Jov.* I. 1, *PL* 23, 221 A, 237).

Perhaps this latter passage, although too late to influence tannaitic usage, offers nevertheless a clue to an earlier stage in rhetorical style at which expressions such as "the Epicurus of our time, ... of our group, ... of our disputation" may have led to the term Epicurus for Epicurean. Sarcastic uses may have aided in this development. In any case, the early Empire already seems to have possessed this peculiar terminology. The Greco-Roman "Epicurus" for "Epicurean" may thus have been the model for the tannaitic usage in preference to more common Greco-Roman terms, since apparently it occured most often in strongly-worded anti-Epicurean statements which were useful to the Tannaim in their struggle. Furthermore, a strongly-worded epithet is more likely to leave its mark on the memory of the listener than a conventional term.

[114] *c*. 100 A.D. Among the few items in his name is a consolation formula of Stoic-rhetoric provenance, *Aboth de R. Nathan* (*AdRN*), Recension A, ch. 14, Schechter, 2nd edition (New York, 1945) p. 59. Ironically, he is apparently the only Tanna who succumbed to a hedonistic way of life, if we can believe this tradition, *ibid*. (See also Bacher's doubts).

¹¹⁵ The syntax is somewhat ambiguous. So also C. Taylor, *Sayings of the Jewish Fathers*, 2nd edition (Cambridge, 1897), p. 40, n. 45 and Marmorstein, *op. cit.*, p. 186. On the habit of the Epicureans to have summaries of their creed readily at hand see below. The parallel *AdRN* A, ch. 17, end, as well as other earlier uses of אפיקורוס, such as Mi. *Sanhedrin* X. 1; Tos. *Sanh.* XIII. 5, p. 434 Z.; *Seder Olam* III. 36, 9a Ratner, offer texts that are neither well established nor perfectly clear nor unaffected by medieval censorship. Still, they vaguely suggest or include similar doctrinal deviationism. The amoraic passages, beginning with BT *Sanh.* 99bf., introduce increasingly definitions that have lost sight of actual Epicureanism.

¹¹⁶ *RAC*, V, 780ff. and Lactantius, *Div. Inst.* III. 17.

¹¹⁷ See Ginzberg, *JE*, I, 304-310; Bacher, *Tannaiten* I, 263ff., 339-342.

¹¹⁸ Actually there is almost next to nothing on any mysticism of Akiba in the crucial treatise on theosophy in BT *Ḥagigah* 11b-16a; on the contrary, his exegesis of Gen. 1:1 is quite realistic (*peshaṭ*) and grammatically correct, although the narrative setting is a walk with his antagonist Ishmaʿʿel, such perambulatory discussions frequently being the framework of (later) mystical items (*Ḥag.* 12af.). His disputed exegesis of the "thrones" of Dan. 12 :7 in *Ḥag.* 14a is at first merely messianic, thereafter allegorical and traditional rather than "dualistic", as Eleʿazar b. Azariah, *ibid.*, claims. In *Ḥag.* 14b Yose b. Yehudah, a Tanna who flourished 70 years later, asserted that Akiba was involved in a theosophic discussion the details of which, however, are given only for, and in the name of, other participants in the debate (the claim that there were three such discussions suggests an artificial attempt to connect Akiba somehow with theosophy). Finally, there is our passage of the Four which, in amoraic times, indeed, was understood mystically (regarding Akiba : *Ḥag.* 15bf.). This article, however, is concerned only with the earlier tradition which created this story and by which Akiba became one of the Four.

¹¹⁹ Ginzberg, *JE*, *loc. cit.*

¹²⁰ Opponent : Eleʿazar b. Azariah, Bacher, *Tannaiten* I, 216f.

¹²¹ Opponent : the School of Ishmaʿʿel, BT *Soṭah* 37b, *et al.*

¹²² See the brief Akiba biography in *AdRN* A, ch. 6, p. 29 S.

¹²³ BT *Yeb.* 86b and 16a; *AdRN*, *loc. cit.*, Cp. the differing names of his employer (owner ?) ! The Greco-Roman biographical tradition makes almost all major sages former slaves or lowly workers. The most famous talmudic example, that of Hillel the Elder, is influenced by the cynicizing Cleanthes biography, see *Cynicism*. For a partial list of sage-slaves cf. Macrobius, *Saturnalia* I. ii. § 41f. or Aulus Gellius (c. 123 - c. 165), *Noctes Atticae* II. xviii.

¹²⁴ See n. 128, below.

¹²⁵ The interest in how many students followed a sage is important also in the Greco-Roman academic tradition where the treatment is mostly witty-competitive. In the talmudic sources, it is often legendary, but witty treatments are not absent. More detail in *Cynicism*.

¹²⁶ See the histories and A. Büchler, *Der galiläische ʿAm-Haʾareṣ des zweiten Jahrhunderts* Hildesheim, 1968 [Vienne 906]).

¹²⁷ BT *Pesaḥim* 49b; BT *Kethuboth* 63a.

¹²⁸ Or a proselyte or descendant of proselytes (ולית ליה זכות אבות) according to the commentary of Nisim Gaon, *ad loc. cit.*, who sees him as a descendent of Sisera and quotes BT *Sanhedrin* 96b and *Giṭṭin* 57b as proof.

¹²⁹ Timon in *D.L.* X. 3, cp. X. 7.

¹³⁰ *Disc.* III. vii. 30f.

¹³¹ "Palestinians" we call those who spent decades of their productive years in Caesaria or Bethlehem, such as Origen (Caesaria), Eusebius (Bethlehem and Caesaria?), and Jerome (Caesaria). Origen, *c. C.* III. 49, IV. 36; Jerome, *Contra Rufinum* I. 30; Augustine, *c. Jul.* III. xxxi. 48. Others with Jungkuntz, *op. cit.*, and *RAC*, *V*, 792.

¹³² See Athenaeus, *Deipn.* XII. 588 A : ὅστις [τῆς] ἐγκυκλίου παιδείας ἀμύητος, "... uninitiated, as he is, into a [the] general education..."

¹³³ See DeWitt, *Epicurus*, chapters II and III, and the reviews of the book.

¹³⁴ Especially mentioned as undesirable are thus music, geometry, arithmetic, and astronomy (as starting from false premises which are, among others, ideas, a prioris, and non-empiricism), Cicero, *de fin.* I. xxi. 69f. On music cf. *Usener*, fr. 599 (it is without moral and intellectual value) and A. J. Neubecker, *Die Bewertung der Musik bei Stoikern und Epikuräern* (Berlin, 1956; Berlin Academy), analyzing Philodemus' *de musica*. Astronomy may lead to the re-introduction of "divine" laws or beings and produce fear. Even the use of mechanical devices is objected to, see A. Barigazzi, "Epicuro e gli *organa* astronomici (*Peri Physeōs XI*)," *Prolegomena, 1* (1952) 61-70. Apelles remained "unblemished" of mathematics according to an enlightening tirade of Plutarch against Epicurean ignorance, *Mor.* 1094 D (*Usener* fr. 117). On Zeno's of Sidon attack on geometric proportions see Crönert, *op. cit.*, p. 109. The ban on mathematics was relaxed, however, since Demetrius Laco (*Ueberweg*, via Index). Rhetoric, often called *kakotechnia*, was fought by Epicurus already with his own teacher Nausiphanes, together with all *mathēmata* (i.e., *enkyklios paideia*), see *Usener* fr. 114. DeWitt, *Epicurus*, 61ff., differently. Rhetoric, about the ignorance of which Philodemus complains, was re-introduced by the latter, Crönert, *op. cit.*, p. 99, n. 480. Poetry was likewise rejected (Schmid limits Tescari's overemphasis in his review in *Gnomon, 20* [1944] p. 13), although Lucretius and the Italian school made compromises. Among the best known passages on the Epicurean attitude towards learning is Plutarch's *Mor.* 1094 E according to which Metrodorus is supposed to have encouraged those who did not know details on Hector or the opening of Homer. Of course, the "relaxations" did not affect the stereotype. A good summary also in Sextus Empiricus, *Adv. Mathematicos* I. 1; on music, VI. 27.

¹³⁵ *Usener*, p. 88ff. See Sextus Empiricus, n. 134, above. The ancients criticized his coining of new nouns ending in -*ma*, his use of *Koine* at the expense of elegance, non-avoidance of the hiatus, and repetition of words, cf. H. Diels, "Ein epikuräisches Fragment über Götterverehrung", *Sitzungsber. Berlin (Königl.-Preuss.) Akad. d. Wissenschaften*, 1916 II, 886-909 (888-892). Mildly amusing is a contribution of an anti-semitic character by Cleomedes (after Posidionius) according to which Epicurus fathered his expressions from the Synagogue or among the people begging there and his style was a corrupted Jewish jargon, "indeed, lower than anything that creeps under the sun", *de motu* ii. 1 after Louis H. Feldman, "Philosemitism among Ancient Intellectuals", *Tradition*, I, No. 1 (1958) 27-38, p. 37. Modern opinions are divided on the quality of Epicurus' style. Some praise it as difficult but incisive. According to the balanced judgment of Schmid (*RAC*, *V*, 708ff.) it is somewhere between Aristotle and Polybius regarding the choice of words. Owing to the conservativism of the school the style remained comparatively steady, although that of Philodemus is considered tedious (except the end of *de mortis* and, of course, his epigrams!). See also the defense of Epicurus' style against Plutarch's criticism by Aulus Gellius in *Noct. Att.* II. ix and Theon's (c. 125 A.D.) condemnation (*Progymnasmata*, p. 169, Walz).

¹³⁶ *D.L.* X. 26 : not at all.

¹³⁷ *D.L.* X. 13, *Usener* fr. 123, 232.

¹³⁸ This pretended ignorance must be distinguished from the attempt of the Epicureans to hinder *actively* or forcefully the education of the young. More, below.

¹³⁹ Aelian fr. 39, Hercher. Aelian's gossip, of course, is more important in the formation of such beliefs than historical documents. See also Plutarch, *Non posse*... 1089 F (*Mor.*). Read with Einarson-DeLacy Aristobulus for Agathobulus.

¹⁴⁰ This deserves a fresh investigation.

¹⁴¹ *De vita beata* XIX. 1.

¹⁴² *Piso* 59, end. See Dante, above.

¹⁴³ The same fr. 39; see also Bignone, *op. cit.*, II, 154f. It was, perhaps, this belief which Lucian wanted to counter in his usual anti-anti-Epicurean polemic when in the *Timon*, 10, he has Zeus fling a thunderbolt against the impious Anaxagoras only —irony upon irony— to hit his own temple.

¹⁴⁴ *Non posse...*, 1089 D ff.

¹⁴⁵ *An recte...*, end, 1130 C-E. There is no hint here at the special dangers under which Epicureans frequently lived.

¹⁴⁶ *D.L.* X. 7, 15, 22 and Cicero, Seneca, Plutarch and the papyri. See *Usener*, frs. 122, 138, 177, 190 and Suidas, *s.v.*, "Epikouros".

¹⁴⁷ Jastrow and Levy, *s.v.*, פגע, and all medieval and modern commentators and translators (Rabbenu Hanan'el and Rashi : נטרפה דעתו). BT *Shabbat* 13b is less severe : אין שוטה נפגע, "a fool is not troubled" (Shimeʻon b. Gamli'el) but may have prepared the meaning "insane". Close is also "to be possessed by demons", examples to be found with Jastrow and Levy. And yet, our passage apparently remains a *hapax legomenon*.

¹⁴⁸ *D.L.* IV. 44. Strangely enough, also the basic Greek verb is not as frequent as other terms for insanity and it also has the basic meaning "stricken", see Liddell and Scott, *Greek-English Lexicon*, 9th edition (Oxford, 1940) *s.v.*, παρακόπτω. In view of the many cases of "translation Hebrew" (calque) that have come to light in recent years one is tempted to see an example of it in this semantic group "stricken-insane". On translation Hebrew see A. Bendavid, *Leshon ḥakhamim u-leshon ha-Miḳra'* (Tel Aviv, 1967). In this case, however, caution is advisable since the transition stricken-insane is psychologically natural in view of the habit of many cultures to describe insanity metaphorically-euphemistically.

¹⁴⁹ Adjectives and verbs are even more common. Cf. *RAC*, V, 795f. K. Ziegler, *op. cit.*, p. 429, lists the most emphatic passages in which Lactantius abuses Epicurus and Lucretius. There abound *insania, insanire, delirare, deliramentum, furiosus*, and *stultus*.

¹⁵⁰ In the recent literature on invectives, such as the ample collection of I. Opelt, *Die lateinischen Schimpfwörter...* (Heidelberg, 1965) and the linguistic treatment of D. M. Paschell, *The Vocabulary of Mental Aberration in Roman Comedy and Petronius, Language, Suppl.*, Lang. Diss. 27 (Baltimore, 1939), the special stituation of the Epicureans is not recognized.

¹⁵¹ Cicero, *Tusc.* III. iv-xi (7-25); Seneca, *Epist.* LXXXI. 11.

¹⁵² Whether there were actually historical cases of insane Epicureans is, of course, not decisive for the formation of the academic legend, because there must have been insane philosophers in all camps. Only in the case of the Epicureans does this motif acquire permanency.

¹⁵³ IV. 45, see *Anth. Palat.* vii. 104, φρενῶν ἐκτός. As we have seen, Arcesilaus was no Epicurean but his portrayal borrowed the colors of a biographical tradition of Epicurus.

¹⁵⁴ Jerome learned Hebrew in the desert near Antioch, Syria, 375-378; in 386 he settled permanently in Bethlehem.

155 If not for centuries. A survey in Ziegler, *op. cit.*

156 P. Boyancé, *Lucrèce*..., p. 2, calls it "un assez mauvais roman".

The motif of drinking unmixed wine before death is a part of the Hermippus-based tradition on Epicurus, reported (X. 155) and re-used by *D.L.* in his eulogy on Epicurus (X. 16), see the comparative table Epicurus/Arcesilaus, above, item 10. The general theme "potion before death" is thus represented for all three, Epicurus, Lucretius and Arcesilaus (with Epicurus, though, still being the customary anesthetic).

157 Surveyed by Wechsler, *op. cit.* (n. 94, *supra*), ch. 2, section 1.

158 Our interpretation of this term will be introduced shortly, *infra*.

159 *s.v.*, קצץ, p. 1407.

160 Also quoted by Jastrow and translated correctly by Levy, "verführte die Kinder", p. 362a. For קיצץ in BT he has, however, "verwarf die Ceremonialgesetze"!

161 See Levy, *s.v.*, נטיעה (3) : "Abkömmling, Sprössling, Sohn". In biblical Hebrew, too, the equivalent נטע refers to people : Is. 5 :7, Ps. 144 :12.

162 This probably means that he deprived them of their chance to acquire eternal life by study, for in the story that follows immediately they are all quite alive. The last of the framework stories, however, introduces an entirely different tradition by which Acher denounced Sabbath observers to the Romans which resulted in actual executions. Here the vocable נטיעה seems to have been identified with the related מטע, a metaphor for the righteous in Is. 60.21, also represented by the usage נטיעות "pious ones", in JT *Berakoth* II. 8.

163 Jastrow, *s.v.*, שכח II, Aramaic. The emphasis which JT puts on the elite of the students ("greatest", "succeed") evokes the question whether JT saw in קצץ the meaning "scrape (the gold) off", as in biblical Hebrew, 2 Ki. 16.17; 18.15; 24.13; 2 Chr. 28.24; i.e., Acher misled precisely the "cream of the crop". On the other hand, these superlatives may have been caused by the emotionalism prevailing in the tragic story or may be an explanation of the preposition ב in our item : "he cut down (the best) *among* the shoots".

164 *D.L.* X. 6; Bailey, fr. 33; *Usener* fr. 163. Bailey's rendering : "Blest youth, set sail in your bark and flee from every culture", Hicks : "Hoist all sail, dear boy, and steer clear of all culture", p. 235.

165 E.g., *de fin.* I. xxi. 71f.; *Mor.* 1094 A : "Epicurean boat", *Mor.* 1094 D : "hoist all sail", etc.; *Mor.* 662 C; Quintilian, *Institutio Oratoria*, XII. ii. 24 in a Latin paraphrase.

166 *Usener* fr. 164. This has also been rendered as "education of free men", or "liberating education".

167 N. W. DeWitt, "Organization and Procedure in Epicurean Groups", *CP, 31* (1936) 205-211, p. 207, summarizing A. Olivieri's edition (Leipzig, 1914) of Herculanean *Peri Parrhēsias* fragments by Philodemus (18. 1-2).

168 Lactantius, *Inst.* II. viii. 50, see already Cicero, *de fin.* I. vii. 25, totam rationem everti. Further examples *RAC, V*, 792f.

169 In the case of Acher no immediate punishment is indicated. It had to be supplied by the framework of BT and JT. It is, of course, his loss of a share in eternity (World to Come). More, below.

170 This is also reflected in the text of some of the other versions : נכנס בשלום ויצא בשלום, "he entered in peace and left in peace", JT, *SSR*. So also in BT *Ḥag.* 15b, bottom, a later comment, but not in the initial text 14b. This additional phrase "he entered in peace" would indicate that he had studied the mainline tradition previously and was never exposed to any real danger. It is, however, not utterly impossible that the fuller wording was introduced for stylistic-rhythmic reasons. In either case, it is apparently

later and less satisfying in view of the structure of the story. Tos. has עלה וירד, "he ascended and descended", a formulation which is influenced by the later connection of the passage with mysticism. This is true, too, for BT *Ḥag*. 15b where the ministering angels threaten him and he was spared only owing to his worthiness. According to another amoraic interpretation there he did not make any blasphemous mistakes in his vision and was therefore not at all guilty.

171 *AdRN* A, ch. 6, p. 29 S. : watching water hollow a stone. In ancient academic lore the oracle, most often involving metaphor, is frequently the beginning of the philosophical career of the Sage. The Delphic oracle : Socrates, Diogenes, Zeno the Stoic, Dio of Prusa, etc. Chance oracular utterances of a child to Augustine (the famous "tolle, lege; tolle, lege!" which is interpreted as a divine command to add a book-and-passage oracle, which turned out to be Romans 13 :13, a counterposition to hedonism, *Conf*. VII. xii.); to a proselyte (and later sage) in the Hillel cycle (see *Cynicism*). Differently (reversed) Acher : 13 condemnations! (BT *Ḥag*. 15af.). Epicurus came to philosophy through the chance reading of a schoolmaster (who, like the child, was imagined to be naive), Sextus Empiricus, *Adv. Phys*. II. 19. Akiba discovers in this chance happening a metaphor indicating that even an older man could still study, employing patience and persistence.

172 BT *Nedarim* 50a; *Kethuboth* 62b. His *rich fiancee* would *forego her wealth* and *family* and *follow* Akiba, the *lowly* shepherd, into a *life of poverty*; she *marries against her family's wishes*. All these motemes (italicized) similarly with Crates and Hipparchia, *D.L*. VI. 93, 96f., 87, end. See *Cynicism*.

O. Gigon, "Antike Erzählungen über die Berufung zur Philosophie", *Mus. Helv*., 3 (1946) 1-21, calls the entry into philosophy a decisive and most often paradoxical event (p. 2). He analyzes a great many traditions on several crucial philosopher-sages and demonstrates the existence of several contradictory, mostly invented, narratives on the leading figures (five on Socrates!). Several of these initiation stories are paralleled by *chriae* on Hillel the Elder and Eli'ezer b. Hyrcanus (cf. *Cynicism*).

Both Aristotle (in some hostile traditions) and Akiba enter their respective academies when forty years old! Aristotle is demeaningly called *opsimathēs*, "late learner" (p. 18).

Other important motifs involved in the *vocatio* of the philosopher in Greco-Roman literature have been collected and discussed by Martin Hengel in *Nachfolge und Charisma* (Berlin, 1968), 31-33. Among the recurrent literary elements we find the freedom from (or abandonment of) worldly possessions and/or custom and convention, and the break with one's family (or wife).

173 Cf. Arcesilaus' witticism tantamount to "once a eunuch always a eunuch". That Caesar outgrew his supposed Epicureanism did not become a part of literary consciousness and Cicero's development from admiration for his Epicurean teachers to a strong anti-Epicurean position is expressed only in chance remarks in his work. Horace's complex relationship with Epicureanism was hidden and too individualistic to be effective in subsequent rhetorical literature, and an actual "conversion" may never have taken place. The defection of Timocrates from the original school was precisely this : a defection, and a conversion to another movement is not mentioned by *D.L*. (X. 6; X. 4; X. 23, 28). A famous incident regarding conversion, quite to the contrary, concerns Dionysius of Heraclea, c. 328-248, *D.L*. VII. 37, see *OCD* (8) and *P.-W*. No. 119, who left Stoicism and became a renegade to hedonism (of which type remains unspecified) when during an illness he perceived that pain is not a negligeable matter (*adiaphoron*), as the Stoics asserted. He acquired subsequently the nickname *metathemenos*, "turncoat". The equally famous conversion to the cult of Isis of Apuleius' Lucius in the *Metamorphoses* '('Golden

Ass") does not clearly suggest an Epicurean, nor is the Lucius-Apuleius of the romance a serious representative of the Sage-Scholar class around which all our material centers. Likewise a story of a renunciation of hedonism, that of Polemo, *D.L.* IV. 16, Valerius Maximus VI. ix. 1, *extern.*, does not imply Epicureanism. In the case of Metrodorus of Stratonicea who went over to Carneades (c. 215-130), "being perhaps burdened by his master's excessive goodness", the text indicates no actual conversion (*D.L.* X. 9; the anachronism is his. This Metrodorus is, of course, not the famous early follower of Epicurus.) "Bion's Repentance" of his atheism, *D.L.* IV. 54ff., practically in a last illness, is, again, a different motif: it does not occur during his active lifetime.

174 One item seems to indicate that he repented or that R. Meir thought he did. On this and the legend of the smoke rising from his grave see Büchler, *op. cit.*

175 *Epicurum accepturum fuisse palmam in animo meo nisi ego credidissem post mortem restare animae vitam et tractus meritorum quod Epicurus credere noluit.* The following translation incorporates the caution expressed by Elder, *op. cit.*: "Epicurus could have received the palm (garland) in my (state of) mind (at that time), had I not personally believed that after death life of the soul would remain as well as the extent of merits —which Epicurus would not believe". *Supra, ibid.*, he was in a "deeper abyss of carnal pleasures", similarly, *infra, ibid.*

176 On this general subject see A. D. Nock, *Conversion* (Oxford, 1933) ch. XI, "Conversion to Philosophy"; Festugière, *op. cit.*, p. 37ff., also *Personal Religion among the Greeks* (Berkeley, 1954) ch. I, IV, VII, and especially Gigon as in n. 172, *supra, passim*.

177 Even if "left in peace" has merely the conventional meaning of "left safe and sound", the possibility of his later conversion is implied by his survival. The typology would then-consist of

death - insanity - nihilism - survival (for a new life).

178 *Usener*, p. 409, *s.v.*, *Kēpos*. *D.L.* X. 10, 17. Cicero, *de fin.* V. i. 3; *Att.* XII. xxiii. 2; *de nat. deor.* I. xxxiii. 93; *ad fam.* XIII. i. 3-5; Plutarch, *Mor.* 1098 B; Sextus Empiricus, *Adv. Phys.* I. 64 ("The men of the Garden"), etc. Cf. the cognomen of the later school head Apollodorus, the "Garden Tyrant" (*Kēpotyrranos*), c. 125 B.C. In Cicero's *de nat. deor.* I. xliii. 120 the diminutive *hortulus* is used sarcastically. *Kēpologos*, jocularly, approximately "Garden-brain", is found in the epigram of Phanias, *Anth. Pal.* VI. 307.

179 The origin of the latter, however, was controversial already in ancient times. The "Dogs" may have been named after their teachings or habits, not after their meeting place. *D.L.* VI. 13.

180 There were branches of the school in Antioch, 2nd ct. B.C., and Italy. Most other places mentioned as strongholds or seats of Epicureans or of one important representative may not have had an actual school.

181 Cant. 4:13; Eccl. 2:5; Neh. 2:8. See Jastrow and Levy, *s.v.* The former, however, speaks cautiously of an enclosure in Heaven when referring to *Ḥagigah*. E. E. Urbach, *op. cit.*, has forcefully and rightly denied that anywhere in rabbinic literature *pardes* signifies Paradise, cosmological speculation, the Heavenly Sanctuary or apocalyptic visions, the Garden of Genesis or the Hereafter (n. 54, p. 13). G. G. Scholem had previously raised this issue again in his *Jewish Gnosticism...*, 14-19, on account of newly discovered Aramaic fragments of Qumran and of Enoch 32:2 and 77:3 ("Paradise of Truth"). He combines these with Paul's "being caught up into paradise, whether in the body or not of the body, I do not know...", 2 Cor. 12:2-4, and similar Jewish apocalyptic passages of the ecstatic journey type. Urbach's scepticism as to the use of the Aramaic

fragments is justified : they belong to special circles, may represent translations from Hellenistic Jewish Greek, and be allegorical. T. Wechsler, *op. cit.*, p. 24, who assumes that *pardes* signifies Pythagorean numerical speculation with the letters of the alphabet offers no sources for this assertion.

[182] Jastrow and Levy, *s.v.*, ..., I. 256 and I. 344 resp.

[183] The precise and graphic "entered" is, of course, conditioned by the realistic use of the word "garden". *D.L.* X. 10, written over 500 years after Epicurus, still reconstructs the situation of the past quite realistically : "these (friends) indeed from everywhere came to him and lived with him in the garden".

[184] Too remote is the possibility that this may be an instance of the *'al tiḳra'* type of interpretation, i.e., a replacement of the verb תשבענו, "eat your fill thereof", by תשגענו, "and go insane by it".

[185] A partial treatment in *Cynicism*. More on this genre in G. Highet, *The Anatomy of Satire* (Princeton, 1962); Grube, *Critics*; G. A. Gerhard, *Phoinix von Kolophon* (Leipzig, 1909).

[186] Two passages among several others : BT *Horayoth* 2b; *Soṭah* 49b. B. Azzai, though, is found as visionary in the later Hekhaloth texts, taking Akiba's place, cf. Scholem, *Jewish Gnosticism...*, p. 15, but then this type of literature approves of ecstatic visions.

[187] He ingested more than his fill of "honey", i.e., possibly, cosmological but still Torah-bound speculation.

[188] A customary formula to introduce *testimonia*. On the terminology involved see W. Bacher, *Die exegetische Terminologie der jüdischen Traditionsliteratur* (Leipzig, 1899) p. 90ff.

[189] *SSR, loc. cit.* Tos. and JT, after quoting Cant. 1 :4a add "etcetera". This is common procedure when also the second half of the testimonium is the intended proof (or even only the latter). It is possible that Cant. 1 : 4a, "draw me near, after You we shall run", is supposed to indicate, according to these versions, that Akiba asked for divine permission or acted out of love for the divine.

All testimonia are here translated in the sense of their respective midrashic, i.e., novel, uses.

[190] In JT, however, the scene in the academy in which he drives the students away, is interpolated at this point. Apparently "thy flesh" are here the students (so also commentary *Ḳorban ha-'edhah, ad. loc.*). In concluding, JT uses, in addition, Eccl. 5 :5d, "and spoil the (former meretorious) work of thy hands", referring to Acher's pre-heretical period (so also commentary *Pene Mosheh, ad loc.*). It is not clear whether Eccl. 5 :5b-c are also included as proof and understood thusly : "and do not speak (falsehoods) before the Angel, for this is heresy", thus referring to the heretical statement on Metratron of which he is accused in the BT framework story. It is quite possible, however, that the Metraton item was unknown to JT.

The testimonium in Akiba's warning will be discussed below.

[191] Apart from possible allusions to Epicurus in Aristophanes' comedies the oldest known satirical work on Epicurus, provoked by the sectarian celebrations of the Garden and the quasi-apotheosis of Epicurus is that of Menippus of Gadara, *fl.* 250 B.C., "On the Birthday of Epicurus and the Celebration of the 20 th", *D.L.* VI. 101. See n. 195, below. Aristophanes parodies the apotheosis and cult of deified men, see H. Kleinknecht, "Zur Parodie des Gottmenschentums bei Aristophanes", *Archiv für Religionsgeschichte (AfR), 34* (1937).

[192] E.g., sic fac omnia tamquam spectet Epicurus, "do everything in such a way

as if Epicurus was seeing", *Usener* fr. 211 cf. 210, a maxim which was appropriated by Seneca, *Epist.* XI. 8, XXV. 5.

¹⁹³ In Cicero's *In Pis.* 59 see 46 an Epicurean speaks of Epicurus as of a god in a world from which Epicurus had expelled the gods. Actually, Epicurus' teachings on his passive gods are skillfully anchored in his atomic theory, his ethics, and even his epistomology. The question still arises as to why he found it necessary at all to incorporate a doctrine of the gods —a question of which many answers have been given by contemporary interpreters. Most satisfying is still the view of Koch, *op. cit.*, p. 123 (on Horace's *Roman Ode* I) according to whom Epicurus' system represents a refined rationalized form of Greek Olympic religion transformed and dominated by the aesthetic. The centrality of the perfect Sage in his gradual approximation of the divine, ὁμοίωσις θεοῦ (not to be be-translated by a mere "imitatio dei") is decisive in it, too.

¹⁹⁴ Cp. Plutarch's exposure, *adv. Col.* (*Mor*) 1117 A-B, of the mystic hymn-like language of Metrodorus in praise of Epicurus and Plutarch's sarcastic description of the famous incident in which Colotes began to worship Epicurus in his presence. Although Epicurus returned Colotes' compliment and the entire scene was partly a demonstration of ethical teachings and not a true apotheosis, posterity liked to distort this happening beyond recognition. And yet, Epicurus' self-description is frequently close, —in style— to self-apotheosis, cf. *epist. fr.* 65, lines 29-40, p. 401, Arrighetti. Cf. Cicero, *de nat. deor.* I. xvi. 43.

¹⁹⁵ Epicurus' supposed birthday, the tenth of Gamelion (actually the seventh) and the days of remembrance for him and Metrodorus on the 20th of every month, the wearing of rings with Epicurus' portrait, etc., see n. 191.

¹⁹⁶ Especially V. 1ff. where Epicurus is preferred to the "inventor" gods. Cf. K. Thraede in *RAC*, V, "Erfinder II", cols. 1192-1278. This area of inquiry is frequently called heurematology. Lucretius' Epicurean "hymns" are so extreme that Lactantius could reuse *de rer. nat.* V. 6-8 for God and VI. 24-28 for Christ, *Instit.* III. xiv. 1f., VII. vii. 6, cf. Ambrosius *adv. gentes* I. 38.

¹⁹⁷ W. A. Heidel, "Die Bekehrung im klassischen Altertum ...", *Zeitschrift für Religionspsychologie, 3* (1910) 377-402.

¹⁹⁸ Bailey, *Phases*, p. 29, is close to this view of Epicureanism. Unlike some other types of Greek philosophy, however, which use similar features Epicurus did not believe that the contemplation of Being leads to bliss or that the cosmos is perfect or that the soul remembers an ideal former state.

¹⁹⁹ K. Kerényi, "Religionsgeschichtliches zur Erklärung römischer Dichter", *AfR, 28* (1930) 392-398.

²⁰⁰ The "visions" of Epicurus and Lucretius is the beauty of rationality. So clearly P. Boyancé, "Les Épicuréens et la contemplation", in *In Memoriam Hectoris Bignone* (Genoa, 1959) 89-99. Cornford, as usual a fine and penetrating interpreter of the intricacies of Greek thought, has pointed out that the cause for this sweeping metaphysical language of Epicurus may well have been his inability to lay a solid foundation for his "apprehension" (*epibolē*) of "clear", self-sufficient physical principles which do not come in the way of other sense perceptions, *Principium Sapientiae* (New York, 1965; Cambridge, 1952) p. 29f.

²⁰¹ Although this passage is vaguely reminiscent of the Lucretian mood, Cicero is probably speaking of the rhetorical habits of lesser lights.

²⁰² *Mor.* 1097 C, speaking of *atopia*, oddness, absurdity, and criticizing the exaggerated language for a mere gift (*daimoniōs*, "divinely").

203 The Cyrenaics have tippled from the same jug as Epicurus, etc., *Mor.* 1089 A; the Epicureans play swineherd to the soul, 1096 D, etc., using a cliché of anti-Epicurean vituperative, i.e., the Epicureans as pigs, see DeLacy, "Pigs and Epicureans", *Classical Bulletin, 34* (1958) 55-56. There is mild parody of a Colotes title in Plutarch's essay *non posse...* according to which one cannot achieve a pleasant life with Epicurus,

204 *Praeparatio Evangelica* XIV. xxvii. 9, 782ff, ed. K. Mras, 2 vols. (Berlin, 1956) p. 336f, vol. II.

205 *Op. cit.* 784, § 13, p. 338 Mras. Dionysius' work was entitled *Peri Physeōs*. He died at or before the time of Eusebius' birth, in 264, his *floruit* being perhaps 220. He was thus a younger contemporary of the editor of the Mishnah.

206 *Hellenistische Wundererzählungen*, 3rd edition (Darmstadt, 1956 [1927]) p. 133f.

207 *De somniis* II. xlii. 696 (283ff).

208 In other words, the revolt is one of philosophical-theological opinion, e.i., Epicurean doctrine, not an actual plan of war as in some Palestinian Targumim and Rashi *ad loc.*

209 Accepting Colson's happy rendering of the wordplay. He did overlook, however, Philo's skillful equivocal use of ἐπιχείρημα which is both, "attempt" as well as dialectical proof (or syllogism).

210 246e, see n. 212, below.

211 *De somniis* II. xlii. 697-698 (293f.). Admittedly, Plato's charioteer is introduced because of the preceding metaphor which equates (Epicurean) philosophers with disobedient horses. Nevertheless, the urge to use the weighty Phaedrus apocalypse somehow may well have been the decisive mental stimulus.

212 In the later part of the diatribe Philo drifts into a more general denunciation of the presumptious. Some of the initial accusations may also fit others, such as the Skeptics; and as a whole, Epicureans may here be merely *typoi* for all "materialistic" schools but the syndrome of all details fits the Epicureans best.

213 ἄφθαρτον is an Epicurean term referring frequently to the atoms which according to Epicurus are eternal although the (perishable) world (of ours) has a beginning and an end, see C. Bailey, *The Greek Atomists and Epicurus* (New York, 1928, repr. 1964) p. 276. Philo thinks here of matter generally and not of the formation of the world, a term which he avoids in this passage. He refers to other detail of the Epicurean theory of atoms in *de fuga* XXVI. 567 (148).

214 *de somn.* II. xliii. 696 (283), summarized.

215 *de opif. mundi* LVI. 39 (160) and Gen. R. XIX. 1 on 3.1.

216 In detail: *Part II.*

217 *Anadiplosis* is, of course, a fairly common stylistic device. The basis of the parody is its incongruous use by the Epicureans.

218 This precedes the passage quoted above, No. 5, and is part of a prayerlike sequence which, among other startling phrases, has

tu pater es rerum inventor, tu patria nobis suppeditas praecepta...

Thou, father, art the discoverer of things (as they truly are), thou doest provide us with fatherly precepts... (III. 9f).

III. 12f. and V. 8 are actually closer to *anaphora* (*epanalepsis*). Whether *anadiplosis* ("doubling") or *anaphora* ("carrying back"), the effect is an incongruous pathos.

219 Among the hypotheses are: reference to Greek cosmological speculation as to water as the basic element; heretical talmudic-Pythagorean lore concerning the numerical

value of the consonants of *mayim*, water, and *shamayim*, heaven, and the text of Gen. 1 (Wechsler); the waterlike appearance of marble in mystical ecstasies (Scholem), etc.

[220] That a parody, whether serious-parenetical or merely ridiculing, must by its very nature contain a heavy dose of the parodied text is self-evident. Usener thus carried the Eusebius passage as an Epicurean fragment and Heidel, Regenbogen, Reitzenstein, Schmid and others have followed this precedent. Indeed, not only Epicureans and anti-Epicureans but many a modern scholar fell imperceptibly into this semi-ecstatic style when discussing Epicurus.

[221] The possible reminiscence of *anadiplosis* appears here to have been modified to resemble a biblical *parallelismus membrorum*.

Lucillius, a potegee of Nero, has no less than three epigrams which involve (apart from odd people) Epicurus' atom, *Anth. Pal.* X. 93; XI. 103; XI. 249. The atom, celibacy and childlessness are satirized in Automedon's epigram *Anth. Pal.* XI. 50.

There is a very remote possibility that the text of our warning may have once parodied the inevitable atom rather than the *anadiplosis*. According to the structure of Hebrew loan words from the Greek there is a possibility that "atoms" (sing. τὸ ἄτομον but Epicurus prefering ἡ ἄτομος) would have appeared in Hebrew as *tomosim* with loss of initial vowel as in גזוזטרא for ἐξώστρα and parallel to Hebrew *nomosim* from Greek *nomos*, "law". Since the final letter *mem* was used exclusively in that period, "atoms" would have appeared as טומוסים. With the similarity of *samek* (ס) and *teth* (ט) to *mem* (ם), and of *waw* (ו) to *yodh* (י) in the manuscripts, a misreading *mayim* (*u-*)*mayim* מימומים) may not have been impossible, This, however, cannot be claimed with any degree of certainty.

[222] *Arch*, 247a; *pure*, 250c, etc.; *light*, 250c, *flood*, *pour*, 250c-251e, *passim*; *waters*, 251e. It is strange that the modern interpreters who see ecstatic-mystical meanings in the entire Ḥagigah passage have never considered this Eros apocalypse as its basis. Beyond the keywords, above, there are: *behold*, 247c, 249e, etc; *ascent*, 247a; *difficulty*, 247b; *danger*, 248a-b; *madness*, 249d-e; 253c. Of course, visions, ascents, and flights of the mind are ubiquitous in certain types of Greek philosophy, from the earliest Pythagoreans on (a survey in DeWitt, *Epicurus*, 108ff.). The keywords used in the Phaedrus apocalypse are, however, comfortably close to our passage. Platonic bits have been used in Midrashic material, see *Story*, and R. Meyer, *Hellenistisches in der rabbinischen Anthropologie* (Stuttgart, 1937). A reduction of our Ḥagigah passage to such Platonic elements, however, will not account for all the details of text and context; see the summary at the end of this essay.

[223] Applied to the cosmos already with Epicurus according to F. Solmsen, "Epicurus on the Growth and Decline of the Cosmos", *AJP*, 74 (1953) 34-51, p. 38. Already Athenaeus, *Deipn*. XII. 511 E - 512 A, had claimed that Epicurus' triple division of desires was anticipated by Plato, *Rep*. 559a (*Usener*, p. 295). DeLacy, "Pigs...", p. 56, n. 1, observes that Epicurus occasionally accepted ideas which Plato had discussed but discarded. Comparisons between the religion of Plato and that of Epicurus are made by Festugière, *Epicurus*, p. 62. Other dependencies are mentioned in P. Merlan, *Studies in Epicurus and Aristotle* (Wiesbaden, 1960); C. Jensen, "Ein neuer Brief Epikurs", *Abhdlgn. d. Gesellsch. d. Wissenschaften z. Göttingen*, Philol.-Hist. Klasse, 3rd ser. 5 (Berlin, 1933) 1-10; A. H. Armstrong, "The Gods in Plato, Plotinus, Epicurus", *Classical Quarterly*, 32 (1938) 190-196; F. Solmsen, "Epicurus and Cosmological Heresies", *AJP*, 72 (1951) 1-23. Koch, *op. cit.*, p. 233f., claims that Lucretius' portrayal of Epicurus purposely conjures up Platonic features.

[224] So G. Townsend, "Imagery in Lucretius", in ed. Dudley, *op. cit.*, p. 108.

[225] *Op. cit., loc. cit.* In this he makes Epicurus the recipient of "oriental", i.e., Near Eastern ideas —without offering clear proofs. That some motifs of our passage are found in Ezekiel, as A. Neher, "Le voyage mystique des quatre", *Revue de l'histoire des religions, 140* (1951) 57-82, has shown and that these combine with the Near Eastern apocalyptic theme of a Heavenly Temple is ingenious but not decisive. In determining the full meaning of a passage such as *Ḥagigah* the entire syndrome of keywords, heroes, settings, purpose, time, plot, polemical meaning, etc., must be discussed and determined. The mere existence of biblical or Near Eastern parallels does not explain the re-activation of a theme in talmudic times. In rabbinic literature even themes and quotations that are unmistakably biblical are re-used only owing to a specific stimulus, frequently from outside the culture, and reshaped in the spirit of or in rejection of that stimulus. Thus, e.g., the odd, public, exemplary action of the cynicizing Sage is the pattern for the talmudic Hillel cycle and not the example of the biblical prophets, see *Cynicism*.

[226] Neither do other such earlier warnings of Epicureanism, e.g., *P.A.* II. 14 (18); Mi. *Sanh.* X. 1.

[227] Intensive contact with Greek, Greek books, the Roman government, heretics, etc., is *per se* a suspicious and dangerous undertaking in some talmudic views. In the very framework of our story such misgivings are uttered regarding Acher and his Greek readings, and even R. Meir is suspect because of his association with Acher. Of course, this does not affect other views and periods that favored Greek and it does not overly affect the total impact of the Greco-Roman culture on the indigenous tradition. See "Greek and Latin, Rabbinic Knowledge of" in the forthcoming English *Encyclopedia Judaica* (New York, Jerusalem) or the articles in the older encylopedias.

[228] It was, of course, also physically dangerous to be an Epicurean, especially from the middle of the second century on with the increasing religiosity of the period and the increasing fears prevailing in ancient society regarding the safety of the state. These fears focused upon a group who counted as atheist and asocial. See Alexander of Abunoteichos' attack on Epicureans (Lucian's *Alexander* 39-48). It is thus understandable that Epicureans and Christians (in distorted views) were often bracketed together; see A. Simpson, *op. cit., passim.* On the persecutions of Epicureans see Momigliano, *op. cit.*, p. 155.

[229] Punishment of Epicureans was expected by all anti-Epicureans, "pagan", Christian and Jewish. See Lucian's *Philopseudes*, ch. 22 : Epicurus punished in hell, a satire on the expectations of rabid pietists. See Dill, *op. cit.*, p. 476.

[230] See Jastrow, *s.v., ṣuṣ*, 1269.

[231] This coinage (Gen. R. LXXVIII. 12 on 23 :10) using the same alliteration as Caesar's in a witty variant of meaning, is a conscious "ironic" imitation according to Avi-Yonah, *op. cit.*, p. 100.

[232] See Eleʻazar b. Arak and his hedonism, above.

[233] See their biographies in Bacher, *Tannaiten*, and Part III, *infra*.

[234] He seems to have been accepted, before his heresy, by his colleagues. He is quoted authoritatively BT *Moʻed Ḳaṭan* 20a; *P.A.* 4. 20 (4.27); *AdRN* A, all of ch. 24; B, ch. 35.

[235] Such negative legends exist, e.g., on Thales, paralleled by a Hillel item; and on Meir and Beruriah, see n. 226, below, anticipated by "Secundus, the Silent Philosopher", treated in *Cynicism*, summarized in *Story*.

[236] They seem occasionally to originate in folklore according to which even the great

were human. See Thales' and Hillel's forgetting their principles and being reminded of them by common people. Apparently the schools and subsequent rhetoric tolerated and fostered some of this material. Here and there, of course, uncomplimentary mention may originate with a hostile school, see the threefold typology on Alexinus the Quarrelsome, Epicurus the Tactless, and Menedemus the Loquatious by Chrysippus the Stoic, *Usener* fr. 574, from Stobaeus.

[237] Such a list in Pliny, *Nat. Hist.* VII. 1 vi. 191ff. Even these lists were parodied: Athenaeus, *Deipn.* I. 27 D. In detail: Part III.

[238] Usually celebrated by cynicizing *chriae* in talmudic literature. Foremost is Hillel, occasionally together with Shammai; to a much lesser degree Joshua b. Hananiah and Eliʿezer b. Hyrcanus. Summarized in *Story*. The "founder" status is assured for Akiba. B. Azzai and b. Zoma are mentioned as the last great ones of certain catergories of sages —a related Judaic motif— in Mi. Soṭah IX. 15; Tos. XV. 4; BT 49b; JT 24a. Some biographical material and the teachings of Acher center around the school of the young and the psychology of learning. This may have been Acher's original contribution, but lack of sources prohibits more than a guess.

[239] *Pap. Herc.* 1005, col. IV, in F. Sbordone, *Philodemi Adversus [Sophistas]* (Naples, 1947) p. 87. On the problems of the text and on literature see Arrighetti, *op. cit.*, p. 499., fr. 174. The *Tetrapharmacus* is introduced by καὶ δ[ιὰ π[αντὸς ἔστω κ]αὶ π[α]νταχῆι παρε[ιρό]μενο[ν] ἡ τετραφάρ[μα]κος, "and always and everywhere be the *Tetrapharmacus* interspersed". Festugière, *Epicurus*, p. 44, n. 30, reads παρε(πό)μενο(ν), "ready", "at hand". For other reconstitutions of the text, such as the indicative instead of the subjunctive ("... anywhere *is* the *Tetrapharmacus* at hand"), see the apparatus of Sbordone, *ibid*.

[240] *Scriptores Historiae Augustae*, Hadr. xxi. 4; Hel. V. 4f; Alex. 30.6; after *RAC*, V, col. 769.

[241] *RAC*, V, col. 741. The latter three are also mentioned as Epicurus' principal disciples by *D.L.* X. 22-25. Seneca, *Epist.* VI. 6, reports that these three became "great men" not through the *schola* but the *contubernium* with Epicurus.

[242] Liddell-Scott, p. 852, *s.v.*

[243] *P.-W.*, vol. 11 (1907) 142f.

[244] Philodemus ("Lover of people") explains his name as "Lover of (all women called) Dēmō, of whom he specifies four. The latter, however, may have been factual. Besides, the fourfold structure of the epigram is required for the progression of his witticism.

[245] To be sure, there are other such quadruple typologies, numerical sayings, or "inventory"-lists in both cultures that have no connection with Epicureanism (just as there are other tripartite systems in modern philosophy that are non-Hegelian, e.g. Comte's three phases of history). These, however, are not *causes célèbres* and do not provoke parody.

[246] The opinion has been recently ventured that the best ancient literary portrayal of a philosopher is that of Epicurus, surpassing, in its greater unity, the contradictory portrayals of Socrates. It could be added that also his portrait in art is unusually impressive and widely distributed. See *RAC*, V, col. 686f.

[247] In *Story* an attempt is made to show that a number of other Hellenic-Hellenistic rhetorical forms, e.g., those of Greco-Roman consolation literature, were utilized by the Tannaim. In *Studies* an attempt is made to demonstrate that literary motifs from the lore centering around Socrates-Xanthippe-Alcibiades were known to the Talmud.

See also "Epicureans and Epicureanism", "Stoics and Stoicism", "Cynics and Cynicism", and "Socrates", in the forthcoming English *EJ*, as in n. 217, above.

Tannaitic and amoraic teachers do, of course, occasionally employ parodies. Some are found on biblical verses and situations, see Israel Davidson *Parody in Jewish Literature* (New York, 1907 or repr. 1966) p. 2, n. 10 (Davidson treats almost exclusively medieval and modern examples). JT *Ma'aser* III. 10 (51a) parodies *Pirķe Aboth* 5. 22; other parodies exploit talmudic dialectic (Davidson, *op. cit.*, p. 2, and n. 7). The parody of Caesar's saying, *supra*, demonstrates that coinages and situations of the Greco-Roman culture, too, could be subjected to talmudic parody.

NOTES TO PART TWO

[1] Thus if the coinage refers to contemporaneous situations. A translation "there will be no trial and there will be no (trial-) judge" is more appropriate wherever the formula refers to any kind of future.

[2] JT *Ḥagigah, loc. cit.*; Ruth Rabba VI. 4 on 3 :13; Eccl. R. on 7 :8. See n. 95, *supra*.

[3] JT, *ibid.*, following the story on Dt. 22 :7, as a variant tradition.

[4] BT *Ķiddushin* 39 b.

[5] The tongue of the martyr was dragged about by a pig which evokes the additional antithesis : "The mouth that uttered pearls licks the dust", In BT *Ḥullin* 142 a, Acher's exclamation is provoked by seeing Huṣpith's tongue on a dunghill.

[6] To be discussed immediately, below.

[7] This sounds like a *non-sequitur*. Unless the Talmud tries to introduce here as many of these parallel formulae as possible without giving much thought to the precise implications (which, as we shall see, may be the survival of a rhetorical trend), the intention could have been that Acher, seeing no justice in life, concludes that there is no God and consequently no resurrection of the dead. A characterization of Acher as an atheist Epicurean, of course, would be fully in line with the common (but unjustified) accusation of vulgarized anti-Epicureanism, see *RAC*, V, 776-803.

The refutation of Acher's opinion, where it is based on the promises of Dt. 22 : 7, is, according to the Talmud, an achievement of R. Jacob (*fl. c.* 140 A.D.). He happened to be the son of Acher's daughter (BT *Ḥullin* 142 a; *Ķiddushin* 39 b). This refutation is attached to the Acher passages, *ibid.*, and uses Dt. 22.7 as scriptural basis. The irony of the refutation of a heretical opinion by a grandson of the heretic is not concealed from the Talmud.

[8] Athenaeus, *Deipn.*, 593 d, end, and Part I, *supra*, text between n. 95 and n. 100. ... δικαίως οἱ πολλοὶ καταφρονοῦσι τοῦ θείου ὅτε ἐγὼ μὲν τὸν γενόμενόν μοι ἄνδρα σώσασα τοιαύτην χάριτα παρὰ τοῦ δαιμονίου λαμβάνω, Λαοδίκη δὲ τὸν ἴδιον ἀποκτείνασα τηλικαύτης τιμῆς ἀξιοῦται. χάρις, "grace", "favor", "thanks", may here be ironical (just as רחמין in Cain's mouth, see n. 17).

This passage is, of course, a popular piece *on* Epicureanism. A classical Epicurean did not expect interference from blissful passive gods who are enthroned in the intermundane spaces. Nevertheless, the Epicureans may have arrived at such a conclusion not only by physical-metaphysical speculation but also by observations based on life experiences.

[9] The Greco-Roman parallels and the rhetorical nomenclature for these literary devices will be given together with the presentation of the Greco-Roman sources, below.

¹⁰ See the targumic-Aramaic passage, below, line 4, Neofiti I.

¹¹ In more detail, below.

¹² Occasionally hebraized : ...לא דין; אין דין...; once fully aramaized : ...לית דינא; see, below.

¹³ Out of six which paraphrase the biblical story, that is, Pseudo-Jonathan; Neofiti I; Fragmentary Jerusalem Targum; and Targumic Tosephta fragments, whereas Onḳelos and Genizah Targum Yerushalmi (Leningrad No. 739) lack it; see G. Vermès, "The Targumic Versions of Gen. IV 3-16, " *Annual of Leeds University Oriental Society* (*ALUOS*), *3* (1963) 81-114, p. 87. A comparative survey of the parallel texts in form of tables in P. Grelot, "Les Targums du Pentateuque... Gen. IV, 3-16", *Semitica, 9* (1959) 59-88 (Tableaux 6-8).

¹⁴ The Neofiti I text now also in B. Grossfeld, *A Commentary on the Text of a New Palestinian Targum* (*Codex Neofiti I*) *on Gen. I-XXV*, Diss. Abstracts 1969 (Baltimore, Johns Hopkins Ph. D. Diss., 1968).

¹⁵ This arrangement according to short numbered lines is made here for the purpose of discussion.

¹⁶ As the time and place of divine reward and punishment.

¹⁷ These two lines are less structured and evidently belong to the initial section of the fraternal dispute where they are found in the other five versions, see Tableaux 6 and 7, Grelot, *op. cit.*, p. 73, p. 75. Such a transposition may not be a "corruption" but a legitimate shift of emphasis : the לית דין formulation may gradually have drawn all such similar phrases to its orbit.

This is not the place to delve into the intricacies of "the principle of love" (מדת רחמין) and "the principle of strict justice" (מדת הדין), the reflection of these (without the term מדה) in the initial phase of the fraternal dispute (and with Philo), and the difficult and apparently self-contradictory utterances of Cain in some of the versions. (He is a total sinner but agrees to the proposition that the world is governed by רחמין, usually "love", "mercy".) Here it must suffice to say that Cain's statements of this sort are neither questions nor concessions to Abel's beliefs nor uses of רחמין as "caprice" or "favoritism" but rather irony (cf. the use of χάρις in the Danaë item above). The uses of irony, parody, and *spoudaiogeloion* (playful seriousness) as moods or genres have until recently been largely overlooked in the interpretation of talmudic texts owing to a comparative isolation of Near Eastern-Judaic studies from classical-Hellenistic disciplines.

¹⁸ Grelot-Vermès-Grossfeld, and A. Marmorstein, "Einige vorläufige Bemerkungen zu den neuentdeckten Fragmenten des jerusalemischen (palästinensischen) Targums", *Zeitschrift für die Alttestamentliche Wissenschaft* (*ZAW*), *49* (1931) 231-242.

¹⁹ Perhaps best known is thus "Death does not concern us. Whatever dissolves has no perception. Whatever has no perception does not concern us". *Kyriai Doxai* 2 (cf. 17), identical with *Gnom. Vat.* 2, see ed. Von der Muehll, *Epicurus, Epistulae Tres et Ratae Sententiae* (Stuttgart, 1966, repr. of Leipzig, 1922). "We are born once, twice to be born is impossible; not to be throughout eternity is one's destiny..." (*Kyriai Doxai* 14). More elaborately : *Letter to Herodotus*, 81; *Letter to Menoeceus*, 124ff., cf. 125, "... there is nothing frightful in death". (ed. v.d. Muehll).

In summarizing Epicurus' "dogma", Jerome's formula resembles Epicurean as well as Hebraic-Aramaic patterns in word -repetition and brevity (*in Isaiam* VII. 22. 12, Migne, *PL* 24, 272 C):

> Post mortem nihil est
> et mors ipsa nihil est.

20 Usener, *Epicurea*, frs. 359-383. Justice consists in the fact that the sages (the just) possess peace of mind, the unjust will never attain it. Further elaboration of these positions, below.

21 In spite of the many outcries about the suffering of the just (Job, the Suffering Servant passages of Isaiah II, Psalms) final compensatory justice is still expected in this life. See *AdRN*, ch. 5; 13 b (26), A.

22 In later amoraic times when actual Epicureanism (and popular rhetorical anti-Epicureanism) were no longer known, the Sadducees were, indeed, called Epicureans. This development parallels patristic situations in which the equation Sadducees-Epicureans is also found, see *RAC*, V, col. 802, and Jungkuntz, as in n. 5.

Regrettably, other tannaitic passages that treat sectarian situations, such as *AdRN* A, ch. 17, end; Tos. *Sanhedrin* 13.5; *Seder Olam Rabba* III. 36, 9a, Ratner, offer texts that are neither well established nor perfectly clear nor unaffected by medieval censorship with its replacement of sectarian terms. Amoraic passages on sectarians, such as BT *Sanh.* 99 bf., introduce increasingly definitions that have lost sight of actual Epicureanism. Contrary to prevailing opinions, Josephus' two descriptions of Sadduceeism contain no hint whatsoever at Epicureanism (*Ant.* XVIII. i. 4 ⟨16⟩ and *Bell. Jud.* II. viii. 14 ⟨164f.⟩). In detail, Part I, n. 16, *supra*.

23 ויאמר קין אל־הבל אחיו ויהי בהיותם בשדה ויקם קין אל־הבל אחיו ויהרגהו

24 In several manuscripts and editions there is a lacuna at this place, see R. Kittel - P. Kahle, *Biblia Hebraica*, 3rd ed. (Stuttgart 1937) ad loc.

25 So variously Septuagint, Peshitta, Vetus Latina, Vulgate, Hebreo-Samaritan Pentateuch, Ps.-Jonathan, Pal. Targum (Kahle), and Neofiti I, see *Biblia Hebraica*, ad loc.

26 Described with the symbolism of athletics: ἄμιλλα; cf. also the reference to the Pancratium, I. x. 197.

27 σημεῖου cf. σύμβολον, I. ix. 197. In I. ii-iii he quotes as proof for this several other biblical instances in which "field" is an allegory of strife. Devoid of allegory and as a lexical comparison of several biblical passages which mention "field", this idea is found as a Midrash, e.g., in the item on Esau, below, no., 2.

28 ἐν ἁμίλλῃ λόγων I. viii. 196.

29 See P. Wendland, *Philo und die kynisch-stoische Diatribe* (Berlin, 1895); "Studies", *passim*; I. Heinemann, *Philons griechische und jüdische Bildung* (repr. Darmstadt, 1962). The treatment of Philo's Epicurean knowledge in this work of the great master of classical studies is quite sparse compared with his exhaustive analysis of Philo's use of Cynicism. Philo knew a great deal about Epicureanism (including its doctrine of cognition) and was acquainted also with the anti-Epicurean rhetoric of his time, referring to Epicureanism some twenty times in his total work (by name only twice). True, Heinemann was not influenced (as Marmorstein was, *ZAW*, *loc. cit.*) by the writings of Moritz Friedländer, as, e.g., *Der Antichrist...* (Göttingen, 1901), who saw in the target of Philo's polemic a Gnostic sect who followed Cain and identified these "Cainites" with the Gnostics of this name mentioned by the Church Fathers (Irenaeus, *adv. haer.* I. xxxi. 2f.; Epiphanius XXXVII; Ps. Tertullian 7, etc.). Instead, Heinemann took the pejorative "sophist" with Philo quite literally (p. 436, n. 2), in line with other interpreters of Philo, as recently again A. Michel in *Colloque national sur Philon d'Alexandrie*, Lyon, 1966 (Paris, 1967), ed. R. Arnaldez et al., p. 84. This would explain the "disappearance" of a number of Epicurean allusions in Philo, especially in the case of Cain. Here P. Wendland, in his still valuable *Philos Schrift über die Vorsehung* (Berlin, 1892) has made a sounder an-

alysis (in spite of a number of problematic philological suggestions). In truth, Philo participated fully in the cultural life of his time, attacked many targets, religious as well as philosophical, Jewish as well as non-Jewish. For Philo Cain is a symbol of notoriously argumentative Epicureanism and occasionally of all "impious" and sophistic (argumentative) philosophies but not the founder of a sect of Gnostics nor a Sophist in the technical sense of the word (an occasional mention of Protagoras notwithstanding). In fact, certain (marginal or extreme?) Epicureans were called or considered "Sophists" (*D.L.* X. 26).

That Gnosticism and Epicureanism had much in common and were, indeed, compared and even occasionally identified with one another (vituperatively or seriously) in ancient philosophy and patristics (and even in the Talmud) is an entirely different matter. See Part I, *Supra*.

30 Philo can afford this implied anachronism, since he speaks of perennial types and his audience, attuned to him, knew that he castigated simultaneously contemporary situations. He also employed "city-building" as an allegory for "system-building", see *de posteritate Caini*, XIV, end, and was well aware of the fact that there could be no cities yet in that period.

31 Other "Cainite" passages further support this claim: *Quod deus...* IV. 275; *de sacrif.* II. 21-33; *quod deter.* XLIII. 221. Cf. in these passages also the reproach of ignorance which was a common theme in anti-Epicureanism; in detail, Part I, *supra*.

32 Complaint (or praise) of Epicurean argumentative skill is ubiquitous in the ancient world. In detail, Part I, *supra*.

33 The possibility that Philo refers to the exceptional Roman period of Epicureanism in which many leaders were Epicureans (possibly young Caesar, Piso, Cassius, Atticus, etc.) and celebrated poets dallied with it (Horace, Vergil, Ovid, Juvenal, Petronius) is fairly remote. The tentative suggestion may be made here that he is still occupied with the catastrophic role in the fate of Judea (and possibly, Alexandria) which his renegade nephew Tiberius Julius Alexander played, variously as prefect and viceroy of Egypt, procurator of Judea, and general of staff with Titus and to whom Philo's *de providentia* is held to have been addressed. The Alexander in this latter work, especially in fr. 2, indeed, did deny the existence of providence, and Philo's argumentation there is quite similar to that under discussion here.

34 For all technical terms see R. Volkmann, *Die Rhetorik der Griechen und Römer* Hildesheim 1963 or Leipzig 1885); Quintilian, *Institutio oratoria*; H. Lausberg, *Handbuch der literarischen Rhetorik*, 2 vols. (Munich, 1960). Cf. Part I, *supra*, n. 36.

35 Altogether seven ending in -*menoi*; four in -*toi*. A few -*tes* endings are interspersed.

36 Most famous example of ancient literature is Caesar's *veni, vidi, vici*, skillfully parodied in Gen. R. LXXVIII. 12 on 23:10.

37 Philo's tirade, freely rendered here in condensation (all phrases, nouns and verbal forms given as adjectives), runs approximately as follows: *The virtuous*: obscure, despised, lowly, impoverished, underprivileged, subjected, enslaved, filthy, sallow, emaciated, starved, diseased, deathbound (Abel). *The non-virtuous*: honored, wealthy, powerful, praised, prestigious, strong, healthy, robust, revelling, riotous, leisurely, pleasure-loving (allegory of Cain).

This approximate quantitative (syllabic) balance between these two antithetical passages is classified as πάρίσωσις with some ancient critics. The Greek text is given here to facilitate the inter-cultural comparison of such rhetorical-antithetical lists:

οἱ μὲν γὰρ λεγόμενοι φιλάρετοι ἄδοξοι σχεδὸν ἅπαντες, εὐκαταφρόνητοι, ταπεινοί, τῶν ἀναγκαίων ἐνδεεῖς, ὑπηκόων μᾶλλον δὲ καὶ δούλων ἀτιμότεροι, ῥυπῶντες, ὠχροί, κατεστελετευμένοι,

λιμὸν ὑπ' ἀσιτίας ἐμβλέποντες, νοσερώτατοι, μελετῶντες ἀποθνῄσκειν · οἱ δ' αὐτῶν ἐπιμελού-
μενοι ἔνδοξοι, πλούσιοι, ἡγεμόνες, ἐπαινούμενοι, τιμώμενοι, [πάλιν] ὑγιεινοί, πίονεσ, ἐρρω-
μένοι, ἁβροδίαιτοι, θρυπτόμενοι, πόνον οὐκ εἰδότεσ, ἡδοναῖς συζῶντες διὰ πασῶν τῶν αἰσθήσεων
ἐπὶ τὴν πανδεχῆ ψυχὴν τὰ ἡδέα φερούσαις.

[38] The targumic dialogue, however, is somewhat closer to the briefer exchanges in Cicero's *Tusc. Disp.*, see Greco-Roman item no. 3, below. Philo's passage, as we remember, was, in any case, not a dialogue but an antithetical statement of some length.

[39] See the Greek in n. 37.

[40] Neofiti I has one *asyndeton* with Cain; but with Abel all four phrases are connected (*polysyndeton*). The manuscript, however, can not be relied on regarding such minutiae. See a ninefold example of *polysyndeton* in Cicero, *pro Flacc.* II. 5, eightfold in *post reditum* VII.

[41] Since the late renaissance usually called alliteration.

[42] Very frequently with Epicurus himself. As we shall see our לית דין may well have parodied such an Epicurean coinage.

The fact that such etymological word-play is also biblical (Isaiah !) is irrelevant. Our item tries to be rhetorical-anti-Epicurean and to evoke the speech of contemporary Epicureans, not of Isaiah. It is, thus, in mood and intention far removed from biblical reminiscences.

[43] Especially with Apuleius. Also in poetry since Ovid, see J.W. Halporn, M. Ostwald, T. G. Rosenmeyer, *The Meters of Greek and Latin Poetry* (Indianapolis, 1963) p. 71. The requirement for genuine rhyme would include the involvement of two final syllables. On the tendency to introduce "versification" and rhyme elements into prose see also U. v. Wilamowitz-Moellendorff's "Asianismus und Atticismus", now reprinted in ed. R. Stark, *Rhetorika*, (Hildesheim, 1968), 350-401, and, of course, E. Norden, *Die antike Kunstprosa*, (repr. Darmstadt, 1958), 847ff., 861, 878f.

[44] Variant : אוחרן in Abel's rebuttal.

[45] *Torah/sekharah*. This, however, may have been genuine rhyme, since the *ḳamaṣ* may have been closer to an open o than to an ah in that period, the vocalic *waw* resembling, in turn, the *ḳamaṣ*; thus : *toroh/sekhoroh*.

[46] *(ep)anaphora*, or *epanalepsis, epanodos*, iteratio, repetitio, conduplicatio, see Volkmann, *op. cit.*, p. 467. This achieves *gravitas* or *acrimonia*, p. 468. See Cicero, *Cat.* I. 1 : *nihil*, six times; Demosthenes, *de cor.* 121, τί, three times.

[47] Other ancient and modern synonyms are : maxims, gnomes, apophthegms, aphorisms, sayings, idioms, occasionally even *chriae* or *exempla* (which are usually didactic anecdotes) and epigrams.

[48] The frequency of the *sententia* is a characteristic of the Asianic style by which Cicero was more than mildly affected, see H. J. Rose. *A Handbook of Greek Literature* (*sic*, New York, 1960) p. 362f. These *sententiae* often conclude the rhetorical unit (see Acher); in Neofiti I our *sententia* is used midway in the total controversy, in a strategically effective position, introducing the final exchange between Cain and Abel.

Quintilian asserts that some rhetoricians considered the *sententia* the sole merit of a work (*Instit. oratoria* I. viii. 9) and that others overused it (II. xi. 3 and xii. 7). The writing of *sententiae* was a school exercise (I. ix. 3). The *sententia*, of course, is not a proverb (παροιμία, *paroemia*); it is an artful creation of the poet, the school, and the rhetor. Archilochus is praised for his terse and vibrant *sententiae* (X. 1. 60), and Quintilian warns of showing off *vibrantibus concitatisque sententiis* (XII. x. 48). Aristotle, however, had been more willing to recommend the use of gnomes that were close to the rustic and the common and popular with uneducated listeners, i.e., the actual proverb (or its refutation), *ars rhetorica* II. xxi.

⁴⁹ Aristotle, Quintilian, see n. 48.

⁵⁰ Our total targumic homily is quite extensive (so, e.g., in Neofiti I), drawing part of the Lord's speech (Gen. 4 :7) into this dogmatic dialogue. Altogether, the homily is seven times as long as the biblical text.

⁵¹ Lev. R. XXVIII. 1 on 23 :10, Margulies, vol. 3, p. 648f.; Eccl. R. 1.3, 1 and 11.9, 1; *Pesiḳta de Rab Kahana (PdRK)*, *Pisḳa* 8, Buber, 68 b; *Pesiḳta Rabbati (PR)*, *Pisḳa* 18, Friedmann 90 b (merely a reference); Midr. Prov. on 25.20; *Midr. Zuṭa* 1.3, Buber, p. 84, and later collections, such as *Yalḳuṭ Shimeʻoni* and *Midrash ha-Gadol* (see Margulies, *ad loc.*). In most variants the author is Samuel bar Isaac, *c.* 300; some versions have Benjamin b. Levi (probably a confusion with the author of the preceding midrashic item, *ibid.*), Samuel b. Nahman, *c.* 260, or even Yohanan, d. 279, all Palestinians.

⁵² דברים שנוטין לצד מינות. מינות is a general term for heresy but occurs also for actual or supposed Epicureanism. In later amoraic sources מינות and אפיקורסות are synonymous, indicating simply heresy and no longer genuine Epicureanism, see Part I, n. 48.

⁵³ All translations are in accordance with the midrashic view of a verse.

⁵⁴ Whether Ecclesiastes (if at all an integral work) originally intended to portray and then to refute Epicureanism is an entirely different question and refers, in any event, to an earlier period of Near Eastern Epicureanism (see Part I, introduction). In most recent opinions the work is believed to be in line with Near Eastern wisdom literature without the influence of Greek culture.

⁵⁵ הותרה הרצועה: לית דין ולית דיין. Some texts (or manuscripts) make this a question: וכי, "and should then the strap be relaxed?" So, e.g., *PdRK*, see Buber, *ad loc.* Another variant offers אלא, "for (if) the strap..." In the Lev. R. text which Margulies printed, the order of the two phrases is reversed and our coinage is hebraized (לא דין).

⁵⁶ *Ibid.* אמרו יפה אמר שלמה "they said, 'well has Solomon spoken.'" The implication is that this then made Ecclesiastes acceptable as part of the biblical canon.

⁵⁷ That this is so may also be indicated by the midrashic unit which immediately precedes our passage in all variants except Eccl. R. 11.9 and which is almost identical with ours in content and formulation except that Eccl. 1 :3 is the obstacle to canonization : "What gain has man in all his toil which he toils under the sun?" —obviously a reference to the view that there is no divine recompense. There is, however, no mention of our *sententia*. The quotation of ... לית דין with our midrashic unit is actually quite abrupt and somewhat startling. The many forms and actual corruptions of the text (see the apparatuses in all editions) make it possible to suggest that the first item once also had our *sententia* thus bringing out more clearly this double-headed monster of Epicureanism with its hedonism and quasi-atheism.

⁵⁸ τοὺς θεοὺς ἡμῶν ἀφῃροῦντο... Dio is quite an important witness. It will be shown in *Cynicism*, that one *chria* in Dio's formulation is found pratically *verbatim* in the talmudic cycle around Hillel the Elder ("The Rumor").

One is tempted to consider "wiser than all wisdom". σοφώτεροι... τῆς ἀπάσης σοφίας, as a phrase that may have been transferred together with the anti-Epicurean material to the talmudic homily and applied with a serious (non -ironical) connotation to Solomon who had this very reputation in Judaic tradition. Examples of such transformation of the jocular (often *spoudaiogeloiic*) into the serious are not unknown with Plutarch and with the Midrash (see *Cynicism*...); neither are parallels between extended Greco-Roman rhetorical periods and Midrash unknown. One such example of considerable length and several keywords has thus been found in the Hillel cycle (see *Cynicism*..., "Body and Soul").

During his exile from Rome, Dio travelled extensively in the East, thus to Tarsus (*Orat.* 33 and 34) and Alexandria (32), usually from Phrygia and, after his reacceptance to imperial favor, from Bithynia; see H. v. Arnim, ... *Dio von Prusa* (Berlin, 1898), via Index. Unless he preferred the sea to the land route, he may have travelled through Judea. In any case, the effective orations of a famous wandering and cynicizing beggar- "philosopher" may have survived in the Near East, perhaps merely in their outlines (and by keywords). Indeed, the stereotyped nature and ubiquity of rhetorical materials do not really require the actual presence of Dio in Judea proper.

In the case of our Solomonic Midrash, merely the suggestion of possible interdependence (of all detail) with Dio can be offered but no air-tight proof of actual interdependence.

[59] It must never be forgotten that crucial thinkers of the Church spent decades of their productive years in Palestine, cf. Part I, n. 26. They are contemporaries of Judah the Prince (see n. 60), the Greek-speaking Abbahu (*fl. c.* 300, Caesaria), and the editors of the Palestinian Talmud (*c.* 400), respectively. These facts, however, should not suggest mutual borrowing (although this cannot be entirely excluded) but indicate a comparative sameness in some of the circumstances of their lives and education.

[60] Cp. the keywords πρόνοιαν (3), ἡδονήν (4), and the logical tie οἷς ἀκόλουθον, *Philosophumena* (*Refutation of all Heresies*) I. xxxi. 3f., in *Hippolytus, Werke*, vol. III, ed. P. Wendland (*Die griech. christl. Schriftsteller d. ersten drei Jahrhunderte*, vol. 26, Leipzig, 1916) p. 26f. Hippolytus was active from before 212 to 235 and thus a younger contemporary of Judah the Prince, the redactor of the Mishnah (*c.* 135-219).

Another such statement is found in Salvianus (5th ct.) *de gubernatione dei* I. 5 (*Usener*, fr. 363, end), "...qui (the Epicureans) sicut voluptatem cum virtute, sic deum cum incuria ac torpore iunxerunt". Such combined criticisms of hedonism and the doctrine of non-providence must have been part of a general anti-Epicurean tradition and reached as such the Midrashists. The Judeo-Christian polemicists, however, would perhaps be still more inclined to condense such accusations into effective juxtapositions.

[61] vol. III, p. 694, Theodor-Albeck.

[62] באותו הזקן בגעה מדת הדין, אין כאן לא מתן שכר ואין תחיית המתים. Esau heard of Abraham's death when he chanced upon Jacob cooking lentils (the meal of the mourners). The existence of divine providence is reestablished (for the listener or reader) by a forced interpretation of Jeremiah 22:10 on Abrahams' reward and Esau's punishment. Among the (partially) parallel passages, *PR, Piska* 12, זכור, 47b (Friedmann) returns to Esau's denial. The latter says to his brother: "Fool! Do you then believe that once man dies and ends in the grave he will live thereafter?" "And he denied the resurrection of the dead". The last sentence also in *Yalkut Shime'oni, ad loc.*, 110, near end.

[63] It is unlikely that this exclamation is part of the legitimate talmudic controversy that consists in asking whether the world is ruled (or created) preponderantly by mercy or by justice according to the letter of the Law, a dogmatic question around which, as we have seen, some of the Targumim on Gen. 4:8 centered and which is also otherwise referred to in Gen. R. (see the beautiful item XII. 15 on 2:4b: both are active in equal measure). Even if a talmudic opinion would have been inclined to see divine strictness everywhere, this would not render it heretical nor lead to a denial of resurrection. Esau's exclamation, however, is introduced here to make him a thorough heretic (Epicurean) and not to pursue further the dogmatic controversy.

⁶⁴ *Piska* 18, Buber, *et al.* Author : Samuel b. Jonah. Actually the author is uncertain, see Buber *ad loc.*

⁶⁵ Indeed, Samuel b. Isaac, the author of the Midrash on Solomon, above, no. 1, is given as the author of this Midrash on Manasseh in the variant version *PdRK, Piska* 25, 126b.

⁶⁶ See Maximus of Tyre (c. A.D. 125-185), XV. 8, Hobein; Cleomedes (c. 150-200 ?), *de motu...* II. 1, p. 166, H. Ziegler; and Justin, *II Apol. VII.* 3 (of Nablus, but active elsewhere, d. c. 165). See E. Bignone, *op. cit.,* vol. I, 331 ff., 341. The theme of the excesses of Sardanapalus (perhaps the most prominent Near Eastern King in classical culture), before it was used in anti-Epicureanism, was, of course, already active in Greek literature. The ascription of luxury, effeminacy, and degeneracy is first fully developed in Ctesias' version (*Persika*). See also Plato's *Gorgias* 524e-525, where Sardanapalus is alluded to. On the age and veracity of the classical sources since Herodotus see *P.-W., s.v.,* "Sardanapal", *Second Series,* second half-vol. (1920), 2436-2475.

⁶⁷ H. Fuchs, *Der geistige Widerstand gegen Rom* (Berlin, 1964, repr. of 1938). See also "Spiritual Resistance Against Greek and Roman Rule", in the forthcoming English *Encyclopedia Judaica.* New York-Jerusalem.

⁶⁸ *AdRN* A, ch. 32, end, 47a Schecter, see footnote (*ibid.*) for correct text. R. Meir uses only one half of the saying whereas Akiba, Gen. R. XXVI. 6 on 6 : 3, near end, in a slightly different midrashic version quotes in full and refutes in full, using also Ps. 10 :13 as an identical formula.

⁶⁹ Midr. Pss. on 10 :6 (Buber), *Yalk Shim.* II, Pss., § 651 (the only instance where Aramaic is used throughout אינא: לית דינא ולית דיינא, see Buber's important note, *ibid.*).

⁷⁰ *Yalk.* : והלך לו עולמו את הניח הקב״ה. Midr. Pss. adds : בשמים לו וישב.

⁷¹ Details in Part I.

⁷² *Usener,* fr. 340, from Hippolytus, *op. cit.,* I. xxii. 5.

⁷³ It seems that although Epicurus indeed used frequently *paronomasia,* such as the rapid succession of active and passive of the same verb, as in *Kyriai Doxai* 32, see 31 and 33, μὴ βλάπτειν μηδὲ βλάπτεσθαι, or different tenses of the same verbal root, as in *Gnom. Vat.* 14 (both *schēma etymologikon*) or *epiphora,* Οὐδὲν ἱκανόν ᾧ ὀλίγον ἱκανόν, "nothing is sufficient to whom the sufficient is little", *Gnom. Vat.* 68, these effects are apparently produced by the effort to be logical and clear but not by the will to achieve rhetorical effects. He was opposed to rhetoric and its devices, and antiquity found his style often heavy (in detail, Part I, *supra*). Suspiciously close to conscious alliteration is the fourfold *pi* in *Gnom. Vat.* 61, a particularly moving statement. Yet this entire *Gnomologium Vaticanum* has been modified by materials from Metrodorus and, possibly, later sources; see *RAC,* V, col. 697. Philodemus' introduction of rhetoric effected a change (critical discussion in Part I, *supra,* n. 229f.) and must have encouraged (and is typical of) such later Epicurean coinages.

⁷⁴ Esau modifies the talmudic coinage by the interpolated כאן, "here", "in this case". Coinages were thus expandable according to the requirement of their uses.

⁷⁵ To use the *sententiae* of others was, of course, quite commendable. Edition of Lucretius' *de rerum natura* by C. Bailey, 3 vols. (Oxford, 1947).

⁷⁶ Tantalus, Tityos (Tityus), Ixion, and Sisyphus are among those most spectacularly and ingeniously tortured in the Netherworld and the prototypes of punishment after death in Greek mythology. On the complex and varying traditions on these see the standard works on Greek mythology, such as W. Roscher, *Ausführliches Lexikon der griechischen und römischen Mythologie,* 6 vols., 4 suppls. (Leipzig, 1884-1937); H. J.

Rose, *A Handbook of Greek Mythology, Including... Rome*, 6th ed. (London, 1958);
I. Radermacher, *Das Jenseits im Mythos der Hellenen* (Bonn. 1903).

[77] All within III. 980-984.

[78] I.e., "Hell on Earth", *in vita sunt omnia nobis*, 978f.

[79] Written in 43 B.C. Cicero who had heard Epicurean teachers in Athens and counted many Epicureans among his friends, seems to have edited Lucretius' poem, if we can believe Jerome, and once recommended in a letter to his brother Quintus the work of Lucretius. He praised the Epicureans Siro(n) and Philodemus. He became, however, the most prolific, virulent, and durable of the anti-Epicurean rhetorical writers. Details and sources in Part I, *supra*.

[80] Was this the lacuna in Lucretius' poem, III. 1012?

[81] Many of his letters are full of praise and imitation of Epicurus. This passage, too, is favorable to him, cf. the continuation of the letter, 22f. The somewhat flippant *cantilenam* actually pays tribute to the fact that certain Epicurean arguments and doctrines had become commonplace but Seneca does not want to be accused of triteness.

[82] Seneca is referring to Tityus. The formulation is Seneca's (determined, of course, by the preceding parallelisms) but the content is common to classical enlightenment in general and Epicureanism in particular.

The consonant c was still pronounced k in that period. The intention was probably to continue the phonetic effect of x (ks) by reversal of consonants (sk) and further use of k.

[83] *Nemo... puer est* (this is the key thought "fable".)

[84] On this Epicurean doctrine more below.

[85] The ancient critics discussed the use of s and x in rhetoric extensively, see Volkmann, *op. cit.*, p. 514.

Our argument refers, of course, to this strong concentration of rhetorical devices and key words within such a comparatively limited passage, not their occurrence as such. Such intense structuring betrays the stimulus or actual presence of a coinage.

[86] Editions: C. W. Chilton, *Diogenes Oenoandensis Fragmenta* (Leipzig, 1967) fr. 14; I. William, same title (Leipzig, 1907) fr. 16; A. Grilli, same title (Milan, 1960) fr. 15.

[87] The few reconstituted letters and the dittographies of the inscription in all three editions are identical and obvious and therefore not reproduced here.

[88] The alliteration is, of course, by choice, not by necessity. There would have been several other famous "sinners" at the disposal of the writer.

[89] *Inscriptiones Graecae* XIV, ed. G. Kaibel (Berlin, 1890) # 1746, p. 439; also in *Inscr. Latinae Selectae* II. 1, ed. H. Dessau (Berlin, 1906) #8156, p. 881. On Epicurean epitaphs see Part I, n. 69.

[90] Dessau: $Αἶκος$.

[91] Dessau: $Κέρβε[ρ]ος$.

[92] *Tusc. Disp.* I. xli. 98. See also Isocrates, *Orat.* IX. 14f., Plato. *Apol.* 41a, *Gorgias* 523aff. Philo is acquainted with some of the myth surrounding Minos (*de spec. leg.* III. 307 ⟨43⟩) and Triptolemus (*de praem.* 409 ⟨8⟩), the fourth judge who is often mentioned together with the foregoing three. In the latter's case Philo expressly rejects mythlike phantasy ($μῦθον$ $πλάσμα$) and goetic sophistry in favor of true wisdom, regrettably not in connection with Triptolemus' judgeship but with another myth attached to him and without a sign of any permanent coinage.

The playful, satirical portrayals of the Netherworld, including the mythological Judges and usual Sinners, in Lucian's work is in the spirit of this type of Epicurean criticism. Lucian merely uses a different literary form and adds the cynical emphasis on equality and special punishment of the rich; cf. *passim*, *Menippus*; *de luct.*; *dial. mort.*; *catapl.*; *ver. hist.* II.

⁹³ See n. 82, end.

⁹⁴ The Hebrew noun דין has, in any case, a wide sematic range. Its use and translation as "justice" (the abstract quality, *iustitia*) should not conceal the fact that it can also signify (valid) law; (corpus of) law; judgment (decision, sentence, punishment); case (cause, claim); contest, trial, procedure, lawsuit; court of justice, see J. Levy, *Wörterbuch*, *s.v.* All translations of this coinage are, therefore, tentative, and must actually vary according to the context.

⁹⁵ καὶ ἐν τῷ αἰώνιόν τι δεινὸν ἀεὶ προσδοκᾶν ἢ ὑποπτεύειν κατὰ τοὺς μύθους ...

⁹⁶ See also the less detailed passages *Letter to Menoeceus* 125 and H. Diels, "Ein epikuräisches Fragment über Götterverehrung", *Sitzungsberichte... Akademie d. Wissenschaften* (Berlin, 1916) 886-909, p. 904, col. III, beginning, not necessarily by Epicurus. The reconstructed phrase "palingenesis of the dead" is, as Diels recognized himself (p. 907)., somehow too bold, but the reference to the fiction of Plato's sort is well in line with the literary precedents.

⁹⁷ The two Seneca items are thus from letters of consolation, no. 6 is an epitaph.

⁹⁸ The positive coinage (there is...) expresses the shock of unexpected mercy with Manasseh. The item on the Generation on the Flood is too brief for any such conclusion.

⁹⁹ DeWitt, *Epicurus...*; *RAC*, V. K. Ziegler, however, thinks that he was formerly a Stoic, see "Der Tod des Lucretius", *Hermes*, 71 (1936), 421-440, p. 428.

¹⁰⁰ *Div. Instit.* III. xvii. 8; 16-22. *Usener*, fr. 370. The two Epicurean *topoi* "gods destroy their own temples", and "obnoxious animals refute providence" (the latter very frequent), with which the Epicureans challenged the Stoics, were known and dealt with by the Midrash. The present writer hopes to demonstrate this at some future date.

¹⁰¹ See the witty incident in Lucian's *Timon* 10 according to which Zeus is angered by Anaxagoras' impiety but the lightning intended for him struck Zeus' own temple. Lucian strongly sympathized with Epicureanism and uses here an Epicurean-Lucretian idea, see *de rer nat.* II. 101, which, by the way, Lactantius (see n. 100, *supra*), quotes.

¹⁰² This psychologizing and semi-biographical account by Lactantius may not be factual, since it may represent Lactantius' attempt ot explain to himself Epicurus' development. He could not have made such an attempt, however, without the knowledge that the Epicureans did occasionally perceive and discuss this injustice.

¹⁰³ *Usener*, fr. 361, from Aetius, 1st/2nd ct., and fr. 366, from Lactantius' *de ira dei*, as well as frs. 55-57.

¹⁰⁴ "... multa sunt incommoda in vita ut ea sapientes commodorum compensatione leniant, stulti nec vitare venientia prosint nec ferre praesentia?"

¹⁰⁵ *Letter to Menoeceus*, 135, Bailey, p. 90, freely rendered.

¹⁰⁶ So according to Lactantius, *de ira dei* XIII. xix., *Usener*, fr. 374.

¹⁰⁷ Deus, inquit, aut vult tollere mala et non potest, aut potest et non vult, aut neque vult neque potest, aut et vult et potest...

¹⁰⁸ Synesius (Alexandria, c. 400) in his witty *Encomium on Baldness* (p. 63ff., Petavius), countering Dio's famous *Encomium on Hair*, declares that he persuaded himself (in his first regret of having lost his hair) to write an encomium on Epicurus (without sharing his views) if only to anger the gods, and continues "for I said, where are the (signs) of providence in this (that they meet out treatment) contrary to a person's worthiness?" (ἔλεγον γὰρ ποῦ τὰ τῆς προνοίας ἐν τῷ παρ' ἀξίαν ἑκάστου.) Apparently his thought of Epicurus is continued in this complaint (if not systematically-philosophically so perhaps

at least psychologically). Whether this bit is part of Synesius' weak Christian involvement or of his dominant non-Christian leanings cannot be ascertained but the witty and secular theme points to the latter.

The present writer, by the way, has purposely used the terms providence, divine compensatory justice, recompense, and reward and punishment as near-synonymous throughout this article following the usage which prevails in the rhetorical sources as well as the Midrash, without an attempt to distinguish clearly (as systematic philosophies and theologies would do) between terms which are, of course, far from being identical.

[109] Curiously, he is called "Epicurus". Cf. in detail Part I, n. 113, *supra*.

[110] See P. DeLacy, "Lucretius and the History of Epicureanism", *TAPA* 79 (1948), 12-23, p. 18.

[111] Brief mentions in the *Oxford Classical Dictionary*, Oxford (1949), *s.v.*, "Controversia", 233a; "Education", III. 3, 306b. The collection and "codification" of such gnomic materials occurs in both cultures, i.e., the Greco-Roman and the Judaic, in approximately the same period: a first "wave" between 100 and 250 A.D., and subsequently a steady stream to the end of antiquity, of a less "official" character. See *Story*, p. 86, n. 129.

[112] *Eclogue* 3, No. 350 (4th ct. A.D.), R. Kohl, *De scholasticarum declamationum...* Paderborn (1915), p. 87.

[113] Cicero and Plutarch still had an astounding knowledge of Epicureanism but one wonders whether they really understood fully all its true sensitivities and complexities. But who even in modern philosophy has ever been totally understanding when combatting a hostile school?

[114] See *Story, passim*, where an attempt is made to outline the literary forms that are found in both the Greco-Roman and talmudic worlds.

NOTES TO PART THREE

[1] Ed. Lieberman, 6(7).2, pp. 33f.; Commentary (*Tosephta ki-pheshuṭah*), *ad loc.*

[2] Top, Krotoshin. New York (1959): 63b, IX. 1.

[3] The BT version is selected here for the benefit of the non-specialist who may wish to occupy himself further with this material and will find the technical aids, such as lexica, grammars, concordances, translations, commentaries, and monographs, more plentiful for the BT. As shall be seen *infra*, some aspects of the other versions seem to be closer to the Greco-Roman patterns. In the notes only those variants are listed or discussed that are significant for the subsequent treatment.

[4] This formula marks the material as tannaitic (to 200 A.D.).

[5] Significantly, JT, Tos., and *Tanḥuma Pinḥas* on Nu. 27:15 (in some editions ≠10) as well as *Tanḥuma*, ed. S. Buber, *ibid.*, ≠1 (the latter two deal only with the "Halakhah" without b. Zoma's oration) speak simply of crowds. Nu. Rabba XXI. 2, on Nu. 27:15, is still more explicit: "crowds of people" (אוכלוסי בני אדם). The omission of "Israelites)" or the missing Temple Mount, e.g., in Tos., may not represent a textual simplification but rather an original version in which the item had still the general anthropological significance of the Greco-Roman pattern before its adaptation to Judaic culture.

[6] So also a ms. of Tos. (see Lieberman, *ad. loc.*). The major texts of Tos., however, as well as a ms. of BT *Ber.* have כשראה, occasionally continued by היה אומר, and JT

Ber. has כשהיה רואה, i.e., "whenever b. Zoma saw crowds he used to say..." These wordings, however, seem to be influenced by the later halakhization of what was in all probability supposed to have been a one-time event. Moreover, the formulation "whenever b. Zoma saw crowds in Jerusalem (or : on a terrace of the Temple Mount)" does not make sense : he would have said this benediction any place.

[7] See the preceding note. After the Hadrianic War (132-135) the Temple site was prohibited to Jews.

[8] חכם הזרים is missing in JT and Tos. but is, in view of the Greco-Roman material, in all probability, original. More, *infra*.

[9] הוא היה אומר only in BT. The other versions omit this and offer thus a continuous literary unit. This brief introductory phrase in BT is in all probability a result of the later belief that such a blessing was Halakhah (cf. even Halakhah on seeing Gentile crowds in the preceding BT context) and that also b. Zoma thus uttered it, although with the brief addition "blessed be Who created all these to serve me".

One has to recommend caution, however, in analyzing the phrase הוא היה אומר, since it is not utterly impossible that it has a function comparable to the Greek pluperfect, requiring the translation "(for) he had (already previously) said". Unfortunately, a full scholarly inquiry into the use of the tenses of Mishnaic Hebrew and a possible influence of the Greek tense system (most ancient writers and editors of important sections of tannaitic literature must be assumed to have been bilingual) is still a desideratum. In certain periods and localities of Judea, a Greco-Hebrew or Hebreo-Greek jargon may have prevailed even (or just with) the common people, see M. Schwabe, in *Yedi'ot ha-ḥevrah ha-'ivrit la-ḥakirat Erets Yisra'el*, V, p. 86.

[10] JT omits the particle "and" throughout. Both the *syndeton* (with conjunction) as well as the *asyndeton* are found in Greco-Roman rhetoric in such enumerations. Cf. the syndetic continuation in JT in the second section of this item (on garments).

JT has 14 activities, BT and Tos. eleven, as also Mi. *Shabbath* 16.2. On the sequence and the additional activities and their relation to other talmudic-midrashic passages where they may be of technical and geographic significance, see Lieberman, Commentary, p. 106.16. We are here not concerned with these varying details, since we merely attempt to trace the rhetorical substance of the item and believe that the allusions to traditional and geographical situations in our passage were a means to "naturalize" (oicotypify, Judaize) this Greco-Roman *topos*. On the Greco-Roman pattern which made such enumerations *de rigueur*, see in detail, *infra*.

[11] משכים indicates here merely "rising", not rising early, cf. the parallel עומד in Tos. and BT. It is the craftsmen who rise earlier (שוקדות) than the Sages.

[12] Tos. and JT have six and eight activities, resp. See Lieberman, Commentary, *ad. loc.*, and our n. 10, *supra*.

[13] אומניות. אומות ("nations") is a scribal error corrected in R. Rabbinovicz' *Diḳduḳe Sofrim*, *ad. loc.*, and in most printed editions. Tos. and JT have כמה, "how many crafts...;" still clearer, JT adds בעלי, "craftsmen". JT, משכימים ומעריבים, "rise mornings and evenings", seems to be a liturgically conditioned elaboration. The possibility that, after all, the variant "nations" may ultimately derive from another older version of our item in which the (representatives of) *nations* are blessed because of various talents and specialization in supplying the necessities of life, is remote, in spite of the existence of a *topos* "nations as inventors", see "Erfinder II", *RAC*, V, 1204-1208, 1228 (see n. 18, *infra*).

[14] As indicated previously, these are the best-known authors. The theme is, of course,

represented also with anonymous authors, in fragments, spurious works, papyri, etc., cf. the unknown (Sophist?) contributor to the Hippocratian Corpus in *Peri diaitēs*; the (ps.-Platonic?) *Epinomis*, etc.

[15] Sources: "Erfinder II", *RAC*, V (see n. 18), 1226ff.

[16] I 27d-e, partly using Hermippus, fr. 63 K., cf. also I. 25f., and Horace, *Sat*. II. iv. 73ff. and II. viii. 51.

[17] Since Critias. Cf. Pliny's *Natural History*, VII. 191-215 and Hyginus, *Genealogiae* (*Fabulae*), 274, 277, 2nd ct. A.D. See "Erfinder II", *RAC*, V, pp. 1201, 1227, 1273ff. Heurematology is of interest to the Talmud, too, e.g., the question as to who invented the final letters of the Hebrew alphabet, and catalogues are frequent, with the variation that those are listed who first decreed a basic institution or prohibition of the talmudic civilization, see, e.g., Shimeʿon b. Sheṭaḥ, JT *Kethuboth*, VIII, end.

[18] Literature for the entire theme: R. Müller, "Antike Theorien über Ursprung und Entwicklung der Kultur", *Das Altertum*, 14 (1968) 67-79; "Entwicklung" (H. Dörrie), "Erfinder II" and "Euhemerismus" (both K. Thraede), *RAC*, V, 476-504; 1191-1278 (!); VI, 877-890, Stuttgart (1962, 1966). W. K. C. Guthrie, *In the Beginning*, Ithaca (1957), esp. 63-110; W. Spoerri, *Späthellenistische Berichte über Welt, Kultur und Götter*, Basel (1959); Thomas Cole, *Democritus and the Sources of Greek Anthropology*, Cleveland (1967); F. Lämmli, *Homo Faber...*, Basel (1968). On Tzetzes: W. Spoerri, "Über die Quellen der Kulturentstehungslehre des Tzetzes", *Museum Helveticum*, 14 (1957) 183-188.

Still important if not basic: K. Reinhardt, *Poseidonius über Ursprung und Entartung* (*Orient und Antike* 6), Heidelberg (1928); G. Rudberg, *Forschungen zu Poseidonius*, Uppsala (1918); A. Kleingünther, ΠΡΩΤΟΣ ΕΥΡΕΤΗΣ,, *Philologus, suppl. XXVI. 1*, Leipzig (1933); and especially W. Uxkull-Gyllenband, *Griechische Kulturentstehungslehren*, in *Bibliothek f. Philosophie* 26 (Beilage zu Heft 3/4 des *Archivs für Geschichte der Philosophie*, vol. XXXVI), Berlin (1924).

A great number of texts and translations are found in A. O. Lovejoy, G. Boas, *Primitivism and Related Ideas in Antiquity*, Baltimore (1935). On Hermarchus and Porphyry (texts, commentary) cf. K. Krohn, *Der Epikureer Hermarchos*, Berlin (1921, Diss. of 1919).

[19] L. Edelstein, *The Idea of Progress in Classical Antiquity*, Baltimore (1967), ch. 4.

[20] This trend is called primitivism by Lovejoy-Boas, *op. cit.*

[21] The sequence of Greco-Roman passages to be discussed in the following is not chronologically arranged but follows the exigencies of the argument of the principal thesis.

[22] Esp. 369c. Still, our claim is not that the *Republic* is the immediate pattern for b. Zoma. Rather, a number of Greco-Roman sources, to be introduced *seriatim, infra*, will form the profile of a perennial rhetorical theme which is appropriated in the talmudic item.

[23] ... ὅσῳ μέγιστον τὸ τῶν φυλάκων ἔργον, τοσούτῳ σχολῆς τε τῶν ἄλλων πλείστης ἂν εἴη καὶ αὖ τέχνης τε καὶ ἐπιμελείας μεγίστης δεόμενον. The term οἰκειοπραγία (434c) corresponds to our modern "division of labor", the opposite being the filling of different part-time jobs by one man (ἐν παρέργου μέρει, 370 c, cf. 397e) or multiple occupation, called πολυπραγμονεῖν, 433a (this is not the "busybodyness" of cynicizing sources but a Platonic use of the term). Cf. "... to do one's own things (on the basis of the natural differences among men) and not to engage in multiple occupation is justice" (*ibid*., ... τὸ τὰ αὑτοῦ πράττειν καὶ μὴ πολυπραγμονεῖν δικαιοσύνη ἐστί, cf. also 433b).

[24] The singular is authentic in spite of a ms. variant (see Lieberman's text *ad loc*.) that

prefers the "we" formulation. The singular is fully confirmed by the striking parallel of Seneca, *Ep.* 64.6-9, *infra*.

25 That the claim of the talmudic Sage, to be judge, legislator, civil servant, scholar, interpreter of tradition, grammarian, moralist, and theologian, parallels that of the Greco-Roman *Sophos*-Sapiens is briefly outlined in *Story*. Cf., *ibid.*, the examples of heavenly awards and a Heavenly Academy from both cultures, Greco-Roman and talmudic, p. 80f.

26 O. Holtzmann, *Der Tosephtatraktat Berakot*, Giessen (1912), *BZAW* 23, p. 85 f., is comparatively fair, seeing social reciprocity and praise of culture in the passage. Still, he believes that b. Zoma is naive.

27 369c, lines 6f., ed. Burnet. Enlightened selfinterest: οἰόμενος αὐτῷ ἄμεινον εἶναι, line 7.

28 *Passim*, so also 423d.

29 Cleanthes/Hillel the Elder. Cynical sources even claim that all the great Sages were once slaves. In contradistinction to the Sophists, they refuse to take payment for their teaching (rich material in Greco-Roman sources). This attitude characterizes the talmudic Sage, too. To be treated in detail in *Cynicism*. Cf., however, n. 69, *infra*. Cf. n. 123, Part I.

30 On the painstaking effort to be aware of and grateful for all benefits in both *Sophos*-civilizations more *infra*, on b. Zoma's second item (the grateful and the ungrateful guest).

31 Examples in *Cynicism*.

32 Another literary item, tannaitic, anonymous (BT *Sanhedrin* 38a and parallels), which also has our keyword פרצוף (physiognomy), likewise introduces the First Man, and equally stresses the fact that not one person resembles the other, is, however, independent of our item, though likewise not unrelated to Greco-Roman sources. The item compares the divine creation of the great diversity of men in the mold of the First Man with the uniform (and therefore inferior) coining of the mint by man. Precisely this juxtaposition is found with Pliny, *Nat. Hist.* VII. i. 8, as already seen by Sal. Rappaport, *MGWJ*, 78 (1934) p. 309f. ("Plinius und der Midrasch") and "Antikes zur Bibel und Agada", *Festschrift Armand Kaminka* (70th Birthday), Vienna (1937) 71-101, p. 100. Pliny also praises the "power and majesty of Nature", naturae... vis atque maiestas (7) (cf. Hebrew גדולתו של הק״בה, "the greatness of the Holy-One-Praised-Be-He") as manifested in the variety of human physiognomies, inimitable even by the human art of counterfeit. The Hebrew item is derived from Greco-Roman rhetoric ("Popularphilosophie"), as I. Heinemann (note on Rappaport, *MGWJ*, p. 310) rightly suggests, but his reference to Arnim, *Stoic. Vet. Fr.* II, #1163, is unconvincing. The item is ultimately Platonic, not Stoic, and therefore indirectly related to our item.

33 517e, θεραπευτὴν εἶναι, cf. 518b, "wonderful servants of the body" (pl.), ἀγαθοὶ σωμάτων θεραπευταί.

34 Of additional interest is an encomiastic note attached to this treatment of the division of labor. Socrates mentions the benefits of health (the task of the physician), beauty (the task of the trainer), and wealth (the task of the merchant) early in the dialogue (415e-453) and continues (452): "Imagine the men, who create what the author of that (aforementioned) song praised, should suddenly be present: the doctor, the trainer, and the merchant..." and he suggests an imaginary contest to determine whose profession represents the greatest good —which gives Gorgias an opportunity to praise his own, i.e., rhetoric. The verbal forms of ᾄδω (Attic contraction for ἀείδω, "to sing, to praise",

used 451e, lines 2 and 3, and varied in 452, line 2, by the [partial] synonym ἐπῄνεσεν) may be one of the indications that panegyrical elements of some sort became attached to this *topos* of the development of civilization (cf. also Sophocles, n. 35, and Aristophanes, *infra*). Once represented in much of rhetorical tradition, this laudatory element, whether in the forms of *encomium* (on *erga*), *epainos* (greatness of *aretē*), *eudaimonismos*, or *makarismos* (usually for the perfect dead or the gods), was finally transferred to the Hebrew (closer patterns to follow, *infra*). On the laudatory see V. Buchheit, *Untersuchungen zur Theorie des Genos Epideiktikon*, Munich (1960), pp. 158ff.

35 Whether Plato's treatments of our *topos* go back to the Sophist Protagoras is not the subject of this inquiry. That much of this particular literary syndrome is older than Plato is highly probable as Sophocles famous chorus on triumphant man in the *Antigone* indicates (334ff., cf. also the initial list of Greek authors dealing with this topic in general, *supra*). In the *Antigone* we find among man's achievements already *agriculture* (337ff.), *society*-forming skills (354f.), and *protection from rain and cold* (357f.).

36 For some other purpose, i.e., to illustrate the abandonment of the simple satisfactions and the beginning of luxuries which led to vanities, war, and unhappiness.

37 It becomes thus apparent that whether in dialogue, didactic poem, or, as we shall see presently, comedy and the rhetorical genres, the basics of the profile of our syndrome are not essentially affected.

38 Progress in civilization creates unneccessary luxuries, leading to greed, strife, affectedness, effeminacy, urbanization, etc. This is the tenor of the first part of this Epistle (1-19).

39 From 90. 20 on.

40 Omnes istae artes, quibus aut circitatur civitas aut strepit... (90.19).

41 A number of intercalated relative clauses extend the sequence.

42 The passage is extended by Posidonius' demonstration that the milling process was an imitation of chewing and digesting, i.e., a technique learned through the imitation of nature (22/23). Apparently passages on the cobbler and shipbuilder followed.

43 Seneca apparently follows the structure of Posidonius' work.

44 Omnia, inquit, haec sapiens quidem invenit.

45 The mss. vary here somewhat without essential difference in meaning.

46 In II. v. 16 Cicero invokes Panaetius, Posidonius' great predecessor in the reformulation of Stoicism (c. 185-109), as one who at length demonstrated by historical examples that great men could not have accomplished anything without the efforts of other men.

47 In *de natura deorum*, II. lx. 150ff., when demonstrating how providence works for man, Cicero briefly praises again (*quam vero...*) the role of the human hand in creating the crafts and uses again enumerations: agriculture, building, weaving, stitching of garments (150), etc., and, after speaking of the application of manual skill to the inventions of the mind, enumerates shelter, clothing, protection, cities, etc. Here the "we" form is used: ut tecti ut vestiti ut salvi esse possemus, without *syndeton*.

48 ὦ μακάριοι καὶ θεοφιλεῖς οἱ νῦν ὄντες ὑμεῖς, οἷον βίου λαχόντες αἰῶνα καρποῦσθε καὶ νέμεσθε κλῆρον ἀγαθῶν ἄφθονον· ὅσα φύεται ὑμῖν, ὅσα τρυγᾶται, ὅσον πλοῦτον ἐκ πεδίων, ὅσας ἀπὸ φυτῶν ἡδονὰς δρέπεσθαι πάρεστιν.

49 B. Zoma utters these blessings on the deity, Plutarch on his contemporaries. This distinction should not be over-exploited, since such rhetorical motemes wander about also with the Greco-Roman orators according to personal inclinations or requirements of the subject. In Hebrew "blessed" is often applied to man. For such an interpretation of our blessing see the end of the discussion of Cicero's *Tusc. Disp.*, immediately *infra*.

⁵⁰ Or "for thy sake", διὰ σὲ, 160.

⁵¹ Cp. Plutarch's choice of terms : τέχνης ... σοφίας, 993 E. A precise parallel occurs in Poverty's speech, 511 : τέχνην ... σοφίαν.

⁵² The stereotyping in this particular enumeration is achieved by the multiple use of ἀντί, "for a robe but a rug" (without the impetus of poverty), "for a bed a bag... of bugs", etc., 540-545.

⁵³ Cf. Aristophanes' assertion that all the *technai* and *sophismata* were *invented*, εὑρημένα (161).

This parody may also allude to the rising Cynical movement (Antisthenes, c. 455 - c 360) for which praise of poverty was an important theme. On encomia of poverty see W. Meyer, *Laudes Inopiae*, Göttingen (1915, Diss.); J. Hemelrijk, *ΠΕΝΙΑ en ΠΛΟΥΤΟΣ*, Utrecht (1925, Diss.); J. J. van Manen, same title (after Alexander the Great), Utrecht (1931, Diss.); H. Hommel, "Das hellenistische Ideal vom einfachen Leben", *Studium Generale*, XI (1958) 742-751; R. Vischer, *Das einfache Leben*, Göttingen (1965).

⁵⁴ In the ordinary, non-philosophical sense. M. had discussed the Platonic *anamnēsis* immediately before.

⁵⁵ Here Cicero argues that just as the phenomena of this world are divinely created (sine deo non potest), so is their discovery (or reproduction, "imitation", by the human inventor or discoverer, e.g., Archimedes) only possible by (the same or a reflection of the same) divine genius in man (ne ... sine divino ingenio potuisset imitari, 63 end.

"Wisdom" (חכמה) and "secret" (רזא) occur (separately) in Daniel 2 :30 : "As for me, not through any wisdom that is in me more than in all other beings, has this secret been revealed to me..." In rendering the thought of Greco-Roman rhetoric in Hebrew, b. Zoma may have utilized reminiscences of biblical diction but his thought has been generated by the rhetorical stimulus alone. Without it, the Daniel passage would have remained dormant.

⁵⁶ To b. Zoma such detail must have been quite acceptable, since it coincided with indigenous biblical belief: man derived from earth but possessing a creative divine spirit. Cf. also "imposing names on all things" (omnibus rebus imposuit nomina) with Adam's naming of the animals in Genesis. The inventor and discoverer is in Genesis, too, singled out as a culture hero (4 :20ff.).

⁵⁷ Cicero is obsessed with this detail. It is here Platonic (see *Protagoras, supra*) or, possibly, Posidonian, the early Sages being those responsible for progress. See *de oratore* I. ix. 36; *pro Sestio* 91; *de inventione* I. ii.; *Tusc. Disp.* V. ii. 5. According to most opinions Cicero knew Posidonius personally.

⁵⁸ Since the actual state is a somewhat higher and later achievement (62, beginning), this may refer to the tribal organization of life.

⁵⁹ A detail in the description of the invention of writing arrests our attention : the sounds which the few written characters of the alphabet define, seem nevertheless to be of infinite variety (*infiniti videbantur*, 62).

This resembles Pliny's item on the unity within the variety of physiognomies, n. 32, *supra*. Mention of Cicero's strange variation of this theme had to be made, because Cicero's syndrome of themes is extremely close to b. Zoma's and may by itself have supplied the major part of the latter's composition.

⁶⁰ Plato, *Protagoras*, as *supra*. Aeschylus, *Prometheus*, 436ff.

⁶¹ Posidonius : the Sages as the early inventors taught primitive mankind. The latter lived in a state of misery according to Democritus, the Epicureans, Diodorus, and Vitruvius.

[62] Hesiod, Dicaearchus, Aratus, Vergil, etc., also Lucretius V. 925ff., i.e., the cynicizing interlude.

[63] Even to Aratus, primitive man of the Golden Age was already an agriculturist, *Phaenomena* 112, cf. Varro, *de re rustica* III. i. 5; II. i. 3ff; the latter, following herein Dicaearchus, distinguished three early stages : the food-gathering, the pastoral, and the agricultural.

[64] More, *infra*. See L. Ginzberg, *The Legends of the Jews*, vol. V, pp. 83, 105, 109, 113 and the resp. texts in vol. I (Philadelphia, 1913, 1947). H. L. Strack, P. Billerbeck, *Kommentar zum Neuen Testament aus Talmud und Midrasch*, Munich (1928 or 1961), vol. IV. 2 via Index. B. Murmelstein, "Adam", *Wiener Zeitschrift für die Kunde des Morgenlandes* 35 (1928) 242-275 ; 36 (1929) 51-86 (mostly on Iranian and Gnostic concepts).

[65] It seems that this is not too remote from the idea that underlies (much earlier) Euhemerism : that mankind called gods those who benefitted mankind in an exemplary way or on a massive scale.

[66] A wordplay on κοινός : τὰς κοινὰς ἱστορίας ... ὅτι τοῖς ἰδίοις πόνοις ὠφελῆσαι τὸν κοινὸν βίον ἐφιλοτιμήθησαν.

[67] B. Zoma's יגע כמה יגיעות, "how many *labors* did Adam *labor*", lines 10 and 16, is not necessarily an echo of the keyword *laborata* (in the mouth of a later rhetorician), although such transpositions of keywords to another sentence are found. (Details in *Cynicism*). More probable, the theme of harder work of the lower ranks in the subsequent division of labor is here reflected, or the accumulation of tasks preceding that division, and the motif of the strenuous life of early man in general.

[68] Seneca, of course, is grateful for progress in ethical and philosophical knowledge, b. Zoma for progress by the division of labor (which, in turn, created the conditions for the former).

[69] The same vocabulary also in Cicero, *de officiis* I. xlii. 150f. There it becomes quite explicit that the terms used above are used with a negative connotation which their modern English derivatives still possess to this day. Also the general terms for the crafts in Greek have had varying negative connotations either permanently or in limited geographical areas, particular philosophical systems, or historical periods; such as *dēmiourgos, banausos*, but least *cheirōnax*, see P. Chartraine, "Trois noms grecs de l'artisan", *Mélanges de philosophie grecque offerts à Mgr. Diès*, Paris (1956) 41-47. (The term *technitēs*, however, is not treated in the article). Apparently, Hebrew terms, such as ʿeseḳ and seḥorah, are similarly negative for crafts and trade(s) in the mouth of the frequently rhetoricizing Hillel the Elder and Meir, *P.A.* 2.5(6) and 4.10(14). Shimeʿon b. Yoḥai is the author of the often-quoted "the Torah is given for study (interpretation) to only those who eat manna" (*Mekhilta de R. Yishmaʿʿel* on Ex. 13 :17 and 16 :4, *et al*.). On other forceful items of the same tendency by the same author see Bacher, *Tannaiten* II, p. 88.

[70] A brief amusing satire on the "special effects" of ancient entertainment follows.

[71] As previously indicated, Seneca "romanticizes" (cynicizes) in this letter as well as in the 90th in claiming that civilization and its occupations are debilitating. He is grateful for all benefits he receives but to a wealthy equestrian and scholar-politician these benefits are intellectual and pertain to further social advancement.

On the problem of these terms for the arts and the fourfold (or any other) division with Seneca, on parallels with Philo (*de spec. leg.* I. 335f.), Galen, and Philostratus, on the question whether Seneca's hostility to education is here Epicurean, Cynical, or, perhaps, after all, Stoic, and ,finally, on the Posidonian aspect in this letter, see A.

Stückelberger, *Senecas 88. Brief* (Über Wert und Unwert der freien Künste), Heidelberg (1965).

⁷² Not much on our subject can be expected form Aristotle owing to the fact that progress and decline do not figure prominently in his thought which leans toward the phenomenological, teleological and systematic as well as the cyclical and perennial rather than toward the evolutionary and historical. His view of artisans is negative: they are, in most of his outlines, without leisure, without virtue, and undeserving of citizenship. Nevertheless., the juxtaposition of *food* and *clothing* is found in the *Politics* I. viii. 1256b, ≠11, but in reference to the use of animals to man.

⁷³ These get special mention as least respectable together with the entertainers also with Cicero, *de offic.* I. xlii. 150, end. Perfumers are also on Poverty's list in the *Plutus*, 529.

⁷⁴ Ed. P. J. Enk, according to whom this unique poem on hunting was written between 30 B.C. and 8 A.D. Parts of the poem are obviously dependent on Lucretius.

⁷⁵ Other contemporary disciplines may prefer a different nomenclature for this literary terminology, such as social or ethical values, ideas, philosophumena, or even theologumena.

⁷⁶ To be sure, the interest in and frequency of our *topos* in Greco-Roman culture was partly conditioned by perennial problems in ancient civilization. Here, however, as so often in history, the emergence of diametrically opposite opinions must have been helpful. In the case of the division of labor such an opposite opinion was presented by by Iambulus (of uncertain Hellenistic times) in his (travel-)romance of the "Sun State", still excerpted by Diodorus, II. 55-60, and parodied by Lucian in his *True Story* ('Ἀληθής ἱστορία). Thomas Campanella's (1568-1639) "Sun State" is one of the well-known imitations at the threshold of the modern world.

⁷⁷ Gen. R. XXIV. 7, see W. Bacher, *Die Agada der babylonischen Amoräer*, Munich (repr. 1967), p. 13. Rab spent decisive years in Palestine. Eleʻazar (b. Pedat?), died c. 280, who elsewhere quotes an Epicurean slogan, may have been the co-author of the item.

⁷⁸ Rab midrashizes Is. 44:11, חרשים המה מאדם, "the craftsmen being merely human", to mean "the craftsmen —from Adam they stem". Adam is to him also the inventor of the ruling process of the parchment used for the Torah scrolls (*ibid.*), the apparent anachronism being not much of an obstacle for a prophet-clairvoyant.

⁷⁹ Otherwise vegetarianism does not play much of a role in talmudic culture. On vegetarianism cf. Plutarch's passage, *supra*, and also the theory of the food-gathering stage of early mankind. The Pythagoreans and some Academics and Stoics also emphasized vegetarianism (but not the Cynics, and Epicurean austerity is not vegetarianism; so against J. Hausleiter, *Der Vegetarismus in der Antike*, Berlin [1935]).

⁸⁰ Rab in BT *Abodah Zarah* 8 a; JT, *idem*, 39 c; and parallels, see Bacher, *Pal. Amor.*, p. 13, n. 79 and M. Grünbaum, *Gesammelte Aufsätze zur Spruch- und Sagenkunde*, Berlin (1901), p. 130. Adam's mysterious outcry which in the Midrash, *ibid.*, is supposed to be the etymology (midrashically) of *calendae* has been satisfactorily explained by S. Lieberman, *Hellenism in Jewish Palestine*, New York (1962) p. 10f., as κάλον δύε, "set well", presupposing the knowledge of Greco-Roman sun festivals on the part of Rab, and being paralleled in a magical papyrus. In confirmation of Prof. Lieberman's suggestion one could add that his reconstruction rhymes with the cry at the Eleusinian Mysteries (ὕε κύε, see Liddell-Scott-Jones, *Greek-English Lexicon, Supplement*, Oxford [1968], s.v., κύω, p. 90b), i.e. probably: "impregnate, O moisture-bringing Zeus!" (i.e., "Come, O rain!"), used in a rain ritual.

Rab may also have modified a Greco-Roman item resembling Aristotle's *de Caelo* I. 4 in BT *Shabbath* 77b, to the effect that God (and Nature) create nothing in vain (after Bernhard Heller, *MGWJ* 76 ⟨1932⟩ p. 333f., slightly adjusted).

[81] At this stage the present writer is still unable to comment on a possible connection of this theme with the idea of a still disrupted nature in the time of early man, as in the Empedoclean interlude in Plutarch's *de esu carm.*, 993 D/E.

[82] BT *Pesaḥim* 54a. On parallels and textual variants see Bacher, *Tannaiten*, II, 2nd ed., Strassburg (1903) p. 178, n.2. *Maʿalah* can refer to the Deity, see Jacob Levy, *Wörterbuch*, III, *s.v.*, last entry.

[83] Although Plato's doctrine of ideas is represented in the Midrash, e.g., Gen. R. I. 1, the use of *dugmah-deigma* here does not indicate Platonic derivation because of the connection of the term with the heurematological motif in our passage. Rather, *dugmah* is here the semantically attenuated loanword in its meaning "similar to" and not literally "in the pattern of".

Jellinek's contention (*Bet ha-Midrasch* [sic] *V*, 3rd ed., Jerusalem [repr. 1967], Introduction p. XLVIII) that this Midrash represents the Prometheus motif, is equally improbable, since Adam's invention of the fire is approved of (inherently) by the Midrash and occurs rationally-empirically by the rubbing together of two stones (cf. Diodorus I. xiii. 3 and I. viii. 5 : lightning strikes tree; and Vitruvius, *On Architecture* II. i. 1 : storm-tossed trees rub their branches together).

[84] Such a feat must have counted as an invention also with the Stoics. Mentioned *supra*, n. 56. The invention of language by man and the "correctness" of "names" (words) are the problems first discussed in Plato's *Cratylus* in an exemplary and permanently influential manner.

[85] It may have existed in apocalyptic lore.

No complete interdependence has to be assumed, however, to explain the similarity between the setting of b. Zoma's oration and that of the Sermon on the Mount in the version of Matth. 5.1ff., where likewise the vocables "to see", "crowds", and "mountain" occur, followed by *makarismoi*, since the keyword "see" in the Berakhoth versions is supplied by halakhic discussions of blessings that are said when seeing certain phenomena in nature or human life. The "blessed", on the other hand, is supplied by the Greek encomiastic pattern, esp. as with Aristophanes and Plutarch (but also with Cicero and Seneca). The crowds, finally, come with the originally Platonic motif on the variety of human talents (as modified in Pliny). "Temple Mount", finally, is the means for the Judaization of the item.

In many other cases, however, in both Midrash and New Testament, the setting of a one-time event with the central Sage-figure communicating his wisdom before crowds is supplied by the *chria* (χρεία), the Greco-Roman Sage anecdote and favorite literary form of the cynicizing Sage material, as applied to Socrates-Antisthenes-Diogenes--Crates-Cleanthes. In detail cf. *Cynicism*. Only this detail of a chriic setting is common to both Matth. 5 and b. Zoma's passage.

[86] A clear example in Lactantius, *c.* 300, *Instit. Div.* 13-17 (vaguely related to Diodorus I. viii. 1-3) and 18, see Spoerri, *op. cit.*, p. 156ff.

[87] On the possibility that the Hebrew phrasing reflects the Greek pluperfect see *supra*, n. 9. Heb. "thus" is given as "also" in the translation.

[88] Translated in the sense of the midrashic modification of the verse. Thus also in Tos. *Ber.* BT *Ber.* has, in addition, a biblical testimonial on the bad guest from Job 37:24. The use of these two testimonials implies a thorough reinterpretation of the basic verses

which makes them refer to man (and no longer to God). Whether the testimonials also imply that the host is in the place of God can no longer be ascertained, nor whether or not they are b. Zoma's.

[89] Cf. esp. Horace, thereafter Petronius, Iuvenal, and Lucian.

[90] In the sense of the Stoics, i.e., consciously exaggerated, uttered in a controversial, extreme, and unexpected formulation. In detail see *infra*, Section iii.

[91] *Ep.* 81.10 : itaque negamus (we Stoics) quemquam scire gratiam referre nisi sapientem.

[92] Beneficium si qui quibus libet dat, nulli gratum est.

[93] Morbo suo morem gessit, J. W. Basore, *Seneca, Moral Essays*, vol. III. Cambridge (1958), p. 43, suggests that the host followed his "personal weakness", i.e., vanity (n. b).

[94] In the following, four sentences begin with approximately the same phrase (accepi... accepi... accepit ...accepit. Cf. the fourfold Hebrew *kammah* "how many", lines A-C, 12) as well as the threefold *hēbi'* ("he brought", A-C). The term for this frequent rhetorical device was *epanaphora* with the ancient grammarians and critics (also *epanalepsis, epanodos, iteratio, repetitio, conduplicatio*), see R. Volkmann, *Die Rhetorik der Griechen und Römer*, Hildesheim (1885, repr. 1963) p. 467. According to the critics this repetitive element creates *gravitas* and *acrimonia* (p. 468). Other examples : Cicero, *Cat.* I. 1 : *nihil* six times; Demosthenes, *de cor.* 121 : *ti* three times. Cf. No. 9, *supra*, Cicero's *Tusc. Disp.* : *qui* five times.

[95] quam, quot, quanto.

[96] Cf. טורח; טרחות (var.). With Seneca the "labors", however, are on the part of the recipients. Such transpositions of keywords are quite frequent in the reformulation of Greco-Roman materials in the Midrash.

[97] *Aut me.* Some editors have suggested *ita me* instead.

[98] Cf. "this" (*hoc*) twice, here and in 1., as well as II. xxviii. 1, immediately *infra*. The exclamations of the guest are thus highly structured throughout all the examples of our *topos*.

[99] It may be the evil of jealousy which speaks here or an imagined spokesman of it.

[100] The reversal is, of course, a familiar rhetorical device, a subdivision or, rather, special type, of the *amplificatio*.

[101] In Judea meat was not inexpensive.

[102] This tentative statement is made on the assumption that Seneca is not the direct source of b. Zoma but that both, being active within the orbit of rhetoric, had access to similar patterns. In that case, the language of transmission to the Hebrew would have been Greek.

[103] The biblical proof texts which follow each item will be discussed *infra*, n. 121.

[104] What the Stoics would call 'affection", "appetite". Literally, "urge", "inclination",

[105] *AdRN* B re-arranges the sequence : 1, 4, 2, 3. *AdRN* A uses two superlatives. "who is strongest", and in the second position, "who is most humble ?" (Moses). The specific instead of the general and the additional material there have all the earmarks of a late edition.

[106] Literature : Most recent : D. L. Sigsbee, *The Ridicule of the Stoic Paradoxes in Ancient Satirical Literature*, U. of Mich. Diss. (1968). S. Stella, *Paradoxa Stoicorum*, Milan (1937). J. Schmidt, *s.v.*, "Paradoxa", *P.-W., XXXVI. 2*, 1134-37, Stuttgart (1949, somewhat antiquated). H. F. A. v. Arnim, *Stoicorum Veterum Fragmenta*, Leipzig, I (1938), ##216-29; III (1923), ##544-684 (among other materials on the Sage and the Fool).

¹⁰⁷ The passage from Stobaeus *apud* Arnim I, #216, has thus Epicurean formulations (antithetical word plays, p. 53) after the initial Zenonic material (p. 52). In spite of the mutual dislike prevailing between Stoics and Epicureans and in spite of Epicurus' express rejection of the third paradox (all sins are not equal according to Epicurus, *D.L.* X. 120, end), Epicurean descriptions of the Sage were particularly apt to become attached to Stoic materials because also Epicurus preferred the absolute ethical statement in startling formulations (*D.L.* X. 117-21). It goes without saying that Cynical descriptions of the Sage (e.g., *D.L.* VI. 72, beginning; 69, beginning) were easily amalgamated with Stoic materials.

¹⁰⁸ 1. Ὅτι μόνον τὸ καλὸν ἀγαθόν
Quod honestum sit id solum bonum esse.
2. Ὅτι αὐτάρκης ἡ ἀρετὴ πρὸς εὐδαιμονίαν.
In quo virtus sit ei nihil deesse ad beate vivendum.
3. Ὅτι ἴσα τὰ ἁμαρτήματα καὶ τὰ κατορθώματα.
Aequalia esse peccata et recte facta.
4. Ὅτι πᾶς ἄρφων μαίνεται.
Omnem stultum insanire.
5. Ὅτι μόνος ὁ σοφὸς ἐλεύθερος καὶ πᾶς ἄφρων δοῦλος.
Solum sapientem esse liberum, et omnem stultum servum.
6. Ὅτι μόνος ὁ σοφὸς πλούσιος.
Solum sapientem esse divitem.

¹⁰⁹ E.g., Cicero, *de finibus* III. xxii. 75 (sarcastic). Only the Sage is king, *magister populi*, rich, owns everything (Cynical, ascribed to Diogenes the Cynic, *D.L.* VI. 36 and 72), knows how to use things, is beautiful, and free. Another such example in pro Murena 61.

Seneca, *Ep.* 81.10ff., freely: only the Sage is grateful, truly loving, true friend, loyal, has honor. The Sage is, furthermore, objective yet will be inclined to judge anyone in the most favorable light (sed beneficio favebit; in hanc erit partem proclivior), cf. Joshua b. Peraḥiah, *P.A.* 1. 6 (1. 7, Taylor).

The Roman scholar Varro (116-27 B.C.) holds (fr. 245) that the Sage is king, rhetor, beautiful, strong (*fortis*), equitable, etc., and —of particular interest— "of the character (or stamp of) Cleanthes" (quoted in Greek). Cleanthes, the Stoic Sage, often described in Cynical terms and anecdotes and claimed by the ancient Cynics, is one of the models for the anecdotal portrayal of Hillel the Elder, see *Cynicism*.

Other series: Horace, *Epistle* I. i. 106-108; partial: *Satire* I. iii. 124f. Lucian, *Hermotimus* 106, end; *vitarum auctio* 20; *Nigrinus* 1, end. Lucilius, fr. 1225. Iuvenal, *Sat.* VII. 189-94.

D.L. VII. 101 and 119ff. and various examples with the Church Fathers, e.g., Augustine, *de civ. dei* IV. 3.

¹¹⁰ Cf. the entire passage and its continuation, "but we who are not Sages", etc. with Paul's 2 Cor. 6:6-10. A similar but not identical Greek example is found in Lucian's *Nigrinus*, 1: "Does it not strike you as wonderful... instead of a slave, I am free, instead of a pauper, really rich", etc. Another related formulation, *infra*, n. 123.

¹¹¹ This is almost the formal equivalent of the Hebrew if one considers that the words *igitur* and *sapiens* are preponderantly ornaments for the sake of the meter. The rhetorical question, although popular also in the diatribe may have been encouraged by related literary genres, such as the stories dealing with conversion to philosophy in which similar questions are directed to the oracles (who is the wisest; who is most happy, etc.) or riddles and *aporia* (see n. 123, *infra*).

¹¹² This may not be an authentic or even serious formulation of the fourth paradox but just its satirical-parodistic intention brings the literary form clearly into focus. *Sat.* II. iii is a parody of a Stoic diatribe on *paradoxa*; *Sat.* II. vii is entirely devoted to a Stoic paradox, see Sigsbee, *op. cit.*, p. 35. Cf. also his commentaries on the mass of other quotations and allusions to paradoxes in Horace. Horace's material, by the way, happens to be more often close to the Midrash. Several examples in *Cynicism*.

¹¹³ These sources, among others, add to the list "and everything else together", or "everything else there is".

¹¹⁴ On the latter see Sigsbee's detailed treatment of the Roman satirists.

¹¹⁵ Such comparatively precise formulations are, of course, reinforced by more extensive passages and general moods prevailing in antiquity which are not directly connected with paradoxes. Thus Cicero, *de officiis* I. xliv. 155, end, acknowledges that whatever he may have achieved, he achieved through his teachers and their doctrines. The example of Diogenes the Cynic who learned even from a child, or a mouse, was famous and repeated in rhetoric *ad nauseam* (source : *D.L.* VI. 37; VI. 22).

¹¹⁶ *Gibbōr* in *P.A.* 4.1 is, therefore, the original wording. The identical keyword in Prov. 16 :32 and a similar teaching there made the finding of a suitable *testimonium* easy. The stimulus for the coinage of the paradox, however, must be seen in the Greco-Roman model which was fashionable at that time and not in the vaguely similar biblical text. In the Greco-Roman culture, too, there were precursors of the thoughts expressed in the Stoic *paradoxa*, even in early rhetoric, e.g., with Isocrates, *ad Nicocl.*, XXIX, 20d (see Stobaeus, IV, ch. VII, No. 35, p. 257, W.-H.).

Philo, of course, knows and uses *paradoxa* but occasionally extends them into lengthy passages, especially in his *Quod omnis probus liber sit* (That every virtuous man is free !). According to his introduction this treatise is a sequence to a companion piece which demonstrates that every immoral man (*phaulos*) is a slave (*doulos*), I. 1/445. The Sage as leader (*hēgemōn*) or "viceroy" (*diadochos*) appears in III. 20/448. In *de mutatione nominum* XXVIII. 152/601 Moses proclaims that the Sage alone is king; cf. *de sobrietate 57*; *de migratione* 197; *de somniis* II. 244. The theme of self-control appears briefly again in *Quod omnis...* in the concluding chapter (XXII. 158-160) among other virtues of the free Sage but is not formulated as a paradox.

This important item on the triumphant self-control of the Sage re-emerged in Islamic culture. Most often Greek Sages (or Founder-Sages) are given as the authors; e.g., in the ethical collection of gnomes and anecdotes which al-Mubaššir b. Fātik (11th ct.) compiled (see F. Rosenthal, *Das Fortleben der Antike im Islam*, Zurich, 1965). Here we find items closely resembling the earlier formulations of the *paradoxa* (including *P.A.*) under the name of Polemo (? *Aflīmūn*, No. 27, p. 176; on the best ruler) and Heraclitus (No 140, p. 194f.; "sagatious is...").

¹¹⁷ See the extensive material with Sigsbee under this heading and in all the chapters of his thesis. A variant of the item "rich" occurs with Philo, *Quod omnis...* II. 8/445; an adaptation of the thought "satisfied with his lot" appears in IV. 24/449.

¹¹⁸ Omitting three words of rhetorical ornamentation : *vero*, "indeed", and two adjectives defining "riches". The general thought, of course, is common to many philosophical schools that deal with the "Sage". It is Platonic, Cynical, Stoic, and Epicurean alike : Plato, *Phaedrus*, 279b-c, end; Epicurus, *Usener*, fr. 504; 602-603; 474-477; *Gnomol. Vat.* 25. Already Democritus, B 284 : "to be rich diminish desires".

¹¹⁹ The shortest item is also Epicurus' : πλουσιώτατον αὐτάρκεια πάντων, "greatest wealth : self-sufficiency" (*Usener*, fr. 504; Bailey, fr. 70).

Whenever Epicurus wanted to make an incisive statement, he used a *paranomasia* of the same verbal root (*schēma etymologikon*) such as, "... neither hurt nor are hurt", μὴ βλάπτειν... μηδὲ βλάπτεσθαι, *Kyriai doxai* 31f. B. Zoma's "honored/honors" is such a *schēma etymologikon*. The theme of honor is briefly sounded in Philo's *Quod omnis...* XI. 72/456.

[120] The double meaning of the Latin *honestus* —both "virtuous" and "honored"— makes the classification of some brief Latin *paradoxa* somewhat problematic. This very equivocation, however, may have favored the development of the social value according to which whoever is honest will be honorable (cf. a similar relationship between the German *ehrlich*, *ehrsam* and *ehrbar*, *geehrt*).

Once using the *schēma etymologikon* (following the rhetorical pattern and not any biblical precedents) b. Zoma was forced to introduce a somewhat awkward object: "Who is honored ? The (one who) honors *the* (other) *creatures*".

[121] In a very wordy passage, *Ep.* 102. 17ff., Seneca attempted to show how in detail honoring redounds to the honor of the agent, In all probability Seneca had a version of the Epicurean dictum before him. Yet the Senecan passage did not lend itself to easy adaption in rhetoric.

Here, in b. Zoma's fourth paradox, as more often, the biblical proof text is either later or secondary (even if by b. Zoma himself) and did not understand (or on purpose altered) the original meaning of the thought by making God the agent (in this case the bestower of honor : I Sam. 2 :30 : "My honorers I shall honor, and my despisers I shall esteem lightly"). The source of honor, however, must lie *within* the Sage in conformity with the tenor of the other *paradoxa*.

The proof texts for the first three paradoxes of b. Zoma are (1) Ps. 119 :99, "I have become more understanding than (lit., "from") my teachers, which in midrashic fashion, is reinterpreted to mean "from (all) my teachers I have gained understanding"; (2) Prov. 16 :32 (on a warrior-conqueror); and (3) Ps. 128 :2. Although these two latter verses are quite fitting and Ps. 119:99 ingeniously adapted in the midrashic fashion, it is still probable that b. Zoma is not responsible for the proof texts because his work seems to adhere to rhetorical patterns too closely. Another later Midrashist, however, might well have been inclined to adapt he humanistic trend of this paradox on honor to the indigenous God-centered belief. The saying, indeed, does occur in this fashion in the name of Jose, *P.A.* 4.6, (4.10, Taylor) but in reference to Torah (cf. also Eli'ezer, *P.A.* 2.10 [2.14, Taylor], in reference to a friend). The comparative strangeness of b. Zoma's fourth paradox may have been the reason for its substitution by the item on humility in the versions of *AdRN*.

[122] *Ep.* IX. 6. Cf. J. Ferguson, *Moral Values in the Ancient World*, London (1958): "In such passages Seneca combines the Stoic sense of duty with the Epicurean warmth of personal affection" (p. 69).

J. Bergmann, in his pace-setting "Die stoische Philosophie und die jüdische Frömmigkeit", in *Judaica*, Festschrift zu Hermann Cohens 70. Geburtstage (Berlin) 1912 (no editor) 145-166, p. 149, recognized the relationship of *P.A.* 4.1 (4.4) to Seneca(-Hecato)'s "if you wish to be loved, love". In his n. 1, *ibid.*, however, he listed as an illustration further "parallel" sayings which actually promise reciprocity or heavenly reward (just as the testimonial does; he lists JT *Keth.* 31 b; JT *B.K.* 6c; Lk. 6 :37; 1 Clement 13 :2), without fully probing the meaning of the basic text. He also recognized the Stoic coloration of b. Zoma's saying in *P.A.* 4.1 (4.3) —keyword "rich"— but connected it only with Epictetus fr. 172 and 129 (Schweighäuser). He was unaware of the relationship of b. Zoma's sayings to the Stoic *paradoxa*.

¹²³ BT *Tamid* 31b-32a (66a in some editions, occasionally also 32a-b). For a critical text of this passage see Wallach, next note.

¹²⁴ This is a Hebrew-Aramaic version of Alexander's encounter with the Indian Gymnosophists, a theme of Greco-Roman sources, as, e.g., with Arrian, Strabo, and Ps. Callisthenes. L. Wallach, "Alexander the Great and the Indian Gymnosophists in Hebrew Tradition", *Proceedings of the American Academy of Jewish Research*, XI (1941) 47-83, analyzes among others Plutarch's version, *Life of Alexander*, ch. lix. Brief mentions of the Gynmnosophists appear also with Philo in *Quod omnis...* XI. 74/456; *de somniis* II. viii. 56/666; and *de Abrah.* XXXIII. 182/27. The Ten Questions are unknown to Philo.

It seems that Questions 1-3 are actually *aporiae* (*aporia, aporioi*), i.e., (near)-unanswerable questions. So expressly of Question 3 : מלתא דא לית לה פתר ! Questions 4-6 represent *paradoxa*, 5-6 being b. Zoma's second and third, but the answer to Question 4 appears as "wise is who (fore-) sees what comes to pass (this is the usual rendering of הרואה את הנולד). The paradoxes are here preserved in Hebrew whereas most of the context is Aramaic, indicating a variety of sources. Among the questions that follow (the counting is problematic) are three antithetical truly paradoxical items (paradoxical in the modern sense) of a cynicizing ethic, vaguely reminiscent of Cicero's *de Murena* 61 and 2 Cor : 6.8f. A "fill-in" of folk wisdom follows and one question which belongs to the plot of the frame story (differently Wallach).

Strangely enough, in the printed texts of the passage, the Sages repeat the entire (Hebrew) paradoxes inclusive of the questions after Alexander's Aramaic questions, confirming the extraneousness of the source. Moreover, our three paradoxes appear without proof texts; this is perhaps because of the brevity of most other replies (but not because of the presence of foreigners to whom the Hebrew Scriptures are unknown; Question 3 —preceding the paradoxes— does have a proof text !). It is thus not impossible that the true reason for the unqualified statement of the *paradoxa* in this passage is their lack of proof texts in the original source.

¹²⁵ B. Zoma, in his interpretative and legislative function in the realm of Halakhah, belongs to this class. It should not be forgotten that Posidonius, Horace, Dio, Petronius, Apuleius, Plutarch, Arrian, Aelian, Aulus Gellius, and even Lucian as well as Philo, Paul, Hillel, Akiba, Rab, and Abbahu were at one time or another, or principally, civil servants (judges, men engaged in social welfare, administrators, statesmen, active priests, etc.) in addition to Plato, Demetrius of Phalerum, Cercidas, Cicero, the Senecas, Quintilian, the Plinies, and Marcus Aurelius, whose public careers are better known (to mention only those who may have directly or indirectly contributed to the *sophos*-ideology and developed materials which are also found in talmudic civilization).

¹²⁶ The structure of this literary device (which consists of logically *and* stylistically interlocked statements with a final conclusion) is evident in detail from the examples which follow. Sorite or sorites from Greek *sōreitēs*, "heaper", cf. *sōros*, "heap". No true or fully developed example of sorites is found in the Hebrew Bible. Although the Stoics were heavily criticized for a sophistic misuse of sorites (cf. Seneca ridiculing Zeno's syllogisms, *Ep.* 83.9) Greco-Roman rhetoric, Paul, Peter, and tannaitic and amoraic culture did use it but in less technical contexts and almost exclusively for popular ethics and theology.

Cicero, *de fin.*, IV. xviii. 50, thus declares : Iam ille sorites (est), "and this (proof), too, is a sorites",

what is good is to be wished;

what is to be wished is to be desired;
what is to be desired is laudable;
"(and) thereafter (all) the remaining steps (*gradus*) ..."
A fully developed sorites is found in Seneca's *Ep.* 85.2 :
Who is prudent, is temperate;
who is temperate, is content;
who is content, is unperturbed;
who is unperturbed, is without sadness;
who is without sadness, is happy (*beatus*).

Occasionally an additional statement representing some sort of epilogue sums up the reasoning of the entire unit and thus reemphasizes the highest value of the author. Seneca thus concludes : "therefore the prudent one is happy and prudence adequate (as the basis) of the happy life". Cf. the famous nine-(or ten-)link sorites of Phineas b. Yair, c. 200 A.D., Mi. *Soṭah* 9.15, end, *et al.* (see Bacher, *Tannaiten* I, p. 268, n. 2) which begins with caution (prudence ?) and ends with the Holy Spirit and the Resurrection of the Dead. Other examples of sorites of a similar structure and intention : Wisdom of Solomon 6 :18-21; Romans 5 :3-5; 2 Peter 1 :5-7; JT *Sanhedrin* X, 28b, *et al.*; *P.A.* 3.21, Eleʿazar b. Azariah, formulated as an actual sorites with the climax "Torah", in the version quoted by A.I. Katsh, "Unpublished Geniza Fragments of P.A. in the Antonin Geniza Collection in Leningrad", *JQR*, *LXI* (1970) 1-14, p. 11f. Folklore with a theological appendix : *B.B.* 10a cf. Eccl. R. on 7 :26.

[127] Third person instead of the second, probably a euphemism in view of the dire threat.

[128] Indeed, this introduction may be Eliʿezer's but his vineyard seems to be that of Song of Songs (Song of Solomon). The actual sorites in *Tanna debe Eliyahu*, however, must be of later origin. The full text is

רבי אליעזר הגדול אומר כרמו של הקב״ה בית ישראל. אל תציץ בו. ואם הצצת בו אל תרד לתוכו ואם ירדת לתוכו אל תהנה ממנו. ואם נהנית ממנו אל תאכל מפירותיו, ואם הצצת וירדת ונהניתה ואכלתה מפירותיו סופו של אותו [איש] ליכרת מן העולם.

[129] Such a non-technical homiletical condemnation is pronounced, e.g., in *P.A.* 3.7 (3.11, Taylor) against those who interrupt their study in order to look at nature (a tree, a field). Scripture considers them *as if* they forfeited (or endangered or corrupted) their own souls, a considerably less stringent formulation (Shimeʿon b. Yoḥai or R. Jacob). Yet even here where apparently the important rule not to interrupt a discourse is alluded to —important also in Greco-Roman philosophy— modern interpreters have seen allegorical allusions to Gnosticism (L. Wallach, on the grounds of the repeated exclamation). A similar warning not to *forget* a Mishnah is found in *P.A.* 3.8 (3.12).

[130] *P.A.* 4.2 (4.5, *Taylor*). The full text of the statement of b. Azzai (colleague, friend, and occasional co-author of b. Zoma) is as follows :

הוי רץ למצוה קלה כחמורה ובורח מן העברה
שמצוה גוררת מצוה ועברה גוררת עברה
ששכר מצוה מצוה ושכר עברה עברה.

The beginning of this saying, "*Run* to a slight duty as to a grave one and *flee* from transgression", is rhetorical in style in as far as antithetical categorical imperatives are common with both Epicurus and the Stoics, preferring the verbs "to *choose*", and "to *flee*". On the former cf. Epicurus' (lost) book on *Choices and Avoidances (Flights)*, Περὶ αἱρέσεων καὶ φυγῶν D.L. X. 27, on the latter, E. Schwartz, *Die Ethik der Griechen*, Stuttgart (1951), p. 196, τὰ αἱρετέα καὶ φευκτέα. Both the diatribe and the rhetorical letter (Epicurus, Cicero, Seneca) use such grammatical imperatives. For an imperative of "run" see Marcus Aurelius, *Medit*. IV. 51 (*syntomē*, "shortcut", *ibid*., is a slogan of the Cynics).

The meaning of b. Azzai's second dictum, on "duty attracting duty", may be a reversal or correction of "the courage of Epicurus who endures *trouble* in order to *flee more troubles*", Usener, fr. 516, from Origines, *contra Celsum* V. 47, ὑπομένοντος πόνους διὰ φυγὴν πόνων πλειόνων, yet it is also superficially reminiscent of Seneca, *Ep*. 87.24, (sacrilegium) malum est quia multum mali adfert, "(sacrilege) is an evil in that it brings on much evil", a reasoning which is almost immediately followed by the statement that crime is its own greatest punishment (cf. b. Azzai's epilogue). Yet the first proposition has a different task with Seneca : its purpose is to define the essence of evil, which *cannot* be illuminated by its consequences. B. Azzai, however, stresses consequences (perhaps being relieved of stating essences because of the existence of a divine Law). Yet it is nevertheless possible that rhetorical sequences of this kind were transmitted because of their general theme, without a precise coinciding of all terms and syllogisms involved.

The epilogue of b. Azzai's dictum, however, does coincide with the preponderantly Stoic view that virtue is its own reward (and vice its own punishment) and may, indeed, reflect it : "for the reward (or result) of duty is duty (of virtue is virtue) and the reward of transgression (or vice) is transgression". Cf. Seneca, *Ep*. 81.19, "the reward of all virtues is in (the virtues) themselves", virtutum omnium pretium in ipsis est, and *Ep*. 87.24, *supra*. Origen, in the passage quoted *supra*, contrasts the courage of the Epicureans with "that of the Stoics who choose all virtue for its own sake", ἡ τοῦ ἀπὸ τῆς στοᾶς δι' αὐτὴν αἱρουμένου πᾶσαν ἀρετήν. B. Azzai's dictum may thus somehow be related to the Seneca passage of *Ep*. 87.24. Actually, Seneca's mention of sacrilege may be intended to be an instance of the general doctrine of Epicurus on the avoidance of troubles. (As usual, the claim of dependency for an item in tannaitic culture includes possible antecedents or descendents of the pattern item in rhetorical culture).

The humanistic provenance of b. Azzai's dictum has apparently been recognized by a number of Jewish commentators of the High Middle Ages and the Renaissance, naturally, without mention of Greco-Roman affinities (see the literature at the end of this note).

It would be a highly doubtful procedure and possibly anachronistic to project the later traditional understanding of the passage into an inquiry of its original meaning. This later interpretation (possibly already late tannaitic) sees in b. Azzai's statement the promise that in fulfilling duties one becomes either psychologically conditioned (by habit) to do more and more, or Heaven sees to it that one is granted that opportunity, cf. the collections of commentative material on *P.A.* by Samuel de Uceda, *Sefer Midrash Shemuel*, New York (1964/65), and Noah Haim b. Mosheh of Kobryn, *Masekheth Aboth*, New York (n.d.).

[131] Cf. Cicero's euphemism *si vero aliquid etiam...* (*sic*), "if, indeed, something else", *op. cit.*, III. xviii. 43, end. Different *Usener*, fr. 67, who makes the copyist responsible for the omission and leaves a lacuna for (2). But Cicero repeats these euphemisms : cf. *de fin*. II. x. 29, ... quae si appelles honos praefandus sit.

[132] Further sarcastic allusions and summaries of the same sequence : *de fin*. II. iii. 7; x. 29.

[133] In justice to Epicurus' system it must be emphasized that sensations, anticipations, and feelings are important to him epistomologically, as the criteria of knowledge.

[134] One does not have to accept DeWitt's enthusiastic yet unproven reconstruction

of our Epicurean passage as a form of sorites, *Epicurus...*, p. 72f. He claims that this item was once a sorites-like syllogism in narrative form and reconstructs the assumed dialoguic form of it (p. 73), a chain of syllogistic questions and "enforced" answers.

[135] On the other hand, it is possible that this omission occurred in transmission. Yet shorter or longer enumerations, already found with Epicurus himself and with Cicero (cf. the texts quoted *supra*), may have been created by rhetoricians both in the West and the East and may have become the pattern for b. Zoma.

[136] In detail S. Krauss, "Die Versammlungsstätten der Talmudgelehrten", *Festschrift zu Israel Lewy's 70. Geburtstag*, ed. M. Brann and J.(sic) Elbogen, Berlin (1911) 17-35, section 5. The most famous case was that of Yabneh —either a real vineyard or a symbol of the seating order (so BT *Ber.* 68b; *SSR.* on 8:11, *et. al.*). Krauss also mentions Rab's garden in Sura (Babylonia) and our *pardes* of Ḥagigah as proofs for the suggestion that the Palestinian Sages met in the open for considerable periods, at least in Yabneh. He lists opinions which suggest that Greek custom was influential in the Palestinian meeting arrangements (e.g., Neubauer).

[137] Recent treatments: S. Lieberman, "How much Greek in Jewish Palestine", *Texts and Studies I (Biblical and Other Studies)*, ed. A. Altmann, Cambridge, Mass. (1963) 123-141 (137-139). Cf. Lieberman's Text and Commentary volumes on Tos. *Ḥag.*, *ad loc.* E. E. Urbach, *The Sages, Their Concepts and Beliefs*, Jerusalem (1969, Hebrew) 165ff.

[138] Prof. Lieberman, *loc. cit.*, rightly argues that this is the basic text and adduces important hitherto unpublished witnesses.

Major deviations found in the three other versions of the story in the Ḥagigah sections of Tos., JT, and BT will be discussed *infra*, with the translation of Ber. R., and throughout Section V.

[139] Although other stories likewise begin with כבר, see Theodor-Albeck *ad loc.*, and although this word frequently indicates that a problem has *already* been solved by a talmudic authority elsewhere, the vocable *kebar* seems to have been transferred here from line 18, "b. Zoma is *already* gone", in the Tos. text. Tos., JT and BT begin with מעשה ב..., "A happening regarding R. Joshua", which is quite often the introduction of Sage anecdotes and legends. See *Cynicism*.

[140] Var. ms.: "sitting". BT: "On a step of the Temple Mount". Tos.: Joshua walking in the public roadway (*strata*), b. Zoma coming across.

[141] Did not get up in the other's presence: BT.

[142] Actually the version of Tos., מאין ולאין, "whence and whither", makes more sense. The keyword "feet" is needed only for the second question and answer. In detail, *infra*.

[143] Prof. Lieberman, *op. cit.*, p. 138f., interprets this as an evasive answer but gnostically conceived: "Whence do you come?" Answer: "(I am) nothing (who comes) from nothing". Prof. Lieberman is aware of the fact that the basic formulation is Epicurean and believes it to be playfully twisted (n. 24, p. 139) as so frequently in classical literature (as well as Midrash).

[144] Literally: "I call Heaven and Earth upon me as witness".

[145] Cf. הרגלים מוליכות, "the feet carry" someone somewhere, as in BT *Sukkah* 53a *et al.*, in the mouth of Hillel the Elder; as proverb (Aramaic), *ibid.*; cf. Gen. R. 100.3 *et al.* (most often with personal suffix).

[146] We shall contend, *infra*, that this reply likewise alludes to an Epicurean cosmological idea and is a play on the word "feet", and that this keyword was supplied together with other ingredients by a Greco-Roman pattern story.

¹⁴⁷ Note the variants "eagle", Tos. and JT with an additional testimonial (Dt. 32 :11), and "dove", BT. Further variants, such as "on his young", etc., are not essential for the understanding of the passage.

¹⁴⁸ Plato —see *infra*— has "into a well". Such varying detail is characteristic of the *chria*; cf. the varying detail of our talmudic item. For a brief history of the *chria* in Greco-Roman culture see *Cynicism*.

¹⁴⁹ « σὺ γάρ, ὦ Θαλῆ, τὰ ἐν ποσὶν οὐ δυνάμενος ἰδεῖν τὰ ἐπὶ τοῦ οὐρανοῦ οἴει γνώσεσθαι ? »

¹⁵⁰ ... τὰ μὲν ἐν οὐρανῷ προθυμοῖτο εἰδέναι, τὰ δ' ἔμπροσθεν αὐτοῦ καὶ παρὰ πόδας λανθάνοι αὐτόν, also quoted by Iamblichus, *fl. c.* 288 (*Protr.* 14), and Eusebius, *fl.* 300 on whom more below; see apparatus Burnet on *Theaet.*, *ad loc*. The keyword "feet" occurs again in the ongoing Platonic description of the Sage who in the eyes of the jeering rabble resembles a fool, 174c.

¹⁵¹ BT *Ḥag.* 11b, end, a prohibition to ask about "what is above and what below", may have been provoked by such formulas of Greek philosophy and rhetoric (cf. the talmudic continuation "what is before and what after" with Epicurus-Metrodorus' formulation of philosophy, *Gnom. Vat.* 10, end). The Greek formulations were probably instrumental in the revival of similar indigenous formulas, such as Ex. 20:4, "in Heaven above and on the Earth below..." in the controversies of the tannaitic age.

It is obvious that the story is older than Plato not only on account of his reference to it as an existing item but also because of the somewhat strained attempt to make Thales a martyrlike prototype of the serious philosopher out of a persiflage of a Sage who was caught in an absurd contradiction.

¹⁵² *Anthol.*, ed. C. Wachsmuth, O. Hense, 2nd ed., Berlin (1884, repr. 1958), vol. II, p. 7, #20.

¹⁵³ The *delendum* of Meineke is wholly arbitrary.

¹⁵⁴ ... γελοιοτάτους εἶναι τοὺς ἀστρονομοῦντας, οἳ τοὺς πὰρ ποσὶ τοὺς ἐν τοῖς αἰγιαλοῖς ἰχθῦς οὐ βλέποντες τοὺς ἐν τῷ οὐρανῷ φάσκουσιν εἰδέναι.

¹⁵⁵ The contrast and near-*double entendre* is between "man above" (as concept) and "man below" (as flesh-and-blood neighbor). Although adding more witty and even sarcastic remarks Plato is here dead-serious and sees in these contrasts a natural and necessary state of affairs.

¹⁵⁶ Died 212 A.D.; from his *Hypomnēmoneumata*.

¹⁵⁷ The former : Migne, *Patrologia Graeca*, vol. 91, *Loci communes*, p. 853 A., ch. 21 (600), the latter : D. Tschizewskij, *Melissa*, Munich (1968, Semenov edition) p. 206. These collections actually represent more or less the same Byzantine florilegium.

¹⁵⁸ Involving a boss and a servant girl with the former, and Heracles with the latter. Reference is to the *Dyscolus* and the comical tragedy fr. 12, Nauck; cf. W. Süss, *Lachen, Komik und Witz in der Antike* (Zurich) 1969, p. 34.

¹⁵⁹ The *loci classici* for the treatment of the Thales episode are C. J. Classen, *P.-W., Suppl.* X (1965) 930-947, *s.v.*, and L. Sternbach, apparatus in *Gnom. Vatic.* (Berlin) 1963 (*Wiener Studien* 1887-1889), No. 319, p. 252f., from which some of the material discussed here is drawn.

¹⁶⁰ In *Story* as well as *Cynicism* the suggestion is made that the story of Thales is also the basis of Hillel the Elder's forgetfulness at the Passover celebration. There, the motif of the lowly who teach him a lesson, is preserved.

¹⁶¹ Whether "whence and whither" as in Tos. or "whence the feet" as in Ber. R.

¹⁶² Epicurus, *Letter to Herodotus* 38 : οὐδὲν γίνεται ἐκ τοῦ μὴ ὄντος, "nothing comes into being from the non-existent". Later Greek formulations would more closely cor-

respond to the Hebrew, e.g., Marcus Aurelius, *Meditations* IV. 4 : οὐδὲν γὰρ ἐκ τοῦ μηδενὸς ἔρχεται, "nothing from nothing does come".

The later Latin versions, e.g., Lucretius I. 150, *gigni de nihilo nihilum*, or Persius, *Sat.* III. 83f., *de nihilo nihilum*, display greater economy and *paranomasia* (word play; here : repetition of the same root), having made the transition from the technical distinctions of philosophy to the literary requirements of poetry and satire.

What precisely b. Zoma's quotation represents, i.e., a full or apocopated quotation, is difficult to determine. Both ⟨בא or נולד⟩ לא מאין ⟨אין⟩ "not from nothing can anything (arise)", as well as ל⟨ו⟩א מאין, "nothing from nothing", are problematic, since אין as "anything" and לוא as noun are not clearly attested to in our period. With לא as an Aramaizing noun, however, see Levy, *s.v.*, b. Zoma's quotation may have been לא מאין ⟨בא, נולד⟩ "Nothing (comes) from Nothing". Professor Lieberman, too, holds that a substantival לא is possible (see his edition of Deut. R., p. 119, line 7, and n. 2) but interprets it as an equivalent of "Man" ("How Much Greek...", p. 138, n. 2).

If the preserved Hebrew quotation is complete, it would presuppose a late Greek formula, its brevity paralleling the Latin versions. The present author believes to have lost in his papers a patristic formula of this sort, perhaps μηδὲν ἐκ τοῦ μηδενός (but *not* οὐδὲν ἐξ οὐδενός), yet has been uable to retrieve it or find a confirmation anywhere.

For additional quotations cf. *Usener*, p. 374 (Plutarch; Ps.-Plutarch/Eusebius; Servius; and Aristotle's dictum that this is a general opinion of the "physicists").

[163] Of these the talmudic world knew, e.g., the term *automaton*, see Part I, *supra*, and the denial of Providence, see Part II, *supra*. The existence of Epicurus' atomic theory, closely connected with these, must have been common knowledge in the ancient world even among the uneducated.

[164] In line with the explanation preferred here, we must reject the attempt at explaining this phrase in the sense of a mystical trance, or מבחוץ of the Tosephta version as a term indicating that b. Zoma is now "outside" (the confines of accepted doctrine, i.e., a heretic).

[165] Cf. W. Jaeger, *Ursprung und Kreislauf des philosophischen Lebensideals*", *Scripta Minora I* (Rome) 1960 (*Sitzungsber., Preuss. Akad. d. Wiss., XXV*, Philos.-hist. Klasse, Berlin 1928, 390-421). Jaeger believes that this ridicule is, indeed, an expression of the popular disdain for the unwordly early philosophers but that a reformulation of the material ensued (especially after Plato) which amounted to a positive, even heroizing image of the Sage who follows the ideal of the θεωρητικὸς βίος.

[166] ἀταραξία. Among the better known passages is that in the Letter to *Menoeceus* (and *D.L.* X. 133ff.) which among other formulations declares that it is better to follow even the fables of the gods than to be slave to the necessity (*heimarmēnē*) of the "physicists" (natural philosophers), 134.

[167] Τὸ δὲ μέγεθος ἡλίου τε <καὶ σελήνης> added only by Usener⟩ καὶ τῶν λοιπῶν ἄστρων κατὰ μὲν τὸ πρὸς ἡμᾶς τηλικοῦτόν ἐστιν ἡλίκον φαίνεται, *Letter to Pythocles* 91. C. Bailey, *Epicurus*, Oxford (1926), p. 60; Arrighetti, pp. 81 and 83. A logical-physical "proof" from Epicurus' (lost) "On Nature" follows in form of an interpolation (*Usener*, fr. 81; small print in Long's text of D.L.; bracketed by Arrighetti; carried in Bailey's apparatus but not in the main text). Epicurus then continues to say that in reality the sun may be somewhat greater or smaller than what we see or precisely the size of its appearance, since also earthly fires produce the same impression on the senses, i.e., are approximately of the size of their appearance even at great distances.

The reason for this astounding teaching is thus not only Epicurus' all pervading battle against fear (cf. the beginning and end of the letter) but also his complete reliance on only those sense perceptions that can be corroborated, see in detail C. Bailey, *The Greek Atomists and Epicurus*, New York (1928), re-ed. 1964) 258ff.

168 *On Signs* (περὶ σημείων), X. 35 - XI. 9.

169 Modern accounts of Epicurus, whether favorable or unsympathetic, likewise frequently mock at this particular teaching and call it "childish" and "silly".

170 *De finibus* I. vi. 20 includes a translation-like reference to Epicurus' formulation as does *Academica* II (*Lucullus* or *Academica priora*) xxxvi. 82. The former passage includes Cicero's demonstration that Epicurus did even worse than his predecessor Democritus. The third passage is *Academica* II. xxxix. 124.

171 *De fin.*, *loc. cit.* : huic pedalis fortasse.

172 *Academica* II, first item. Quantalus nobis videtur! mihi quidem quasi pedalis. Thereafter : "Epicurus, however, believes that it could be even smaller than it appears but not much..." Translation-like quotation follows.

173 In Greek, πούς, "foot", is both the part of the body and the measure, see Liddell-Scott, *s.v.*, III. In Latin, *pedes*, "feet", and *pedalis*, "a foot long", are related and reasonably close to one another.

174 Of course, b. Zoma (or the author of our item) must have known a certain measure of Greek when using Greco-Roman situations for jesting. This, however, is not unusual. Abbahu of Caesarea used to joke in Greek.

175 "Two to three", literally "two and three", Gen. R., but "three" in BT Ḥag. It is, of course, possible that this expression signifies merely "a few" as it does in b. Azzai's item on humility, see Appendix I, #11 and n. 228. This would approximate a foot more closely. Yet the *Ḥagigah* versions of our story took the measurements quite literally.

176 טפח, "a hand's breath", i.e., four fingers, Tos. The version of JT Ḥag. is מלא פותח טפח, "the full opening of a fist"; see Levy, *Wörterbuch*, vol. IV, *s.v.*, פותח and vol. II, *s.v.* טפח. No better text is available in Ratner's variant readings of the Vilna edition.

177 Or of Plato's "man above" and "man below".

178 Aristides adheres to this belief for the same reason as Epicurus (without mentioning him) : to fight ("Chaldean") astral worship. Theophilus uses it in a variant of a well-known simile which is also represented in Xenophon's *Memor*. IV. iii. 14; IV. vii.6; and *Barnabas* V. 10 : if man cannot face the sun (Theophilus : a very small heavenly body), he certainly is unable to face the glory of God. Similarly R. Joshua before Hadrian, BT Ḥullin 59b (the sun is here merely one of the myriad *servants* of God, cf. Xenophon, *loc. cit.*). To repeat : our self-same Joshua appears in an anecdote in which he defeats an Epicurean who had uttered a (partial) denial of divine providence in a contest of gestures before Hadrian, BT Ḥag. 5b. It seems that R. Joshua has a knack for running into Epicureans.

179 Tertullian : *adv. nat.* II. 4, *Usener*, preamble to fr. 342; Arnobius : *adv. gent.* ii. 58ff. Valerius Maximus has Socrates express similar sentiments about the uselessness of such questions, "to set down and prove the measurements of the sun, moon... and star", *Factorum* ... III. iv., *extern.* 1 (written after 27 A.D.). His passage seems to be dependent on the socratic statement on astronomy with Xenophon, *supra*, *Memor*. IV. vii. 6.

180 Other authors resemble (or anticipate ?) b. Zoma in this : see Gen. R. IV. 3; IV. 5; BT Ḥag. 15a. Also b. Azzai stresses the minimal space available to the Divine Voice between the Cherubim of the Ark, *Sifra* Lev. 1.1. (4a), see Bacher, *Tannaiten* I, p. 418f. On b. Azzai's relation to b. Zoma more *infra*.

¹⁸¹ If b. Zoma had, indeed, adhered to this belief, he would not have been too unorthodox either. V. Aptowitzer, in "Die Seele als Vogel", *MGWJ, 69* (1925), 150-168, has collected valuable material which illustrates that the soul (of humans and of the stars but also the "Evil Urge") is envisaged as capable of flight or similar to birds in talmudic literature (and in Plato) as are Soul and Logos with Philo (p. 166). According to Aptowitzer our passage may be the source or, at least, a parallel to Mt. 3:16, Mk. 1:10, and Lk. 3:22 (p. 163, Hl. Spirit as dove). For patristic parallels cf. *ibid.* p. 164, nn. 5-6. The underlying idea of most of these beliefs in talmudic culture seems to be that the non-material can fly. Cf. also "Flügel (Flug) der Seele I", *RAC, VI* (fasc. 57, 1969) 29-65 (P. Courcelle).

¹⁸² Many examples in the BT *Ḥagigah* context.

¹⁸³ On the other hand, one version of the Thales anecdote ends with his actual death: he falls over the edge of a precipice (*D.L.* II. 4, "Letter of Anaxagoras to Pythagoras")· It is not very likely, however, that this version was frequent. It is now a *hapax legomenon*. Laertius does not mention it when treating Thales' death nor does Suidas (Suda) in his lexicon. Above all, this version does not leave room for the concluding witticism (or would render it quite cruel). This witticism, however, is essential to the genre. Finally, b. Zoma does not die then and there but after a short interval

¹⁸⁴ To be followed up *infra*.

¹⁸⁵ Earlier Judaic demonstration models usually dealt with a messianic state.

In the Roman rhetorical culture, the use of the state as an ideal model is revived following some earlier Cynic and Stoic precedents, as is evident from Cicero and Seneca, but it is then the ideal universal state which encompasses god, world, and man, and does not seem to represent a reflection of the Roman Empire; on the contrary, it betrays a measure of disappointment with it (all this partly anticipating Augustine).

¹⁸⁶ Some of this, of course, stems from the lore of hostile schools.

¹⁸⁷ Another form of such self-criticism occurs, e.g., in the well-known story in which Moses foresees and marvels at the subtleties which Akiba would in a later age detect in Mosaic laws (BT *Menaḥoth* 29b, by Rab. Later elaborations: *PdRK, Parah*, 39b, Buber, *et al.*). Cicero, similarly, is amazed at Chrysippus and other Stoics because of their rationalizations and allegorizations which make the early poets out to be Stoics. (Cicero, however, put this into the mouth of an Epicurean, *de natura deorum* I. xv. 39-41). The half humorous criticism of scholarly exegesis of this sort may thus be Epicurean in spirit in either culture.

¹⁸⁸ Cf. BT *Sanhedrin* 17b (together with b. Azzai); JT *Maʿaser Sheni* 53 d, top. In *AdRN*, A, ch. 40, p. 128, Schechter, b. Zoma is a symbol of wisdom. In mss. variants b. Azzai's (piety) and b. Zoma's characteristics are exchanged, cf. n. 15, *ibid*. Occasionally, b. Zoma is among the *Zeḳenīm* (Early Sages): Tos. *Sanh.* 3.5.

¹⁸⁹ *AdRN* as in n. 180, *supra*; BT *Ber.* 57b; Tos. *Ḳiddushin* 3.9.

¹⁹⁰ BT *Ḳiddushin* 49b.

¹⁹¹ W. Bacher, *Tannaiten* I, p. 406, ch. 15; cf. text and n. 4.

¹⁹² B. Azzai created much Halakhah, b. Zoma a comparatively modest amount. On Elisha see *supra*, Part I, n. 224.

¹⁹³ Almost all of his major utterances are treated in this essay including some of those in which he appears together with b. Azzai as co-author or alternate author (details: Bacher, *Tann.* I, sections 15 and 16, beginnings). An item in a late Midrash, Ex. R. 30.19, shows no trace of Greco-Roman patterns (on shame).

¹⁹⁴ This refers to early Midrash, created and formulated in tannaitic and early amoraic

times (to c. 350 A.D.). Later Midrashim become quite lengthy and display a different style. On this phase of the Midrash cf. S. W. Baron, *A Social and Religious History of the Jews*, vol. VI, Philadelphia (1958), ch. XXVIII.

195 See Appendix I, *infra*. B. Azzai's "Epicureanism", of which he was probably unaware, could have been a personal preference in the selection of general Greco-Roman rhetorical materials which did not bear the philosophers' name (as in some of the early Senecan letters) without access to actual Epicurean sources. His appearance in the Story of the Four may have been due to his celibacy; cf. *supra*, Part I.

196 Mi. Soṭah 1.15; Tos. 15.4; BT 49b; JT 24a, cf. JT *Nedarim* 40 d, bottom; JT *Kiddushin* 64c, top.

197 Usually understood as exegetes or preachers. See W. Bacher, *Die exegetische Terminologie der jüdischen Traditionsliteratur*, Darmstadt (repr. 1965) *s.v., Darshan*. Among the few so called are the teachers of Hillel the Elder, Shemaʻiah and Abṭalion. Bacher points to materials (p. 28 and n. 1) which equate this term with the spokesman and popularizer who accompanied some of the scholars and offered his exegesis in a more precious style and with better vocal effect. As such he is sometimes identical with the מתורגמן (or אמורא), an assistant of the scholars, and often the subject of persiflage because of a rendering that was too loud.

198 Among others in Gen. R. V. 4 on 1:9.

199 These items begin with the phrase שאלו את בן זומא. BT *Ber.* 41b; 43a; BT *Ḥag.* 14b; 15a (not a part of our stories); BT *Yoma* 30a-b; JT *Soṭah* I. 2.

200 מזכירין יציאת מצרים בלילות (i.e., including Nu. 15.37-41), Mi. *Ber.* 1.5; Tos. 1.10ff; *Sifre* Dt. 16:3, #130; *Mekhilta* Ex. 13:2. Reference is to the evening prayer. "*All* the days of your life", Dt. 16:3, means days *and* nights, as. b. Zoma "interpreted it" (דרשה).

201 E. D. Goldschmidt, *Haggadah shel Pesaḥ*, Jerusalem (1960), p. 118.

202 Constant repetition of the basics of their belief was one of the principles of the Epicurean School, cf. *Letter to Herodotus* 36. The *Letter to Menoeceus* closes (135) with the admonition "Occupy yourself therefore in these and related things *day and night*, ἡμέρας καὶ νυκτὸς...., together with a companion congenial to yourself", cf. *P.A.* 1.6(7) "and acquire to yourself a companion".

The professional ethics of the ancient scientist (very often coeval with the scholar--Sage) concurs : "... untiring in his search not only *day and night* but all his life long..." (Erasistratus, physician, 3rd ct. B.C., quoted by Galen, 129 - *c*. 199, cf. L. Edelstein, *The Idea of Progress in Classical Antiquity*, Baltimore (1967), p. 150.

On the widely accepted practice of examining one's conscience morning and/or evening see I. Hadot, *Seneca*, Berlin (1969), 67ff. (Cicero, Seneca, Epictetus, Galen, Porphyry). Some of this may have been originally Pythagorean but had become part of the general *sophos* culture.

As a matter of method it is important not to consider talmudic institutions or teachings which claim to be biblical or quote the Scriptures as necessarily indigenous *in toto*. The mere existence of a biblical precept or formulation does not generate by itself its renewal, reapplication, or reinterpretation in the Greco-Roman period. A special stimulus is needed to awaken it from its dormant state. In this particular instance the duty "to talk of them... at thy lying down and thy rising up", Dt. 4:7, or the model of the pious and studious man praised in Ps. 1:2, who "meditates in His Law day and night", may have been re-inforced or implemented or taken literally only from the Hellenistic Period on under the impact of a new ethos. The ethos of the Greco-Roman Sage, who represented an efficient scholar-philosopher-bureaucracy, which dominated the administrations, academies, and sciences, must have frequently furnished the impetus for the reinterpretation or reuse of biblical passages. The existence of an earlier indigenous Near Eastern Sage culture facilitated, of course, the adoption of the Greco-Roman Sage culture. (The case of Ps. 1 is more complex : it may be proto-Pharisaic and already affected by Hellenism. Yet to the Talmudists it was Davidic).

[203] Gen. R. IV. 6 on 1 :7 : זה אחד המקריות שהרעיש ‹בהן?› בן זומא את העולם (in connection with the creation of the firmament). This phrase "shook the world", "put the world in an uproar", is usually reserved for the Deity, e.g., Haggai 2 :21; BT Taʻanith 20b.

[204] N. I. Weinstein, *Zur Genesis der Agada* II, Frankfurt (1901), 198ff., has argued for b. Zoma's dependence on Alexandrinian speculation and sees in all these passages concerned hints at the Greek idea of water as primeval matter. B. Zoma's mention of a bird in his exegesis of Gen. 1 :2 (see *supra*) alludes according to Weinstein to a Greek myth of a breeding process by which the world was created out of water (p. 199 and n. 122). Similar views are still preferred by H.-F. Weiss, *Untersuchungen zur Kosmologie des hellenistischen und palästinensischen Judentums*, Berlin (1966).

[205] So Nahmanides, see Theodor-Albeck *ad loc*. Likewise the translator of Ḥagigah in the Soncino translation of BT, *ad loc*. (London, 1938; I. Abrahams).

[206] No solution is given to the textual difficulty which b. Zoma points out.

[207] Cf. Is. 29 :6, Ez. 3 :12, and n. 189, *supra*.

[208] *D.L.* X. 9 : ταῖς δογματικαῖς αὐτοῦ σειρῆσι ... *P.A.* 2.14 (18, Taylor) is also aware of the persuasiveness of the Epicureans ("know what to answer" him). "Siren-like", of course, is used also elsewhere in Greco-Roman culture as a description of persuasiveness in philosophy and poetry. Other examples for such epithets : *D.L.* X. 8; Athenaeus, *Deipn.* 278f.

[209] Actually comparatively little of b. Zoma's preserved Haggadah deals with cosmology. There is one more item of his in Gen. R. V. 4 on 1:9, *et al.*, in which he together with b. Azzai considers "the voice of the Lord" as a *metator* (מיטטור, so rightly M. Jastrow, *A Dictionary of the Targumim, the Talmud Babli*, etc., 2 vols., New York (1943) *s.v.*), i.e., having the function of a surveyor, or boundary assigner. This simile, taken from the technological aspect of the Roman administration, seems to be a demythologication of Gen. 1 :9 and Ps. 29 :3, "the Lord's Voice over the waters", rather than dangerous speculation. Apparently some interpreters, both medieval and modern, have been misled by faulty readings of the passage, as e.g., מטטרון (Metraton), the Chief of the Angels, instead of *metator*.. Similarly, a reference to Dt. 32.49 does not belong here, see *Midr. Pss.* 93,5, end, where our passage appears without it (cf. Bacher, *Tann.* I, p. 425, n. 6). *Midr. Pss.* 93.5, beginning, has a modification of b. Zoma's "narrow space" motif with b. Azzai as co-author, but the item appears to be a later amplification and not originally b. Zoma's.

[210] For examples see "Erfinder II", *RAC*, V, p. 1239 (4).

[211] In *Cynicism* examples of playful *chriae* will be cited which were misunderstood and became the basis of Halakhah. Cf. *Studies*, p. 392, and n. 1 (e.g., Hillel and the chriic episode of the "Female Bull" as Halakhah).

[212] On the complex question of origin and redaction of the Tosephta see A. Spanier, *Die Toseftaperiode in der tannaitischen Literatur*, Berlin (1936).

[213] Also Akiba in the item on the Four is the young Akiba before his "conversion".

[214] Possible Epicurean elements in b. Zoma's Haggadah endorsement of cultural progress; "honor honors the honorer", "day and night", the formal use of an Epicurean sorites— are counterbalanced by Stoic elements: three *paradoxa*, and "gratitude"

(unless also Epicurean). Herein he most of all resembles Seneca whose death preceded b. Zoma's lifetime by approximately a generation.

215 Eleatic, Hedonist, Ps.-Hippocratic, Empiricist, and Aristotelian.

216 Some aspects of Greco-Roman rhetorical literature, however, must be similarly described, especially elements deriving from Platonism, Pythagoreanism, and Posidonian Stoicism as well as much of the thought of Seneca and Epictetus.

NOTES TO APPENDIX

1 In presenting this Appendix it must be emphasized again that similarities and interdependencies of many sorts prevailing in Greco-Roman philosophical literature present a formidable problem to any such analysis. Short of a minute investigation of all pertinent details this vexing and problematic assignment of a talmudic item to the teachings or the mood of a particular school or movement (within or beyond rhetorization) in the later Hellenistic-Roman Age (i.e., the declining Roman Republic and the first few centuries of the Empire), is here tentatively made according to these methodological considerations (the *ultimate* origin of an item not to be investigated except where a tradition of long standing has to be emphasized):

1. when content *and* form (literary genre, keywords, style, syntax, etc.) point to a particular school;
2. when a related or identical item of a particular school is conspicuously prominent in rhetoric from 100. B.C. - 300 A.D;
3. when the immediate context of the talmudic item concerned deals with or has clear reference to a particular school;
4. when a talmudic author has some clearly attested philosophumena of a particular school to his name that are related to the item to be analyzed.

2 It is self-understood that b. Azzai would not deny that sacrifice is a divine command, but it is a command for the sake of man, to fulfil his needs. However, even Epicurus-Velleius-Cicero admit: "Whatever is highest receives (or possesses) its *due* veneration" (habet... venerationem iustam).

3 Other Greek philosophies were either hostile to the sacrificial cult (Cynicism) or gave different reasons for its value (Stoicism). Of course, Plato, *Laws* 905d, and, centuries earlier, Hebrew prophetism, likewise rejected the possible *do ut des* aspect of the sacrifice. The argument preferred here is, as always, the uniqueness of the syndrome/no bribe/no food/natural or beneficial/to us, to you/, which is indicative of a new intercultural discussion of an age-old problem.

4 From this the following motifs must be distinguished:
1. laughter, cheerfulness, when philosophizing, likewise Epicurean (*Gnom. Vat.* 41);
2. the laughing and the weeping philosophers Heraclitus (Cynic hero) and Democritus (his opposite, Cynic cliché).

Cf. the talmudic story of the laughing Akiba and three weeping companions in Rome, Lam. R. V. 18, #1; BT *Makkoth* 24a, et al.

5 In the Hellenistic sources: last will, admonitions to friends, servants, and family, (mention of) last sacrificial offerings, etc. The motif of halakhic discussion in talmudic death scenes of the Sages (*Derekh Ereṣ Rabba* I, et al.) is anticipated in *Phaedo* 117 by Socrates' playful question as to the necessity of a libation from the cup of poison. Plato's

last hour was filled with active study (*agitatione studii*) of Sophron's mimes (of which he was, indeed, inordinately fond) according to Val. Max. VIII. vii., *extern.* 3. It is regrettable that the text does not clarify whether serious inquiry or light-hearted study is implied by this "fact", a detail worth knowing since *Factorum* ... was an influential rhetorical aid book from the Tiberian rule on.

Philosophical readings and discussions (often on the immortality of the soul) as well as eloquent dictation are Greco-Roman motifs which are not too remote from halakhic discourse, Cf. Plutarch, *Cato Minor* LXVIII. 2 - LXX. 4, 793f.; Tacitus, *Ann.* XV. 62-64 (on Seneca) and XVI. 34f. (on Thrasea Paetus), all in connection with enforced suicide. While friends sitting with Solon in the hour of his (natural) death are engaged in academic discussion, Solon *lifts his* drooping *head,* and when asked why, replies "that when I understand what it is you are disputing, I may die", Val. Max. *loc. cit., extern.* 14. Tacitus mentions actual libations and, in the case of Seneca, joy (Helvidius is safe) and the *turning of Thrasea's eyes toward Demetrius* (the respected Cynic philosopher). Cf. this particular detail with b. Azzai's *direction of his eyes* at death in *AdRN*. B. Azzai's sayings in *AdRN* are here interrupted for a second time (p. 80) by details on the death of Eliʻezer b. Hyrcanus (whose biography is also elsewhere affected by Greco-Roman motifs). Cf. Eliʻezer's elaborate proof that he is *not* deranged (שנטרפה דעתו...) with Cato's the Younger similar proof (παρανοίας). Cf. the involvement of their sons (no removal of the phylacteries/no tying of Cato's hands). Cf. the *tour de force* of several readings of the *Phaedo* with that of resolving a great number of halakhic problems. Cf. the keyword 300 in both accounts (Plutarch, *op. cit.,* LXXI. 1 and *AdRN*, p. 81).

On the Sage as an actual martyr: S. Lieberman, "*Roman Legal Institutions in Early Rabbinics and the Acta Martyrum*", *JQR*, 35 (1944-1945) 166-186; H. A. Fischel, "Martyr and Prophet", *JQR, 37* (1947) 256-280, 363-386; A. Delatte, "Le sage-témoin dans la philosophie stoïco-cynique", *Acad. royale de Belgique, Bulletin* de la classe des lettres..., *5th ser., 39* (1953). Cf. also *RAC, VI* (1966), *s.v.,* "*Exitus illustrium virorum*", 1258-1268 (Ronconi).

⁶ The parallel Senecan and Ciceronian passages, *infra,* and their contexts are essentially descriptions of the Sage. For this reason the translation "aspect" would actually be preferable here (for *sīmān*). It could also be satisfactorily rendered as "a good example", or "pattern", see S. Krauss, *Griechische und Lateinische Lehnwörter...*, II, Berlin (1899), p. 386ff., entry 10. Krauss mistakenly lists the *AdRN* occurrences under entry 9, "omen". The Greek σῆμα or σημεῖον from which the Hebrew loanword *sīmān* seems to derive, however, as well as the latter, do not only refer to things of the future but also of the past and present. In the famous *Phaenomena* (translated from the Greek by Varro and Cicero!) of Aratus (died 276 B.C.) —in the section often subtitled *Diosēmiai, et al.* (733-1154), which deals with the "signs" that indicate weather and other meteorological phenomena— this frequent term refers variously to any of these three tempora. Presentic use is also apparent in Hippocrates' *Aphorismoi*, e.g., IV. 56, 74, 78, 81, 83 (verbs) and VII. 10 (noun). (Some Hippocratic material was known to the Talmud, cf. *Cynicism*). It is assumed here that b. Azzai's statement is thus presentic-preterite but not prognostic. The same is true, e.g., of JT *Yoma* VIII. 5, 45b (of a mad dog). Unfortunately, the article in *P.-W., Series II,* vol. II. 1, Stuttgart (1923), *s.v.,* "Semeion (Nota)", 1339ff., is quite unsatisfactory in that it does not deal with the phenomenon sketched here and thus omits the mention of a literary convention which could be called "semiotics", the aphoristic form of which is represented in all the sources quoted *supra*. This convention may have been transferred from the empiricist natural sciences to other disciplines. Prognostic

use, however, may have to be assumed in a later, anonymous variant of our basic passage in BT *Kethuboth* 103b (i.e., indicating future reward or punishment).

⁷ Similarly *AdRN* A, ch. 25, beginning; yet "urge", "affect", instead of body, and positive and negative signs *seriatim*. A mention of *cupiditates*, which would correspond to the Hebrew *yeṣer* of *AdRN*, follows in the Ciceronian text, quoted immediately *infra*.

⁸ This thought is introduced by a gnomic *parallelismus membrorum* that resembles the "house divided by itself" of Luke 11:17. Repetitive words have been underlined in order to indicate the high degree of structuredness in both the Latin and the Hebrew.

Seneca becomes more expansive and explicit in a reformulation of his item with a tripartite structure (without reference to Epicurus) in *Ep.* 75.8-15, where he introduces *adfectus*, "the affects", into this scheme. Cf. preceding note.

⁹ Treated in Part I, *supra*.

¹⁰ Although b. Azzai's reasoning is halakhic, i.e., that women should know that merit will delay their punishment (in the case of adultery established by ordeal, see Nu. 5:11-31), his attitude is nevertheless unconventional vis-a-vis the strong opposition against *all* education of women by Eliʻezer and Joshua, *ibid*.

Apparently b. Azzai meant by Torah also Rabbinic law, since the law or belief that merits delay punishment is not biblical.

¹¹ Biblical books that were temporarily under the suspicion of having been declared inspired only after prolonged debate (and certainly those actually rejected) could have been attacked for late authorship, after ben Sirah, or Alexander the Great, or "the last prophets". Yet Canticles and Ecclesiastes counted as Solomonic. There is, further, no problematic Halakhah in them, another possible reason for rejection. The reason for the presumed temporary rejection of Canticles and Ecclesiastes could then well have been the suspected heresy indicated above. Even modern interpreters have suggested Epicurean sources for Ecclesiastes, although this work is really closer to a pessimistic strain of Ancient Near Eastern Wisdom Literature. R. Akiba's indignation at those who used Canticles secularly-hedonistically at inns or symposia also speaks for the existence of a view according to which this work was sensual-hedonistic (Tos. *Sanh.* 12.10).

¹² *Sifra* 1.1, 4a Weiss, reports b. Azzai's claim that even the angels cannot see the divine glory. This statement eliminates the essential ingredient of early Jewish mysticism: the seeing of celestial mysteries. B. Azzai rejects the suggestion that he is occupied with (mystical) esoterics in *SSR* on 1:10 and Lev. R. XVI.

¹³ Parallels: JT *Nedarim* 41c; Gen. R. XXIV. 7 on 5:1.

¹⁴ See *Story*, p. 72.

¹⁵ This is anti-Stoic in detail. Cicero, *de nat. deor.* I. xviii. 46ff. The body of the gods is only *quasi corpus* (49). Cf. frs. 352-355, *Usener*.

¹⁶ He gives two examples, one in Latin and one in Greek. Gen. R. I. 12 on 1:1; Midr. Pss. 18:36; *Tanḥuma* Buber, *Bereshith* 4; *Tanḥ., ki tissa'*.

¹⁷ For חרוב as "dried" see the dictionaries, *s.v.* Cf., immediately *infra*, Seneca *Ep.* XVIII. 7: hard (*durus*) bread, etc., and *Ep.* 87.3, "dried figs" (and/or bread). The attempt at "austerity" (a fairly comfortable one) described in the latter epistle is followed by the expectation that general opinion will call the ascete mad: *insanitis, erratis*..., 87.5, cf. b. Azzai's "fool". If Seneca is, indeed, somehow b. Azzai's pattern, it must be borne in mind that the austerity prevailing with Seneca is Epicurean in the very delight with which he considers dried figs as a relish or even as the main dish (87.3); cf. Epicurus' self-conscious "Send me some potted cheese so that when I wish I can lavishly feast

(*polyteleusasthai*)", *Usener*, fr. 182, end; *ibid.*, fr. 181 : "I burst with the pleasure of the little body, using but water and bread". Even Seneca's seat is lowly : a mule-driven farmer's cart, 87.4, cf. b. Azzai's lowly posture. Seneca, however, is his own Sage, as it were, although, admittedly, he declares himself still a learner, 87.5, (cf. b. Azzai's "door of the Sages").

[18] More, *infra*.

[19] Cf. the stylistic antitheses "mere words"/"tested truth" and "fool"/"Torah".

[20] There is a long tradition of this use of "pallet" in Greek literature (connected, by the way, with the portrayal of primitive man) which cannot be treated here.

[21] Literally "two and three" steps, the phrase used also for the distance between the Waters, *supra*.

[22] This proposal of Seneca introduces the actual Epicurean fragment but is itself quite Epicurean.

Ben Azzai's pattern is thus hardly the NT parallel, Lk. 14 :8-10 (nor is any earlier Rabbinic tradition, e.g., Hillel in Lev. R. I. 5, necessarily the pattern of Luke) but both, Luke and b. Azzai, may here have been stimulated by Greco-Roman rhetorical patterns. The mention of the elevation in rank which follows the humbling of oneself with Luke and b. Azzai is available with Seneca only as a general preamble (XX. 6) which speaks of the elevation of moral perfection (*ad summum*) that follows self-restriction. In contradistinction to Seneca both Midrash and NT prefer the tersely formulated anti-thesis, cf. Lev. R. I. 5; BT *Erubin* 13b; *Midr. Hallel* on Ps. 113 :4; BT *Tamid* 32a (among the ten Gymnosophist items); Bacher, *Tannaiten* I, p. 5f.; Strack -Billerbeck I, 774 on Matth. 18 :4 (and 23 :21; Lk. 14 : 11 and 28 :14b).

[23] We suspected already *supra* that b. Azzai was aware of Epicurus' principle of avoidances, see #9.

[24] Some of these in Seneca, *Ep.* XX. 12f. It is unlikely that b. Azzai accepted all these or even knew of them. Cf. however, the next item.

[25] *P.A.* 3.1 (three basic statements); *AdRN* A, ch. 19, p. 69; B, ch. 32, p. 69 (four basic statements as also *Der. Er. R.*). On the many parallels and variants as well as the question of authors see Schechter, *ad loc.*, A.

[26] Drop, liquid, etc. (*ṭippah, lēḥah*).

[27] Or ashes and maggots, etc. Other sets of later variants list twice "darkness", and "uncleanness".

[28] Thus both Hebrew and Greek. Likewise, one metaphor for birth and two for death in all texts.

[29] These demeaning passages must be distinguished from those Greek views according to which the origin of life is water, and semen moist for this reason, a proposition that is devoid of any value judgment (Thales, Aristotle, etc.). See W. K. C. Guthrie, *A History of Greek Philosophy*, I, Cambridge (1967) 61f.

[30] Others : *Gnom. Vat.* 14 and 60 (on birth and death).

[31] Thus Epictetus, *Disc.* IV. xi. 9ff., mentions bodily functions with some disgust, such as "mucus to flow... this being man's constitution (mixture)", (9). IV. i. 142f. has the associative sequence : "man a worm"/"intercourse". "Paltry (little) body" is found *passim*, so *ibid.* 153 (*sōmation*).

Even the questions as to whence man comes and whither he goes are not only Gnostic but also rhetorical; thus Seneca, *Ep.* 120.15, "for whoever remembers wherefrom he comes, knows whereto he will exit".

[32] 46b, Friedmann; vol. II, p. 97, Lauterbach. The text is difficult; for details and parallels see Friedmann *ad loc.*

³³ "And free will is given (granted)" is out of place as either redundant, out of sequence before the testimonial, or altogether not fitting. It is missing in the two similar formulations of this thought by b. Azzai which precede our item and may have been trasferred here by scribal addition from Akiba's saying, *P.A.* 3.15 (3.24) which deals with a similar theme.

³⁴ The Greek is equally difficult and actually requires a detailed treatment of all inherent problems. Also Epicurus apparently speaks here of man's inclination and practical choices and not of his rational free will (which has to be developed through philosophy, of the Epicurean brand, that is).

³⁵ See H. A. Wolfson, *Philo*, I, Cambridge, Mass. (1948) 446ff.

³⁶ See Wolfson, *loc. cit.* As a talmudic parallel add *P.A.* 4.5 (4.8), contemporaneous with b. Azzai.

³⁷ Ut iam universus hic mundus una sit communis deorum atque hominum existimanda.

NOTES TO EPILOGUE

¹ The item on lavatory manners, BT *Ber.* 62a, may have Hellenistic precedents (Cicero). Furthermore, he denounced those in fine linen garments among his listeners (Cynicizing or referring to colleagues? *AdRN* A, ch. 25. See Bacher, *op. cit.*, p. 414, n. 4).

² See "Celibacy", *supra*, and toilet manners, preceding note. He had seen, or used, a version of the Ascension of Isaiah or related material, unless it was really, as claimed, a genealogical roll (BT *Yebamoth* 49b); he knew details of Greco-Roman myth or art (JT *Abodah Zarah* III. 3); he interpreted the biblical *lex talionis* as implying monetary compensation (*Mekh. de R. Shimeʿon b. Yoḥai* on Ex. 21:24). The problem of the contradictory reports of his supposed martyrdom in the Hadrianic persecutions has never been resolved (see Bacher, *op. cit.*, p. 409). His lack of ordination and yet high esteem have been mentioned together with b. Zoma's similar status, *supra*.

BIBLIOGRAPHY

The usual bibliography has been replaced by the indexes. The INDEX OF REFERENCES will help in tracing text editions or other sources of information used in this monograph. In most instances the lowest page number appearing in the indexes will lead to the pertinent statements on editions in the main text or the notes of this book.

Similarly, the titles of books and articles by modern authors can be found through the INDEX OF MODERN AUTHORS. The first entry as well as all starred entries (*) thereafter opposite the name of an author represent his different works as used in this monograph. Under "Highet, G.," e.g., one finds "101, *101, *101, 122." "101" signifies the first item of his on p. 101, i.e., "Petronius, the Moralist", *TAPA* 72; the first starred entry which follows, "*101," refers to "The Anatomy of Satire," Princeton 1962; the second starred entry which happens to be again p. 101, signifies "The Philosophy of Juvenal," *TAPA* 70. The final "122" refers to any one of the former items, found on page 122.

INDEX OF REFERENCES

["all" refers to the mention of a work without specification of a particular passage]

HEBREW BIBLE, APOCRYPHA AND PSEUDEPIGRAPHA

[listed according to the most common traditional masoretic sequence. Biblical verses which appear as part of a midrashic location and are not germane to this inquiry, are entered under "RABBINIC LITERATURE" within their respective midrashic location. Thus, e.g., Gen. R. on 24:3 will be found under Genesis Rabba].

Genesis
Ch. 1   125
1:1   93
1:2   85, 160
1:7   87
1:9   160
4:3-16   129
4:7   133
4:8   36
4:20ff. 143
6:3   42
9:6,7   110
11:1ff. 29
34:8   108

Exodus
20:4   155

Numbers
15:11-31 163
15:37-41 159

Deuteronomy
4:7   133
22:6f.   11, 35, 128
32:49   160

1 Samuel
2:30   150

2 Kings
16:17   119
18:15   119
24:13   119

Isaiah
5:7   119
29:6   160
44:11   145

Jeremiah
22:10   134
37:24   146

Ezekiel
3:12   160

Haggai
2:21   160

Psalms
1:12   159
10:13   42, 135
25:14   108
29:3   9, 160
107:7   31
116:15   23, 24, 90
119:99   150
128:2   150
144:12   119

Proverbs
16:32   49f.
25:6   23, 24
28:7   94
31:25   90

Job
18:4   74
36:24   66

INDEX OF REFERENCES

Canticles (Song of Songs)		Nehemiah	
all	152, 163	2:8	121
1:4	24, 106, 122		
4:13	121	2 Chronicles	
		28:24	119
Ecclesiastes			
all	133, 163	Ascension of Isaiah	
1:3	133	all	165
2:5	121		
5:5	24, 106, 122	1 Enoch	
11:9	40f.	32:2	121
12:13	97	77:3	121
Daniel		Sap. Sal. (Wisdom of Solomon)	
2:30	143	6:18-21	152
12:7	116		

NEW TESTAMENT AND RELATED WORKS

NT		Romans	
all	146, 164	5:3-5	152
		13:13	120
Matthew		Ephesians	
3:16	158	all	103
5:1ff.	164		
18:4	164	Colossians	
23:21	164	all	103
		2:4	30
		2 Corinthians	
Mark		6:8ff.	72, 148, 151
1:10	158	12:2-4	121
		2 Peter	
Luke		1:5-7	152
3:22	157		
6:37	150	Barnabas	
11:17	163	5:10	157
14:8-10	164		
14:11	164	1 Clement	
28:14	164	13:2	150

EXTRA-RABBINIC JEWISH LITERATURE

Josephus		C. Ap.	
Antiquities		II.19; 180f.	102
X.xi.7; 277f.	102, 106		
XVIII.i.4; 16	102, 130		
XIX.i.5; 32	102	Philo	
Bell. Jud.		*de Abrah.*	
II.viii.14; 164f.	102, 130	XXXIII.182/27	151

INDEX OF REFERENCES

de fuga		II.viii.56/666	151
XXVI.567	124	xxxvii.244/691	149
de migr.		xliii/696f.	124
197	149	*de spec. leg.*	
de mut. nom.		I.335f.	144
XXVIII.152/601	149	III.307	136
de opif. mundi		*Quod det. pot. ins. sol.*	
LVI.39	124	i.191f.	38
de plant.		ii.f.	130
159	63	viii.196	38, 130
de post. Caini		ix.197	38, 130
XIV, end	131	x.197f.	38, 130
de praem.		xlii.221	131
409 (8)	136	*Quod deus*	
de prov.		IV.275	131
fr. 2, all	131	*Quod omn. prob. lib. sit*	
de sacrif.		I.1./445	149
II.21-23	131	II.8/445	149
de sobr.		III.20/448	149
57	149	IV.24/449	149
de somn.		XXII.158ff.	149

RABBINIC LITERATURE

Aboth de R. Nathan (AdRN)		*Baba Bathra (B. B.)*	
A5, p. 26	130	10a	152
A6, p. 29	116, 120	*Berakoth*	
A11, p. 46	93	6b	96
A14, p. 59	115	27b	15
A17, end	116, 129	41b	159
A19, p. 69	164	43a	159
A23, p. 75	70	57b	158
A24, all	126	58a	51
A25, p. 79f.	90, 162f.	62a	165
A25, p. 81	94	68b	154
A32, end	135	*Erubin*	
A40, p. 128	158	13b	164
B32, p. 69	164	*Giṭṭin*	
B33, p. 72	70 (*paradoxa*)	57b	116
B33, p. 72	74 (sorite)	*Horayoth*	
B35, all	126	2b	122
		Ḥagigah	
Babylonian Talmud (BT)		5b	107, 157
[alphabetically arranged for the convenience of the non-specialist]		11bf.	116, 155
		12af.	116
Abodah Zarah		13a	110f.
8a	145	14a	116, 159

170 INDEX OF REFERENCES

14b	4ff., 10, 17, 19, 22f. 24, 85, 110, 116, 119	30b	97
		77b	146
15a	78f., 112, 120, 157	*Soṭah*	
15a (*sic*)	159	4b	107f.
15b	12, 116, 119f.	37b	116
16b	107	49b	107, 122, 127, 159
Ḥullin			
59b	157	*Sukkah*	
142a	112, 128	53a	154
Yebamoth		*Taʿanith*	
49b	165	20b	160
63b	108, 110	*Tamid*	
86b	116	31bf. (66a)	151, 164
Yoma			
30af.	159	*Derek(h) Ereṣ Rabba*	
Kethuboth		I (III)	95, 161, 164
62b	120		
63a	107f., 116		
103b	162		

Jerusalem (Palestinian) Talmud (JT) [alphabetically arranged, cf. Babylonian Talmud, *supra*. For easier orientation most passages are listed as quoted in the text and notes, *supra*, i.e., the different systems of quoting JT and the varying paginations of the editions have not been synchronized]

Ḳiddushin			
39b	112, 128		
49b	158		
Makkoth			
24a	161		
Megillah		JT	
9a	107	all	105, 134
37b	116	*Abodah Zarah*	
Menaḥoth		39c	145
99b	107	III.3	165
99bf.	116	*Baba Ḳamma*	
110a	90	6c	150
Moʿed Ḳaṭan		*Berakoth*	
20a	126	II.8	118
Nedarim		13c,IX.2 (K.) = 63b,IX.1 (N.Y.)	51
50a	120		
Pesaḥim		*Ḥagigah*	
49b	116	9a, II.1 (N.Y.)	113
54a	146	77a (9a, N.Y.) II.1	78ff., 113
Sanhedrin		77b, II.1	12, 13, 19, 21ff., 106, 110, 112
14a	109		
17b	158	77c	112
38a	141	*Kethuboth*	
59b	64	31b	150
92a	109	VIII, end	140
96b	116	*Ḳiddushin*	
99b	130	64c, top	159
Shabbath			
13b	118		

Ma'aser (Sheni)	
51a, III.10	128
53, top	158
Megillah	
I.9	107
Mo'ed Ḳaṭan	
81c, III, beg.	19
Nedarim	
40d, end	159
41c	163
Sanhedrin	
28b, X	152
Shabbath	
3c, I.6	107
Soṭah	
I.2	159
24a	127, 159
Yebamoth	
2b, I, beg.	19
Yoma	
45b, VIII.5	162
Megillath Ta'anith	
all	105
Mekhilta (de R. Sh. b. Y.)	
on Ex. 13:2	159
on Ex. 21:24	165
on Ex. 25:26	95
Mekhilta de R. Yishma''el	
on Ex. 13:17	144
on Ex. 16:14	144
Midrash ha-Gadol	
all	133
Midrash Hallel	
on Ps. 113:4	164
Midrash Pss.	
I,22 Buber	106
Ch. 9	108
on 10:6	135
on 18:36	163
Ch. 93	110
93:5	160
Midrash Prov.	
on 25:20	133
Midrash Rabba	
[Cf. note under "JT," *supra*]	
Genesis Rabba	
1:1	146
1.12 on 1:1	163
2.4 on 1:7	78
4.3	157
4.5	157
4.6 on 1:7	160
5.4 on 1:9	110, 159, 160
12.15 on 2:4	134
24.7 on 5:1	145, 163
26.6 on 6:3	135
62.2, 3 on 25:8	90
63.11 on 25:29	41
78.12 on 23:10	126, 131
100.3	154
Exodus Rabba	
30.19	158
Leviticus Rabba	
1.5	164
16.4 on 14:2	9
16.7 on 5:1	163
28.1 on 23:10	92, 133
Numbers Rabba	
XXI.2 on 27:15	138
Deuteronomy Rabba	
all	156
Song of Songs Rabba (SSR)	
I.4, No.1	106, 113
I.4	19, 20
on 1:10	163
on 8:4	154
Ruth Rabba	
6:4 on 3:13	110, 112, 128
Lamentations Rabba	
on 2:2	108
V.18, No.1	161
Ecclestiastes Rabba	
1.3,1	133
11.9, 1	133
on 5:14	78
on 7:1	106
on 7:6	110
on 7:8	112, 128
on 7:26	151
Midrash Song of Songs (G.)	
5b	108
Midrash Zuṭa	
1.3 (Buber 84)	133

INDEX OF REFERENCES

Mishnah
 [alphabetically arranged]
 Berakoth
  1.5 — 159
 Pirḳe Aboth
  all — 105, 149
  1.6 (7) — 148, 159
  2.10 (14) — 150
  2.14 (18) — 14, 107, 126, 160
  3.1 (1) — 164
  3.7 (11) — 152
  3.8 (12) — 152
  3.15 (24) — 165
  3.21 (Katsh) — 152
  4.1 (1-4) — 70-73, 149f.
  4.2 (5) — 152
  4.5 (8) — 165
  4.6 (10) — 150
  4.20 (27) — 126
  5.22 (32) — 128
 Sanhedrin
  10.1 — 116, 126
 Shabbath
  16.2 — 139
 Soṭah
  1.15 — 159
  3.4 — 92
  9.14 — 107
  9.15 — 127, 152
 Yadayim
  2.14 — 92
  3.5 — 92

Pesiḳta de R. Kahana (B.)
 Parah, 39b — 158
 Pisḳa
  8, 68b — 133
  18 — 42, 135
  25, 126b — 135
Pesiḳta Rabbathi (F.)
 Pisḳa
  12, 47b — 134
  18, 90b — 133
Seder Eli(y)ahu Rabba (F.)
 8 (7), p. 43 — 74, 78
Seder Olam (R.)
 III.36, 9a — 116, 130

Sifra (Weiss)
 1.1 (nedabah) 2.12, 4a — 110, 157, 163
 Lev. 19:18, 89b — 92
Sifre (Numbers)
 Nu. 28:8, No. 143 (F). — 90
 Behaʿalothek(h)a 103 (H.) — 110
Sifre Deuteronomy (Friedmann)
 67b, No. 12 — 107
 Dt. 16:3, No. 130 — 159
Tanḥuma
 Ki tissaʾ — 163
 Pinḥas, Nu. 27:15, No. 10 — 138
Tanḥuma (Buber)
 Bereshith, No. 4 — 163
 Pinḥas, No. 1 — 138
Tanna debe Eliyahu
 all — 152
Targumim
 Fragm. Targ. (J II)
  Gen. 4:8 — 37
 Neofiti I
  Gen. 4:8 — 36, 112
 Targ. Jonathan
  Dt. 1:12 — 107
Tosephta
 [alphabetically]
 Abodah Zarah
  1.20 — 107
 Berakoth
  1.10ff. — 159
  3.4 — 91
  6(7).2 — 51, 138
 Ḥagigah
  2.3-4 — 106
  2.6 (L., p. 381ff.) — 78
 Ḳiddushin
  3.9 — 159
 Sanhedrin
  12.10 — 163
  13.5 — 116, 130
 Soṭah
  15.4 — 127, 159

Yalḳut Shimeʿoni
 all — 133
 Gen. 25:29 — 134
 Ps. 9 — 108
 Pss., No. 651 — 135

GRECO-ROMAN LITERATURE

Aelian(us)			27 D	127, 140
fr. 10 (H.)		16	V.215 Bf.	110
fr. 39 (H.)		117, 118	VII.278f.	160
			280Af.	76
Aeschylus			XII.511E-512A	125
Prom. 436ff.		143	546E	76
			588A	117
Aesopus			XIII.578B-583D	112
No. 40 (Perry) or			582A	112
No. 78 (Hahn)		82	584B, Df., F	112
			585A, D, E	112
Anthol. Palat.			588B	112
VI.307		121	593B-D	11
VII.104		118	593D	128
172		81		
IX.44		112	Aulus Gellius	
X.93		109	*Noct. Att.*	
			II.ix	117
Aratus			xviii	116
Phaen.			IX.v.8	47
112		144		
733-1154		162	Cicero	
			Acad. priora (Lucullus)	
Aristophanes			II.xxxvi.82	84, 157
Clouds			xxxix.124	157
225-233		81f.	*ad Att.*	
Plutus			VII.ii.4	109
160ff.		59f., 143	XII.xxiii.2	121
511		143	*ad fam.*	
525		63	II.ix.3	101
529		145	XIII.i.3-5	101, 121
530		63	*Cat.*, see *in Catal.*	
540-545		143	*de fin.*	
593 E		143	I.v.13	101
			vi.20	157
Aristotle			vii.25	101, 119
Ars rhet.			viii.27	101
II.xxl		113	xviii.59	101
de caelo			xxi.69ff.	117
1.4		146	xxi.71	27, 119
Polit.			II.iii.7	153
1253a, No.15, end		97	x.29	153
1256b, No.11		145	xv.49	101
			xxf., 97-99	81
Athenaeus			xxv.119	101
Deipn.			III.xxii.75	72, 148
I.25f.		140		

IV.xviii.50	151	*Tusc. Disp.*	
xxiif.74-44	70ff.	I.v-viii	44
V.1.3	121	xxi.48	28
de leg.		xxv.61f.	60, 143
I.viii.22f.	97	xli.98	136
de nat. deor.		III.iv-xi.7-25	118
I.viii.18	27	xiii.41	77
ix.23	49	xiii.43	77, 153
xv.39-41	158	xix.46	77
xvi.43	123	IV.iii.7	101
xvii.45	90	V.ii.5	143
xviii.46ff.	163	xxxii.89	101
xxxiii.93	121		
xliii.120	121	Cleomedes	
II.lx.150ff.	142	*de moto*	
III.iv.-xi.7-25	118	ii.1	117, 135
de offic.		Demosthenes	
I.xiii.150	145	*de cor.*	
xxviii.98	58	§ 121	132, 147
xxx.107f.	58	§ 258	114
xxxi.113	58		
lxii.150f.	144	Dio Chrysostom (of Prusa)	
lxiv.155	149	*Encomium on Hair*	
II.iii.11ff.	57f.	all	137
v.16	142	*Orat. 12 (Olympic)*	
de orat.		28ff., 32	65
I.ix.36	143	36f.	41, 46
Ep. ad Att., see *ad Att.*		*Orat. 32-34*	
in Catal.		all	134
I.i	132, 147		
in Pis.		Diodorus (Siculus)	
XVI.57	115	I.i	62
XX.46	123	viii.1-3	146
XXV.59	30, 115	viii.5	146
	118, 123	viii.7	61, 63
Parad. Stoic.		viii.18	146
all	70ff.	xiii.3	146
33, 40	72	II.55-60	145
51	73		
pro Flacc.		Diogenes Laertius	
II.5	131	*Lives (D. L.)*	
pro Mur.		all	3
61	71, 148, 151	I.34	80
60-66	70	II.4	158
pro Sest.		7	83
91	143	IV.16	121
Rep.		28-45	109
I.xviii.30	81	28, 30, 33	8

INDEX OF REFERENCES 175

34	109	31	8
37, 38, 40	8	35-138	103
41ff.	8	117-121	148
43	8, 109	118	104, 109
44	8, 118	120	148
45	118	133ff.	156
54	121	155	119
VI.13	121		
22	149	Diogenes of Oenoanda	
28	81	fr.14(Ch.)=16(W.)=15 (G.)	45, 136
36	148	fr.53(Ch.)=64(W.)=63 (G.)	114
37	149		
51	93	Epictetus (-Arrian[us])	
69	148	*Disc.*	
72	148	III.vii.19	109
96-98	108	vii.30ff.	116
101	112, 122	IV.i.142f.	164
VII all	108	i.153	164
VII.37	120	xi.9ff.	164
40	75	*fr.* 129 (Sch.)	150
101	148	*fr.* 172	150
119ff.	148		
IX.21	22	Epicurus	
X.1-28 (*"Vita Epicuri"*)	108	[See also Diogenes Laertius, *Lives* X, *supra*]	
"V.E.", beg. (X.9)	8	*"Choices and Avoidances"*	
1	114	all	152
3	33, 114, 116	*Diaporiai*	
4	13, 113, 120	all	7
5-7	112	*Epist. fr.* (Arrighetti)	
5	8, 112	fr. 65, p. 401	123
6f.	8, 119f.	*Fragments* (*"Usener"*)	
7	76, 116, 118	[Only those passages appear in this index which are quoted without indication of their location (or parallels) in classical and patristic literature, i.e., which are quoted merely as *Usener*, fr. x]	
8	160		
9ff.	8, 17, 113 121, 160		
10	122		
11	94		
13	117		
15, 16ff.	8, 118	*fr.* 19	109
17	121	55-57	137
19	12	63	17
22-25	127	67 (*peri telous*)	76, 153
22	91, 118	74	91
23	120	81	156
25	112	94	109
26	117, 131	114	117
27	152	122, 138	118
28	120	141	26

INDEX OF REFERENCES

164	119	*L. to Menoeceus*	
177	118	124f.	90, 129
181	94, 164	125	137
182	164	134	156
190	118	135	137, 159
206	94	*L. to Pythocles*	
207	31	91	156
210, 211	113	*Peri Physeōs*	
340	135	all	7
352-355	163		
358a	104		
359-383	130	Grat(t)ius Faliscus	
361, 366	137	*Cyn.*	
409	121	2-12	63
434	91		
474-477	149	Himerius	
475	73	*Ecl.*	
504	149	3, No. 350	138
526, 551	109		
574	127	Hippocrates	
599	117	*Aphor.*	
602	73, 149	IV.56, 74, 78, 81, 83	162
Gnom. Vat.		VII.10	162
all	135		
2	129	Horace	
10	26, 95, 155	*Carm.*	
14	135, 164	I.xxxiv.2	17
16	96	*Ep.*	
17	106	I.i.106ff.	72, 148
25	149	iv.6	115
32	73	*Sat.*	
36	26	I.iii.124f.	148
41	161	II.iv.73ff.	140
60	164	vii., all	149
61, 68	135	vii.83	71
Kyriai Doxai (Ratae Sententiae)		viii.51	140
all	3, 104	III.iii.158	72
II	90, 129		
VI	113	Hyginus	
XIV, XVII	129	*Genealogiae (Fabulae)*	
XXXI-XXXIII	135, 150	274, 277	140
Letters			
all	3	Iamblichus	
L. to Herodotus		*Protr.*	
36	159	14	155
38	155		
81	47, 129	*Inscriptiones Graecae (Kaibel)*	
		XIV, No.1746, p. 439	136

Inscriptiones Latinae (Selectae, Dessau)
II.1, No.8156, p. 881 — 136

Isocrates
ad Nic.
29 (20d) — 149
Orat. IX
14f. — 136

Iuvenal
Sat.
VI.461-464 — 101
471-473 — 101
VII.189-194 — 148

Julian
Letter to a Priest
301 C-D — 105

Lucian
Alexander, the False Prophet
all — 3
25 — 16
39-48 — 126
47 — 22
bis acc.
34 — 81
Catapl.
all — 137
de luct.
all — 137
Dial. of Courtesans
all — 112
dial. mort.
all — 137
Hermotimus
6 — 72
106, end — 148
Icaromenippus
6-7 — 84
Menippus
all — 137
Nigrinus
I — 72, 148
Philopseudes
Ch. 22 — 126
Piscator
35 — 71

Timon
10 — 118, 137
Ver. hist. ("*True Story*")
all — 145
Book II, all — 137
Vitarum auctio
20 — 72, 148

Lucilius
fr. 1225 — 148

Lucretius
de rerum natura
I.72ff. — 26
150 — 156
II.101 — 137
109 — 87
767 — 27
1113-1142 — 31
III.12f. — 30
16ff. — 27
828f. — 18
978-1023 — 44ff.
978 — 136
980-984 — 136
1043f. — 27
IV.1078 — 18
1117 — 18
1173-1184 — 101
V.1ff. — 123
6-8 — 123
8 — 30
165-169 — 190
195-234 — 48
564-591 — 83
925ff. — 144
975f. — 65
1350-1378 — 56
1395-1435 — 31
1457 — 56
VI.24-28 — 123
160 — 87

Macrobius
Saturnalia
I.ii, § 41f. — 116

INDEX OF REFERENCES

Manilius
  Astron.
    I.66   65

Marcus Aurelius
  Medit.
    IV.4   156
    51   153

Maximus of Tyre
  XV.8 (Hobein)   135

Ovid
  Tristia
    III.iv.25   101, 109

Papyr. Hercul. (Sbordone)
  1005, col. IV   127

Persius
  Sat.
    III.83f.   106, 156

Petronius
  Sat.
    132, end   101

Philodemus
  de mortis
    end   117
  de musica
    all   117
    Usener, fr. 143   90
  on Signs
    X.35-XI.9   157
  peri Parrhēsias (O.)
    18.1-2   119

Plato
  Apol.
    41a   136
  Crat.
    all   146
  (*Ps.-*)*Epin.*
    all   140
    974dff.   63
  Gorgias
    415e-453   142
    464d-e   63
    517eff.   55, 63, 141
    523aff.   136
    524e-525   135
  (*Ps.-*)*Hippias Maior*
    281c, 283a   83
  Laws
    905d   161
  Phaedo
    117   161
  Phaedrus
    246e   124
    247ff.   31
    247a-253c   125
    279bf., end   149
  Prot.
    321dff.   55f.
  Rep.
    369cff.   54f., 140f.
    372a-d   31
    397e   140
    423d   141
    433a, b   140
    434c   140
    559a   125
  Theaet.
    173c, 174a   80
    174c   155
    176b   22
  Timaeus
    77c-81d   31

Pliny the Elder
  nat. hist.
    II.v.18f.   61f.
    V.xv.73   101
    VII.ii.8   141
      vi.191ff.   127
      vi.191-215   140
      lv.188-190   2

Plotinus
  Enn.
    II.ix.15   111

Plutarch
  (*Life of*) *Alexander*
    IX   150

INDEX OF REFERENCES

(*Life of*) *Cato Minor*
    LXVIII.2-LXXI.1   162

Moralia
[In most instances the traditional titles of the individual tractates will be found in the text and notes, *supra*]

398 B	102
548 B	115
548 B- 568	49
662 C	119
928 E	115
993 Af.	58f.
D-E	146
1086 C-1130 E	104
1089 C	104
D	115
F	117
1094 A	119
C, D	20, 117
D	119
E	117
1096 D	123
1097 B	113
C	123
1098 A	124
B	121
1100 A-B	113f.
1117 Af.	123
B	26
1121 E-F	8
1123f.	17
1123 A	109
B	17
1126 F	113
1128ff.	109
1130 E	118

Placita (Ps.-Plutarch)
    all   104, 156

Quintilian
  Inst. Orat.

all	131
I.viii.9	132
ix.3	132
II.xi.3	132
xii.7	132
X.i.60	132
XII.ii.24	119
x.48	132

Sallustius (4th ct., Nock)
    Ch. XIV, XV   90

Scriptores Hist. Aug.

Alex. 30.6	127
Hadr. 21.4	127
Hel. 5.4f.	127

Seneca
  ad Marciam de cons.
    19.4   46
  de benef.

I.xiv.1f.	67f.
II.xxvi.1ff.	68
IV.xix.1f.	28

  de otio
    III   61
  de vita beata

XII.4	112
XIX.1	118

  Ep.

1.18	100
2.5	73
6.6	127
9.6	150
11.8	123
18.7	94, 163
18.10	94
20.6	164
11	115
12	164
24.18	44
22	136
25.5	123
26.8, 9	95
64.6-9	141
7	62
66.18f.	90
45	91
45-47	27
75.8-15	163
81.10	71, 147f.
11	71, 118
13ff.	66, 71, 73
19	153

180 INDEX OF REFERENCES

83.9	151
85.2	152
87.3-5	163f.
24	153
88.21ff.	62
90, all	54, 144
90.1-19	142
15	63
19	142
20ff.	57, 142
102.17ff.	150
120.15	164

Sextus Empiricus
adv. log.
I.17	75

adv. math.
I.1	117
VI.27	117

adv. phys.
I.64	121
II.19	120

Sophocles
Antigone
334ff., 337f.	142
354f., 357f.	142

Statius
Silvae
II.vii.76	18

Thebais
IV.282	65

Stobaeus (Ioannes)
Anthol. (W.-H.)
vol II, p. 7, No.20	80
p. 8, No. 22	80

Suidas (*Suda*, Lexicon)
s.v., "*Epikouros*"	118

Tacitus
Ann.
XV.62-64	162
XVI.34f.	162

Theon
Progymn.
p. 169 (Walz)	117

Valerius Maximus
Factorum...
III.iv., *ext.* 1	157
IV.ix., *ext.* 1	121
VIII.vii., *ext.* 3	162
ext. 14	162

Varro
de re rust.
II.i.3ff.	144
III.i.5	144
fr. 245	148

Vergil
Ecl.
V.64	30

Vitruvius
On Architecture
II.i.1	146

Xenophon
Memor.
IV.iii.14	157
vii.6	83, 157

PATRISTIC LITERATURE

Ambrosius
adv. gent.
I 38	123

Anonymous
De recta in Deum fide
II.19	111

Aristides
Apol.
IV.2	85
VI.1-3	85

Arnobius
adv. gent.

INDEX OF REFERENCES

II.58ff.		57, 85	*Epistola*	
60		30	XXIII, end	115
			in Is.	
Augustine			VII.xviii.1	111
ad Diosc. epist.			xxii.12	129
118.21		105		
c. Jul.			Justin	
III.xxxi.48		117	*II Apol.*	
Conf.			VII.3	135
VII.xii		120		
de civ. dei			Lactantius	
IV.3		148	*de ira dei*	
			XIII.xix	137
Clement of Alexandria			*div. inst.*	
Strom.			II.viii.50	119
II.23		109	III.xiv.1f.	123
			xvii	116
Epiphanius			xvii.8	137
Haer. (Panarion)			VII.vii.6	123
XXXVII		130	XIII-XVII	146
			Maximus Confessor	
Eusebius			*Loci communi*	
Praep. evang.			Ch.21(600), p. 853A	155
XII.29.4		81		
XIV.27.9, 782ff.		123	Origen	
784		124	*c. Cels.*	
			IV.54	21
Hippolytus			V.47	153
Ref. omn. haer. (Philosophumena)				
I.1.4		81	Salvianus	
31.3f.		134	*de gubern. dei*	
			I.5	134
Irenaeus				
adv. haer.			Synesius	
I.xxxi.2f.		130	*Encomium on Baldness*	
II.xxxii.2		111	p. 63ff. (P.)	137
III.xviii.1		111		
xxiv.2		111	Tertullian	
			adv. Marc.	
Jerome			I.xxv.3	111
adv. Jovin.			V.xix.7	111
I.1		115	*adv. nat.*	
adv. Ruf.			II.4	85, 157
I.30		117	*Ps.-Tertullian*	
III.30		115	7	130

TERMS AND KEYWORDS

GRECO - ROMAN

[In most instances, these entries follow the first appearance of the item, whether in the original script or in transcription. "Etc." following an entry indicates that several derivatives of the basic word are included; e.g., "*chria*" includes *chriae*, *chreia*, chriic, chriization, etc. Greek vowel length in terms that are also English loanwords is not always indicated. Greek upsilon is rendered as "y" except in diphthongs (*ou*, etc.)]

acrimonia 132, 147
adiaphora 120
αἱρετέα / φευκτέα 152
altercatio 107
ἅμιλλα 130
amplificatio, etc. 38f., 69, 147
anadiplosis 124f., cf. "*diplosis*"
anaphoron, etc., see "*ep-*"
anamnēsis 143
ἀνδρός, ἀνδρεῖος 72
antistrophē, see "*epiphora*"
apaideusia 15
apatheia 109
aphalkē 109
aphrodisia 109
apolauston 90
apophthegma, etc. 12, see also "*chria*"
aporiae, etc. 87, 148, 150
aretē 142
asyndeton, etc. 39, 59, 60, 132, 139
ataraxia 93, 109, 156
ἄτομον, τό; ἄτομος, ἡ 125, see also "atom", General Index
atopia 123
αὐτοματισμός, etc. 10, 106, 156
ἄφθαρτός 26, 124
banausos 144
beatus 152
bioi 4
bona 73, 91
cheironax 144
chria, χρεία, etc. 7, 12f., 78-89, 92, 103, 109-112, 120, 127, 132, 146, 155, 160
clinamen 9
controversia 138

contubernium 25, 92, 127
deigma 146
delirare, delirium, etc. 17, 118
dementia, etc. 17, see also "*insania*"
dēmiourgos 144
diadochos 149
διαμάχη 38
diplosis 30
dissipare 20
dissolvere 20
dives 73
doulos 149
ἐγκύκλιος παιδεία 15, 62, 116f.
eikadistae 112
eikōnas 93
εἰρήνη 22
encomium 142
epainos 142
epanalepsis 124, 132, 147
epanaphora 39f., 68, 77f., 124, 132, 147
epanodos 132, 147
ἐπῄνεσεν 141
epibolē 123
Ἐπίκουρος, ὁ 115
epiphora 40, 135
ἐπιχείρημα 124
ἐρώμενον 8
eudaimonismos 142
evertere, etc. 20
exempla 132, see also "*chria*"
ἡμέρας καὶ νυκτὸς 159
fabri 61
fortis 172
furor, etc. 17f., 118

gnomē, γνώμη 50, 132f., 149, cf. also General Index, s.v.
gravitas 132, 147
heimarmēnē 156
hetaera, hetaira, etc., see General Index, s.v., "courtesans"
hedonē etc., 134, cf. General Index, s.v., "Hedonism," "pleasure"
hēgemōn 149
hērōs 25
hēsychē 22
hiatus 117
homoioteleuton, etc. 39, cf. Greek entry, infra
honestus, etc. 150, cf. also "honor," General Index
hortulus 121
hortus 22f., cf. "kēpos," infra, and "Garden," General Index
hystera 112
θεός etc. 26
θεραπευταί etc. 141
imitatio dei 92f., cf. ὁμοίωσις ..., infra
indoctus 15
insania, etc. 118, cf. General Index, s.v., "insanity"
intermundia 9
investigat occulta 60
ἰσχυρός 72
καθηγεμόνες 33
kakotechnia 117
κάλον δύε (and "calendae") 145
κενός 10
kephalaia 92
kēpologos 121
kēpos 22f., 121, cf. "Garden," General Index. Cf. "hortus," supra
kēpotyrannos 121
koinē 117
koryphaios 80
λάθε βιώσας 109
lex talionis 165
liberales 62
libidines 72, cf. "affect(ion)s," General Index
ludicrae 62
-ma 117
magister populi 148

μακάριοι, etc. 58, 142, 146, cf. "macarismus," General Index
malum, etc. 91
marmor, etc. 27
mathēmata 117
mente captus 17
metathemenos 120
mihi laborata sunt 62, 144
μόνος 70
μῦθος 26, cf. "myth," etc., General Index
οἰκειοπραγία 140
οἷον, ὅσα, etc. 58
ὁμοιόπτωτον 39
ὁμοιοτέλευτον 38f., cf. "homoioteleuton," supra
ὁμοίωσις θεοῦ 93, 110, 123, cf. "imitatio dei," supra
opsimathēs 120
otium 57
Paian Anax 113
paideia 20
paradoxon, etc. 70ff., cf. "paradox," General Index
paraenesis 4, 6
παρακόψας, etc. 17, 118
parallelismus membrorum 125
parēchesis 38f., 43f., 45
parisōsis 39, 69, 131
paroemia, etc. 132
paronomasia 39, 46ff., 135, 150, 156
pater veri 101
pedalem, etc. 85, cf. "foot," etc., General Index
peroratio 40
πηχῶν 84
phaulos 149
πλούσιος 73
πολυπραγμονεῖν 140
polysyndeton 39, 46, 55, 132, cf. "syndeton," infra
pornē 47
portenta 44
πούς 157, cf. "pedalem," supra
progymnasmata 50
προκύψας 31
pronoia 47f., 134, cf. "providence," General Index
protrepticus 22

184 TERMS AND KEYWORDS

pueriles 62
sapiens, etc., see "Sage," General Index
schēma etymologikon 39, 135, 150
sententia 40-50, 108, 132f., 135
σῆμα, etc. 162
similiter cadens 39
similiter desinens 38
sophismata 143
sophos, etc., see "Sage," General Index
sordidae 62
sōmation 164
sōreitēs, etc. 151, see also "sorite(s)," General Index
σωτήρ 26
spoudaiogeloion 23, 129, 133
stadia 84
stultitia, etc. 17, 118, see also "fool," General Index
suasoria 50
summum bonum 77
syndeton 139, 142, cf. "*polysyndeton*," *supra*

synousiē 109
syntomē 153
σύστασις 38
technē, etc. 59, 143f.
τέλειος, etc. 26
testimonium, etc. 5f., 23f., 31, 122, 149
Tetrapharmakos 33, 127
theophileis 58
topos, etc. 61, 63f., 69, 81, 139, 142, 145, 147
tribunalia 46
tyrannos 46
usus, utiles, etc. 58ff.
ut famast 44
veni, vidi, vici 32, 126, 131
vocatio 120
volgares (vulgares) 15, 62
ὕε κύε 145
φρενῶν ἐκτός 118
χάρις 129

HEBREW AND ARAMAIC

[Transcribed items are listed according to the English alphabet]

acher, Acher 12
'al tiḳra' 122
Alphabethoth de R. Akiba 106
Am ha-Areṣ 15
Apiḳuros, etc., אפיקורוס 14, 24, 106, 114ff.
baraithoth 105
darshan, etc. 87, 159
derek(h) 'ereṣ 67
dugma 146
'eseḳ 144
gemara 108
ḥakham 3, and *passim*, see "Sage," General Index
ma'alah 146
mayim 125
Midrash 23, see also General Index, *s.v.*
pardes, "Paradise," 5, 22f., 121, 154, see also General Index, *s.v.*
peshaṭ 116
seḥorah 144
shamayim 125
sīman 162

Tosaphoth 108
yeṣer 163
Zeḳenim 158

אומניות / אומות	139
ב[ר]אי בעית אימא	108
אין	156
אית דין	36
אמורא	159
אפיקורוס	133
גבור	70, 72
גן	23
דוגמה של מעלה	65
דעה	65
הוא היה אומר	139
הציץ	5, 31f., 106
וחמדה וחמדה ונסבה	32
חכם הרזים	51f., 60, 139
חכמים	86
חשקה נפשי	8
טהור	27, 29
טובה	95

TERMS AND KEYWORDS

מתורגמן	159		טפח	157
נבט	32		טרח	147
נטע	119		יגע	144
נכנט בשלום	21		יצא בשלום, לשלום	22
סכל	32		כבר	154
עלה וירד	120		כל האדם	97
פגע [נפגע]	17, 110, 118		כלל גדול	92
פקר	114		כמה	58
פריש הוה	108		לא, לוא	82, 156
פריה ורביה	108		לחטיא	24
פרצוף	141		לית דין ולית דיין	35-43, 129-137
קבל	109		לשמשני	58-64
קיצץ בנטיעות	6, 19, 49		מאין	82, 154
ראה	32		מבחוץ	83, 156
רגילים	154		מדת הדין / מדת הרחמים	129
רחף	85		מטטרון	160
רעש	87		מטרטר	110
שוקדות	139		מיטטור	110, 160
שיש	27, 29		מילא	112
שכח	119		מינות	133
שמח	73		מעשה ב	154
תלמידי חכמים	86		משכימים ומעריבים	139

GENERAL INDEX

1. Entries of classical and Rabbinic authorities are in addition to the Index of References.
2. No book titles appear in this index.
3. "Etc." after an entry signifies derivatives of the same basic root. Thus, e.g., "Legend, etc." includes legends, legendary, legendarization.
4. Quotations of hyphenated pages, e.g., 40-46, or 6f., 8ff., do not necessarily indicate a continuous treatment of the subject in question.
5. The Preface, pp. IX-XII, is not covered.]

Abbahu 103, 134, 151, 157
Abel 36-38, 132, see also "Cain and Abel," *infra*
Above and below 155, 157
Abraham 41, 134
Absent-minded, etc. 9, 78-85, 155ff.
Abṭalion 159
Abuyah (father of "Acher") 114
Academy (Platonic) 22, 145; New —, 49 (see also "Arcesilaus", *infra*)
Acher, see "Elisha b. Abuyah," *infra*
Acheron 44, cf. "Hades"
Adam 51-65, 69, 142-146, cf. "Early Man," *infra*
Aeacus 45
Aelianus (Aelian) 4, 16, 53, 104, 117, 151
Aeschylus 52
Aesthetic 110
Aëtius 104, 137
Affect(ion), etc. 147, 163
Afterlife (Hereafter) 14, 23, 37, 43-48; cf. also "Denial...," "Eternal," "Hades," "Hell," "Immortality," "World to Come," *infra*
Aggadah, see "Haggadah," *infra*
Akabiah b. Mahalal'el 95
Akiba (R.) 4ff., 14ff., 20-24, 28, 31-34, 42, 92, 106, 116, 120, 122, 127, 135, 151, 158, 160, 163, 165
Akiba's bride 21, 108
Akiba's daughter 108
Alcibiades 127
Alexander of Abonuteichos 3, 126
Alexander Polyhistor 104

Alexander the Great 73, 151, 163
Alexandria, etc. 39, 96, 131, 134, 137, 160
Alexinus 87, 127
Allegory, etc. 2, 29, 38, 75, 92, 116, 122, 130f., 152, 158
Alliteration 36, 43, 45ff., 47, 132, 135f.
Amafinius (Epicurean) 1, 101
Ambrosius 104
Ammonius Saccas 111
Amora, etc. 4ff., 15, 24, 32, 105, 108ff., 115, 128ff., 133, 158
Anaxagoras 52, 80, 83, 91, 118, 137, 157
Anaximander 10
Anecdote, etc. 4, 7, 9ff., 32, 80, 83, 85, 103-106, 109, 112, 114, 132, 146, 148f., 154, 157f., see also "*chria*", Terms and Keywords
Angel, etc. 9, 110, 122, 163
Anger of the gods 16, see also "Fear of ...," *infra*
Anthology, etc. 4
Anti-Epicurean, etc. *passim* (virtually every page)
Antigonus of Carystus 104
Antinomian 24, cf. "Gnostic," "Heretic," *infra*
Anti-mystical 5
Antioch 118, 121
Antiochus IV (Epiphanes) 2, 16
Antipater of Sidon 81
Antiphon (*OCD* 1) 53, 91
Antisthenes (the Cynic) 143, 146
Anti-Stoic, etc. 3, 163, cf. "Epicurean," *infra*

Antithetical (style) 11f.
Antonius Monachus (Melissa) 81
Apelles 20, 117
Aphthonius 50
Apocalypse, etc. 24, 26, 29, 31, 34, 121, 125 (Platonic), 126, 146
Apollonius (the "Garden Tyrant," Epicurean) 121
Apuleius 2f., 120, 132, 151
Aramaic 34, 36ff., 39-42, 46ff., 108, 113, 119, 133, 151, 156
Aratus 53, 144, 162
Arcesilaus 7f., 17, 18ff., 118ff.
Archelaus 52
Archilochus 132
Archimedes 60, 143
Arete (woman philosopher) 109
Aristides (Christian apologist) 85, 157
Aristippus 109, 115
Aristobolus (brother of Epicurus) 16, 33, 118
Aristophanes 53, 122, 142f., 146
Aristotle, etc. 2f., 10, 22, 53, 103, 114, 117, 120, 132f., 145, 156, 161, 164
Arnobius 30, 101, 104
Arrian(us) 7, 102, 151
Artisan, see "Craftsman," *infra*
Ascent 19, 24, 26, 28f., 125
Ascete, etc. (including "austere", etc.) 8, 76, 93f., 163
Asclepiades (Epicurean physician) 1, 103
Ashes and maggots 164
Asianic, etc. (style) 132
Asocial 126
Astral worship 157
Astrology 83
Astronomy 60, 79-85, 88, 116
Atheism, etc. 25, 41, 111, 121, 126, 128, 133
Athenaeus 53, 76ff., 110
Athenion 53
Athens, etc. 1f., 4, 113, 136
Atom, Atomism, etc. 9f., 28, 37, 123ff., 156
Atticism 132
Atticus (Titus Pomponius, *OCD* 1, Epicurean) 1, 16, 22, 100, 131
Augustine 17, 21, 53, 158

Augustus 52
Aulus Gellius 47, 151
Autodidact 15
Automedon 125
Avoidance of Sin 93, of Trouble 93f., 152f., 164

Bar Kokheba 5, 14, 108
Ben Azzai (Shimeʿon) 4-8, 23f., 32-34, 75, 86ff., 90-98, 108, 110f., 122, 127, 152f., 157-165
Benediction, see "Blessed," *infra*
Benjamin b. Levi (Amora) 133
Ben Sirah 163
Ben Zoma (Shimeʿon) 5f., 8f., 23f., 32, 51-89, 96ff., 107f., 127, 138, 142f., 146f., 150-160, 165
Beruriah (wife of R. Meir) 109, 126
Bethlehem 116-118
Bible, etc. 8f., 50, 65, 143; cf. Index of References, and "Canon" (in parts) and "Midrash," *infra*
Bilingual 139
Biography, etc. 4, 7, 10f., 14, 18, 34, 87, 110, 112ff., 116, 118, 127, 137, 162; cf. "*bioi*", Terms and Keywords
Bion (Cynic) 80, 82, 121
Birth and death 164
Birthday (of Epicurus, etc.) 122f., cf. "Eikadistae," Terms and Keywords
Blessed, etc. 55-64, 69, 142, 146, see also "Macarismus," *infra*
Brothers of Epicurus (Neocles, Chaeredemus, Aristobolus) 16, 33

Caesar, see "Julius Caesar," *infra*
Caesarea (Palestine) 3, 103, 117, 134, 157
Cain 36f., 42, 48, 128-132
Cain and Abel 30, 36ff., 42
Cainites 130
(Ps.-) Callisthenes 151
Calque 118
Campanella, Thomas 145
Canon, etc. (lit.) 8, 15, 23, 92, 133, 163
Canticles (Song of Songs, of Solomon, canonized) 92
Carneades 104, 121
Carthage 3

GENERAL INDEX

Cassius (the Tyrannicide, *OCD* 6) 1, 16, 100f., 131
Catalepsy 26
Catechetic School 3
Catius (Epicurean) 101
Cato the Younger 162
Celestial World (Epicurean) 26-31
Celibacy, etc. 6-8, 16, 91, 108, 159, 165
Celsus 21, 103
Cercidas (Cynic) 151
Cerberus 44f.
Chaeredemus (brother of Epicurus) 16, 33
Charioteer 124
Charon 45ff.
Child raising 7
Chrysippus 109, 127, 158
Christianity, etc. 4, 10, 14, 17, 34, 99, 105, 109, 111, 115, 123, 126, 138
Church, see preceding entry
Church Fathers 10, 15, 34, 53, 104, see also "Patristic," *infra*
Cicero 1, 3, 7, 16f., 20-22, 27, 30, 47, 53, 61, 75, 83, 101, 118, 120, 123, 132, 136, 138, 143, 146, 151-154, 158f., 161ff., 165
Civil servant 141, 151
Cleanthes 116, 141, 146, 148
Clement of Alexandria 7, 109
Cleomedes 117
Client 67-69
Clothing 54-64, 93f. (invented); cf. also "Ascete," *supra*
Colotes (Epicurean) 2, 17, 100, 123f.
Comedy 17, 25, 67, 81
Comic relief 25
Constantinople 18
Contemplation 26, 123
Continence 6f., cf. "Celibacy," "Ascete," *supra*
Conversion (to Epicureanism) 2, 7, 16; (to philosophy) 22, 120f., 148; (to Torah) 21f., 24
Corruption of youth 19f.
Cosmos, Cosmogony, Cosmology, etc. 9f., 83, 88, 96f., 121f., 123f., 154f., 160
Courtesans (and Harlots, Hetaerae) 8, 11f., 14, 47, 112; cf. "Danaë," "Gnathaena," "Laodice," "Leontion," "Metaneira" and "Thais," *infra*

Crafts, — men (and artisans) 19, 51-64, 139-146
Crates (the Cynic) 109, 120, 146
Creation 54, 60, 79, 93, 160; cf. "cosmos," etc., *supra*
Critias 53, 140
Ctesias 135
Culture hero 65, 143, cf. "Inventor," *infra*
"Cutting of the Plantings," see ḳiṣeṣ (Hebrew Section), Terms and Keywords
Cynic, Cynicism, etc. 22, 34, 38, 55, 57, 70, 80, 88f., 92, 94, 106, 108f., 116, 121, 126ff., 130, 134, 136, 141, 143-146, 148f., 151, 153, 158, 161f., 165
Cynosarges 22
Cyrenaic, etc. (philosophy) 109, 124

Danaë 11f., 36, 48, 112, 169
Daniel 102
Dante 14, 118
Daphnis 30
Day and night 159f.
Death (sudden or slow) 16-18, 22f., 48, 85, 88
Death of no concern, nothing 43ff., 90, 129
Death of the Sage 90f., 161f.
Delphic Oracle 120
Demetrius Laco(n) (Epicurean) 100, 117
Demetrius of Phalerum 151
Demiurge 10
Democritus 10, 52, 83, 109, 143, 149, 157, 161
Demosthenes 93
Demythologization 160
Denial (of the existence of divine justice, providence, recompense, reward and punishment) 8, 10f., 12-16, 36f., 41ff., 44-48, 83, 92, 102, 113, 128, 131, 133f., 137, 156f.
Desires 125
Diadoche, etc. 4, 105
Diaries 104
Diatribe, etc. 2-4, 7, 15, 17, 25, 38, 80, 124, 148f., 152
Dicaearchus 35, 143
Dio Chrysostom (of Prusa) 53, 120, 133f., 151

Diocles of Magnesia 104
Diodorus (Epicurean) 16, 18f.
Diodorus Siculus 53, 143
Diogenes Laertius 3, 18, 26, 53, 87, 103, 109, 112ff., 158
Diogenes of Apollonia 52
Diogenes of Oenoanda (Epicurean) 2, 26, 45, 53, 114
Diogenes the Cynic 108, 120, 146, 148f.
Diogenianus (*OCD* 1, Epicurean) 3, 103
Diogenes (Epicurean epitomist) 104
Dionysus (epitaph of) 110
Dionysius (Bishop of Alexandria) 28, 30, 124
Dionysius of Heracleia (*OCD* 8) 120
Dionysius the Elder (Syracusan tyrant) 82
Diopeithes (seer) 79
Discoverer, see "Inventor," *infra*
Displacement of thematic items 13
Diversity (of man) 141
Divinity (and near-divinity) of Epicurus 25f., 28, 30, 113, 122f.
Divine Glory, see "God," *infra*; — Guidance 76; — Presence 107
Divine Voice 157; — Spirit 79, 85, 143
Division of Labor 51-65, 140-145
Divorce 6, 108
Domitian 102
Double entendre 12, 80-85, 155
Doxography 4, 87, 105
Dream voyage 24
Dust and worms 95, 164

Early (First, Primitive) Man 51-65, 141-146
Ecclesiastes 40, 92
Ecstasy, etc. 19, 24, 26, 30f., 75, 121f., 125
Economy of words, brevity 11, 143
Education 14, 20, 103; see also "*enkyklios paideia*, "Greek Section, Terms and Keywords; "Students," *infra*
Egypt 2f.
"Elders of the South" 73
Eleatic (philosophy) 161
Eleʿazar b. Arak 14, 110, 126
Eleʿazar b. Azariah 87, 116

Eleʿazar b. Pedat(h) 109, 145
Eliʿezer (b. Hyrcanus) 15, 74, 110, 114, 120, 127, 150, 152, 162f.
Elisha b. Abuyah ("Acher") 5f., 10-14, 19ff., 24, 32, 35, 40, 48, 86, 106, 111-114, 119f., 126ff., 158
Elisha b. Abuyah, daughter(s) of 111, 128
Empedocles 52, 146
Empiricism, etc. 25, (non- —) 117, 161f.
Engagement (betrothal) 108
Ennius 81
Epictetus 2, 4, 7, 15, 17, 159, 161
Epicurus, Epicurean, Epicureanism, *passim* (virtually every page)
Epicurus, father, mother, of 114
Epigram 17f., 25, 33, 105, 109, 117, 121, 125, 127, 132
Epimetheus 55f.
Epistomology (Epicurean) 123, 153
Epistular style 3
Epitaph 7, 18, 45, 109f., 137
Epitome, etc. (Epicurean) 3, 33, 103f.
Erasistratus 159
Esau 41, 48, 130, 134f.
Esoteric, etc. 19, 24, 31, 34, 87f., 163
Eternal life, Eternity 119, 121; cf. also "Afterlife," *supra* and "World to Come," *infra*
Ethic, etc. 6, 76, 86f., 92, 95, 104, 110, 123, 144f., 148f., 151, 159
Euhemerus, Euhemerism 53, 140, 144
Eunuchs (metaphor) 7f., 110, 120
Euripides 52
Eusebius 3, 18, 28, 30f., 53, 103, 116, 124, 155f.
Evil, etc. (*malum*) 49, 76, 153
Evil Urge 158
Exodus from Egypt 87
Ezekiel 111, 126

Fable (fox —) 78
Fate of Epicureans 4ff.
Favorinus 104
Fear of gods (and stars) 25, 28, 53, 157; of Underworld, of punishment 37, 44-48
Fire, discovered 65, 146
Fire, surrounding 9, 110f., 113f.

First Man, see "Adam," "Early Man," *supra*
First person (style) 69
Florilegia 82, 155
Food, primitive 54-64, 93f., 163f.; see also "Ascete," *supra*
Fool, etc. 44, 49, 71, 86, 93, 118, 134, 147, 163f., cf. "*stultus*," Terms and Keywords
Foot, etc. 79-85; cf. "*pedalem*," "*pous*," Terms and Keywords
Forty Years (biographical moteme) 14
Founder Hero 26, 28; cf. also "*hērōs*," Terms and Keywords, "Inventor," *infra*
Founder-Sage 7, 32, 127, 149
Four (in Epicureanism) 33
"Four Who Entered Paradise" 4f., 9f., 14f., 19, 23, 32, 85, 88, 112, 116, 159f.
Free, Freedom 70-73, 83, 94; freedom of choice, will 96, 148f., 165
Friends, Friendship 8, 71, 148, 161f.

Galen 103, 144, 159
"Garden," the (Epicurean domicile) 12, 22f., 32f., 78, 101, 121
Garden of Eden (as Hereafter) 23
Garden of Genesis 23, 121
Gemara 86
Generation of the Flood 42, 137
Genesis, Book of 10, 65
Genizah 40
Glutton 67
Gnathaena 112
Gnome, etc. 104, 138, see also Terms and Keywords, *s.v.*
Gnomology 3, 82
Gnostic, Gnosticism 10, 24, 75, 84, 95, 111, 130f., 144, 152, 154
Gnosticism, Sethian 111; Simonian 111
God (the Deity, The Holy-One-Blessed-Be-He, etc.) 5, 41f., 74, 93, 97, 142, 145ff., 150, 153, 157, 160, 163
God, gods (Greco-Roman) 10, 16, 26-33, 37, 41-49, 93, 107, 113, 117, 123, 128, 137, 142, 144, 156, 163
Golden Age 53, 61, 143

Golden Rule 93
Good, the (*summum bonum*) 76, 151
Gratitude 65-69, 160
Greek books 107, 126; — wisdom 107
Gregory of Nazianzus 103
Gregory Thaumaturgus 103
Guardian (Platonic) 54
Guest 66-69, 146f.
Gymnastics 55
Gymnosophists 151

Hades 16, 43ff., 135f.
Hadrian, etc. 2, 12, 33, 35, 47, 84, 102, 104, 107, 139, 157, 165
Haggadah, etc. 14, 85f., 160, see also "Midrash," *infra*
Ḥakham, etc., cf. "Sage," *infra*, and Hebrew Terms, *s.v.*
Halak(h)ah, etc. 15, 55, 86f., 138f., 146, 151, 158, 160-163
Hanan'el (Rabbenu) 118
Ḥananiah b. Hezekiah (Tanna) 111
Handbook (Greco-Roman) 4
Happy, etc. 151f.
Harlot, see "Courtesan," *supra*
Harmonization 6, 23f.
Heavenly Academy 141; — Sanctuary 121; — Temple 126
Hebrew, biblical 23
Hecataeus of Abdera 53
Hecato 150
Hedonism, etc. 12-14, 25, 30, 41, 50, 77, 92, 115, 120f., 126, 133, 161, 163
Hek(h)aloth Literature 106, 122
Hell 126; "— on Earth" 44, 136
Hellenistic-Jewish 122
Helvidius 162
Hemon 109
Heracles 155
Heraclitus 149, 161
Herculaneum, etc. (papyri) 1, 34, 99, 103, 119
Heresy, etc. 11, 13, 16, 24, 30, 40, 42, 88, 92, 124, 126, 128, 133f., 156, 163
Hermes 55
Hermippus 53, 105, 110, 119, 140
Hermogenes 50
Herod 2

Herodotus (a former Epicurean) 113; —
  (historian) 53, 135
Hetaera, etc., see "Courtesans," *supra*
Hesiod 15, 52, 144
Heurematology, etc. 32, 51-65, 123, 140, 146
Hierocles (Stoic) 47
Hillel (brother of Judah II) 3
Hillel the Elder 108, 110, 116, 120, 126f., 133, 141, 144, 148, 151, 154f., 159f., 164
Himerius 50
Hipparchia (woman Cynic) 109, 120
Hippolytus 41, 43, 47, 81, 134f.
(Ps.-) Hippocrates, etc. 140, 161
Holy Spirit 152, 158
Homer 8, 15, 117
Honor, etc. 70-73, 76, 148, 150, 160
Horace 1, 99, 120, 131, 147, 149, 151
Host 66-69
Humility 164
Ḥuṣpith the Interpreter (Tanna) 35, 112, 128

Iamblichus 81, 155
Iambulus (author of "*Sun State*") 145
Ideas, doctrine of 146
Ignorant, etc. 14-16, 20f., 117f., cf. "Am ha-Areṣ" Hebrew Terms
Illness (of Epicureans) 16f.
Image of God 92f.
Immortality (soul) 49, 162; cf. "Afterlife," *supra*
Imperative (style) 152f.
Impulse 70-73, 76
Incantation 13, 20, 112
Inconsistency (Epicurean) 8
Initiation (into philosophy) 22; — rite 26
Insanity, insane, etc. 8, 17f., 22f., 83, 85, 110, 118, 121, 125, 162f.
Interrupted study (or discourse) 152
Intermundane spaces (Epicurean) 27, 128
Invective 17f., 19, 118
Inventor 25, 32, 53-65, 123, 139-146; cf. "Heurematology," *supra*
Iranian 144
Irenaeus 10

Irony, etc. 16, 35, 44, 118, 128f.
Isaiah 132
Ishma"el 116
Isis 120
Islam 149
Isocrates 53
Israel, etc. (people) 42, 74f., 107
Italy 2, 121
Ixion 44f., 135

Jacob 134
Jacob (R., Tanna) 110, 128, 151
Jargon 139
Jeroboam 24
Jerusalem 17-19, 101, 111, 116, 118, 136
Jews, the 113; cf. "Israel," *supra*
Job 130; —, Sumerian 50
Jonathan b. Uzzi'el 110
Jose (R., Tanna) 150
Jose b. Ḥalafta (Ḥalaphta) 65
Josephus 2, 102
Joshua (b. Ḥananiah) 79-85, 107, 110, 114, 127, 154f., 157, 163
Joy (at death) 162
Judah the Baker (Tanna) 12, 35 (also "Yehudah")
Judah the Prince, see "Yehudah ha-Nasi," *infra*
Judaic Tradition 133; cf. "Talmud(ic)," "Rabbinic," *infra*
Judea 114, 134, 139, 147
Judge, Justice, etc. 35-41
Judgment, Final 37, 95
Julius Caesar (as Epicurean) 1, 16, 32, 100f., 120
Julian(us), Emperor 4, 105
Justin (Martyr) 3, 103
Juvenal 1, 101, 131, 146

Lactantius 17, 48, 53, 101, 104, 123, 137
Lampsacus 113
Language, invention of 146
Laodice 11, 36
Last will 13
Latin 1, 27, 104
Laughter 90, 161; — and weeping 161 (of philosophers, Sages)
Lavatory manners 165

Lavishness, see "Luxury," *infra*
Law, the, see "Torah," *infra*
Learning (from anyone) 149
Legend, etc. 10, 14, 18f., 21, 32, 34, 85, 92, 107, 110, 113f., 116, 121, 154
Leontion 11f., 112
Leucippus 52
"Live unobtrusively" ("quietly," etc.) 8, 101, 109; cf. *"lathe biōsas,"* Greek Terms; *"ḳbl,"* Hebrew Terms
Logos 158
Loss of Eternity 76
Love 7, 18, 73, 101, 109; — potion 110
Love of learning 8, 108
Lowly foods (bread, cheese, figs, water; acorns) 163f.; lowly posture 163f.
Lucian 3, 136f., 147, 151
Lucilius (satirist) 109; — (Seneca's friend) 103, 115
Lucillius (Epigrammatist) 125
Lucius (of the *Golden Ass*) 120
Lucretius 1, 17f., 25, 30, 34, 43, 48, 53f., 56f., 99, 101, 104, 106, 110, 117, 119, 123, 136, 145
Luke 164
Lupus Rutilius 50
Luxury, etc. 8, 38, 57, 94, 135, 142
Lyceum 22
Lysias (Tarsan tyrant) 2, 109
Lysimachus (Thracian ruler) 113

Macarismus 58f., cf. "Blessed," *supra*, and *makarioi*, Greek Terms
Machon 112
Madness, see "Insanity," *supra*
Maecenas 1, 101; —, metaphor (vulgar) 67
Magical formulae 26; — papyri 145
Maimonides 115
Manilius 53
Manasseh 42, 135, 137
Manna 144
Man's origin 95
Marble 24, 27, 31, 125, cf. *"marmor,"* Greco-Roman Terms
Marcion 10
Marcius Fadus (Epicurean) 101
Marcus Aurelius 2, 22, 95, 102, 151

Marius (Epicurean) 101
Marriage 6f., 108f.
Martyr, etc. 12, 35, 108, 155, 162, 165
Materialism 25, 63, 124
Mathematics 20, 100, 117
Matius (Epicurean)
Maximus Confessor 81
Medicine (medical art) 55, 103
Medieval censorship 116
Meir (Meïr, R.) 21, 42, 55, 109, 114, 121, 126, 135, 144
Memento mori 95
Memmius 101
Memorization 3, 104
Menander 82
Menedemus 127
Menippus 84, 112, 122
Merkabah speculation 9, 110
Messianic, etc. 14, 116, 158
Metaneira 112
Metatron 110, 122
Metrodorus (Epicurean) 11, 26, 33, 100, 103, 112, 114, 117, 123, 135
Metrodorus of Stratonica (former Epicurean) 121
Midrash, etc. 30, 40ff., 61, 65, 75, 86, 91, 98, 105, 114, 122, 125, 130, 134, 137, 139, 145f.
Milesian, Miletus 79, 110
Minos 44ff., 136
Minucius Felix 104
Mishnah, etc. 40, 51, 69, 105, 112, 139, 146-154, 158f., 164
Mithaccus (culinary writer) 63
Mithras (Mithres, ruler) 113
Moderation 101
Monotheism 89
Moschion 53
Monster kings 42
Moses 107, 147, 149, 158
al-Mubaššir b. Fātik 149
Mule (introduced) 65
Musonius Rufus 53
Mystery 26; Mysteries (Eleusinian) 145
Mystic, Mysticism, etc. (Jewish) 5, 8f., 14, 19, 24, 31f., 34, 83, 85, 88, 92, 106f., 110f., 116, 120, 125, 156, 163

Myth, Mythology, etc. 44-48, 83, 87, 135, 136, 160, 165
Mytilene 113

Nablus 3, 135
Nachmanides 160
Naming 143, 146
Naples 1
Nature 26, 48, 54, 57, 77, 140-143, 152
Nausiphanes (teacher of Epicurus) 117
Near East, etc. 1ff., 16, 42, 64, 101f., 104, 125, 129, 133-135, 160, 163
Neocles (brother of Epicurus) 13, 33, 114
Neofiti I 36f., 131-133
Netherworld, see "Hades," *supra*
New Comedy 53
Nicasicrates (Epicurean) 102
Nickname 12
Nicolaus of Damascus 2
Nihilist, etc. 20, 22, 121
Nisim Gaon 116
Noah Haim b. Mosheh 153
"Nothing (from Nothing)" etc., 79, 106, 111, 154, 156
Numerical speculation 122, 124f.

Obedience 96
Odor (of sacrifices) 13
Oicotypify 139
Old Comedy 53
Olympichus (fictional) 49
Oracle 21, 120, 148
Oral Law 7, 14; see also "Mishnah," *supra*, and "Rabbinic," "Talmud(ic)," and "Torah," *infra*
Orate, etc. 4
Ordain, etc. 86, 88
Ordeal 163
Origen 3, 21, 103, 116, 153
Ovid 1, 101, 131f.

Pagan temples 13
Pain 91
Palamedes 91
Pallades 105
Pallet 164
Pamphila 105
Pamphilus 103

Panaetius 142
Pancratium 130
Paphlagonian Epicureanism 3
Parables 23
Paradise 5, 19f., 20, 22, 32, 34
Paradox, Paradoxa, etc. (of the Stoics) 17, 67, 70-73, 76, 147-151, 160
Parasite 67, 69
Parents 7
Parmenides 22
Parody, etc. 3f., 4, 6, 25, 27f., 30, 32ff., 53, 59, 88, 104, 122, 124, 127ff., 131, 145, 149
Passover 87, 155
Patristic, etc. 21f., 26, 41, 43, 50, 65, 82, 84, 131, 156, 158
Patron 67-69
Paul 3, 30, 103, 121, 151
Payment (for teaching) 141
Peace (through scholarship) 22
Peripatos 22
Persuasiveness (of Epicureans) 8, 87, 131, 160
Peshiṭṭa 130
Peter 151
Petronius 1, 91, 101, 131, 146, 151
Phaedrus (*OCD* 3, Epicurean) 1, 101
Phanias (Epigrammatist) 121
Pharisees 37
Pherecrates (Old Comedy) 53
Philemon the Elder (New Comedy) 53
Philo (of Alexandria, Philo Judaeus) 2, 29f., 38ff., 53, 96, 102, 124, 129-132, 150, 158
Philo of Byblos 53
Philodemus 1, 26, 33, 83, 99-102, 112, 117, 119, 127, 135f.
Philonides (Epicurean) 2f., 16, 102
Philostratus (Flavius P.) 104, 144
Phineas b. Yair (Tanna) 151
Physicists 9, 156
Physiognomy 141, 143
Plato 29, 53, 80ff., 86, 103, 124f., 137, 142, 146, 151, 155f., 158, 161
Platonic, Platonism 7, 22, 31, 89, 99, 103, 109, 125, 141, 143, 146, 149, 161
Pleasure, etc. 38, 41, 63, 77f., 101, 121, 164, cf. "Hedonism," *supra*

GENERAL INDEX

Pleroma 10
Pliny the Elder 2, 53, 101, 143, 146, 151; — the Younger 151
Piso (*OCD* 5, Epicurean, father-in-law of Caesar) 1, 16, 30, 99f., 112, 131
Plotinus 10
Plutarch 2f., 7, 16, 20, 53, 58f., 61, 102, 104, 110, 114, 117f., 123, 133, 138, 142, 145f., 151, 156
Plutos and *Penia* 59f.
Poet, etc. 27, 31, 44, 46, 71, 100, 117, 132, 156, 158, 160
Polemo 121, 149
Politics 8
Polyaenus (Epicurean) 33
Polybius 53, 117
Polygenesis 40
Pompedius (or Pomponius) 102
Porphyry 53, 159
Posidonius 53f., 57, 62, 65, 117, 142ff., 151, 161
Post-Socratic 86
Poverty 38, 59, 143
Pre-Socratics 104
Primeval matter 160
Primitive Man, see "Early Man," *supra*
Prodicus 53
Progress of civilization 52-65, 142-147, 160
Prometheus 55f., 146
Proof text 23f., cf. "Harmonization," *supra*, and "Testimonium," Greco-Roman Terms
Prophet, etc. (biblical) 126, 161, 163
Proselyte 14, 116
Protagoras 52, 131, 142
Proverb, etc. 40, 132f.
Providence 134, 137f., 142, see also "Denial of …," *supra*
Pseudapocalypse, etc. (Epicurean) 4, 26, 29ff.
Ptolemies 2; Ptolemy I 130
Public worship 8, 25
Pun 12
Punishment (of Epicureans) 16, 32; — after death 135; —, delay of, 49
Pure, etc. 5, 27, 125, see also "Stones," *infra*

Purification rites 13
Pythagorean, etc. (and Neo —) 24, 89, 94, 122, 124f., 145, 157, 159, 161
Pythocles (Epicurean) 20

Qualities of the Sage 70-73, 148; see also "Sage," *infra*
Quintilian 20, 132f., 151
Quintus (brother of Cicero) 101, 136
Qumran 101, 121

Rab (Abba Areka, Amora) 64, 145f., 151, 154, 158
Rabbinic, etc. 15, 87, 105f., 121, 125, 163f.
Rabirius (Epicurean) 101
Rain ritual 145
Rashi 113, 118, 124
Rational, etc. 25f., 49, 110, 123, 146, 158, 165
Reason 97
Recompense, Retribution, Reward and Punishment 14, 35ff., 41-49, 96, 137f., cf. "Denial of …," *supra*
Reinterpretation 5, 23, 74f., 146, 159f.
Religion, etc. 99, 126
Resistance literature 42
Resurrection 36f., 152
Rhadamanthus 44ff.
Rhetoric, etc. 2ff., 7, 9, 15ff., 29, 31, 34, 37-42, 50f., 56, 65, 69f., 73, 76, 78, 82f., 86-98, 100, 102-108, 113-117, 123, 127f., 130-137, 147-155, 158-164
Rhetorical devices ("figures," etc.) 37-40, 54-64, 69, 140-144
Rhyme (and near-rhyme) 36, 39, 132, 146
"Rich," etc. (Sage) 70-73, 148
Roman emperors 102; — government 126
Romance (lit. genre) 145
Rome (City) 1f., 42, 101
Ruling of parchment 145

Sabbath 12, 90, 112f.
Sacrifice, etc. (cult) 90, 161
Sadducees 14f., 37, 102, 130
Sage, etc. 3, 6f., 9, 12f., 15, 17f., 23, 25, 37, 49f., 52, 54-65, 70-73, 78, 80f., 86ff.,

90-98, 108-117, 120, 123, 126f., 130f., 141-150, 154-164
Sage's wife 108
Samaritan 130
Samuel b. Isaac (Amora) 133, 135
Samuel b. Jonah (Amora) 135
Samuel b. Naḥman (Amora) 133
Samuel de Uçeda 153
Sapiens, etc., see "Sage"
Sardanapalus 42, 135
Satire, etc. 3, 7, 17, 25, 59, 67, 72, 88, 104, 122, 126, 144, 149, 156
Scholar-bureaucracy 34, 50, 159
Sebaste 22
Secrets 51f., 60f., 143, see also "Mystery,", *supra*
Secundus, "the Silent Philosopher," 109, 126
Security (Epicurean goal) 16
Self conquest (control, criticism) 70-73, 94, 149, 158f., 164
Semen 95, 164
Semiotics 162f.
Seneca 1, 16, 18, 27, 47f., 54, 67, 91, 100, 103, 118, 136f., 142, 144, 146-153, 158f., 161-164
Seneca the Elder (*OCD* 1) 50, 151
Senses, sensations 38, 76ff., 123, 153, 156ff.
Sententia, cf. Terms and Keywords, *s.v.*
Septuagint 38, 87, 130
Serenus 81
Sermon on the Mount 146
Serpent 30
Servius 156
Sex(ual license) 10; — legislation 108
Sextus Empiricus 1, 117
Shammai 127
Shemaʿiah 159
Shepherd (Akiba) 14, 120
Shimeʿon b. Azzai, cf. "Ben Azzai," *supra*
Shimeʿon b. Gamliel (II) 118
Shimeʿon b. Laḳish ("Resh," Amora) 15
Shimeʿon b. Yoḥai 144, 152
Shimeʿon b. Zoma, cf. "Ben Zoma," *supra*
Shimeʿon ha-Temani (Amora) 110

Sibylline Oracles 42
Sidon 110
Signs, see "Semiotics," *supra*; *sīman*, Hebrew Terms
Sinaitic 110
Siren, etc. ("beguiling speech") 21, 30, 87
Siro (Epicurean) 2, 136 (or Siron)
Sisera 116
Sisyphus 44f., 135
Skeptic, Skepticism (philosophy) 7, 49, 89, 124
Slaves 141
Smoke (from the tomb) 114
Socrates 55, 81, 83, 91, 120, 127, 141, 157, 161
Socratic Tradition 22
Solomon, etc. 40ff., 48, 133f., 163
Solon 162
Solstice 65
Sophist, etc., Sophism 29, 52, 130f., 136, 140, 142, 151
Sophocles 52, 142
Sophos, etc., see "Sage", *supra*
Sophron 162
Sorite(s), etc. 74-78, 97, 151, 154, 160
Sosicrates (of Rhodes) 104
Sotion 104
Speculation, etc. 9, 16, 75, 82, 85 87f. 121f. 124, 128, 160
Stars 83
Stoa, Stoicism, etc. 17, 22, 47ff., 61, 67, 70-73, 75f., 83, 87, 89, 93-95, 97, 99, 103f., 120, 127, 137, 141f., 146-149, 158, 160f.
Stobaeus (Ioannes) 22, 72, 80, 104, 127, 148f.
"Stones of pure marble" 5, 24, 31
Strabo 151
Students 8, 14, 19f., 84, 116, 119, 122
Style (Epicurean) 15, 25, 27, 29f., 117, 123, 128, 135, 144f.
Succession (of philosophers) 104, cf. "Diadoche," *supra*
Suetonius 18
Suffeius (Epicurean) 101
Suffering Servant 130
Suicide 8, 16, 162

Suidas (*Suda*) 158
Sun (foot-sized) 9, 27, 81-85, 156f.; — festivals 145
Superstition, etc. 13, 25
Symposium, etc. 4

Table manners 65-69
Tacitus 91, 162
Talmud(ic), etc. 5f., 10, 14, 23, 32, 34, 41, 49f., 54f., 67, 69, 73, 76, 78, 88, 93, 102-116, 126f., 131, 137, 139-145, 151, 155f., 158-161
Tanna(itic), etc. 4, 6, 15 24 33, 63, 87f., 105, 127f., 130, 138, 151-153
Tantalus 44ff., 135
Targum(ic), etc. 30, 36-47, 124, 129-134
Tarsus 2, 109f., 134
Taurus (teacher of Aulus Gellius) 47
Temples 48, 118, 137
Ten Questions 151
Tertullian 10
Textual transmission 34
Thais 112
Thales 80-85, 88, 126f., 155, 158, 164
Thearion the Baker 63
Theodorus (the Atheist) 113
Theon 50
Theophilus 85, 157
Theophrastus 53, 104
Theosophy 20, 24, 83, 88, 116
Thrasea Paetus 162
Three hundred (lit. moteme) 162
Thrones 27, 116
Thucydides 53
Tiberius 162
Tiberius Julius Alexander (nephew of Philo) 131
Timasagoras (Epicurean) 102
Timocrates (former Epicurean) 113, 120
Timon 114, 116
Titus 101, 131
Tityus 44ff., 135f.
Torah 9, 12, 14, 19f., 35, 76, 90, 93, 108, 110f., 113f., 144, 150, 152, 163; —, Prophets, Hagiographa 114
Tosephta 69, 88, 105
Tower of Babel 29
Tragedians 15

Trajan 2
Tranquility of soul 27
Translate, etc. 77
Triple entendre 12
Triptolemus 136
Typology, *Typoi*, etc. 4ff., 10, 16, 21f., 31ff., 121, 124, 127, 131
Tyrant 86
Tzetzes (scholar) 53

Unanswerable, see "Ten Questions," *supra*
Uncultured, see "Ignorant," *supra*
Universal State 158

Varro 53, 162
Vegetarian, Vegetarianism 58, 64, 145
Velleius (fictional Epicurean) 27f.
Vergil 1, 53, 100, 131, 144
Vetus Latinae 130
Vineyard (metaphor) 74, 78; — (meeting place) 154
Virtue, etc. 38, 57, 62, 70-73, 75, 93f., 148f., 153
Visionary, etc. 19, 24, 26, 31f., 120-125
Vitae 4, cf. also "Biography," *supra*, and "*bioi*", Terms and Keywords
Vitruvius 53, 143
Void, the (Epicurean concept) 10, 27f.
Vulgate 130

Walls (of the World) 27ff.
Water, etc. 9, 87, 125, 164; — Upper, Lower 79, 82f., 160, see also "*mayim*," Hebrew Terms
"Water, water" 5, 24, 30f.
Whence (and whither) 79, 154, 164
Wine, unmixed 8
Wisdom Literature 50, 133, 163
Wit, witticism, etc. 25, 28, 33, 47, 80, 84, 110, 112, 116, 120, 127, 137f., 155, 158
Withdrawal (Epicurean) 100
Woman, etc. 56, 92, 163
Work of Creation 82f.
World to Come 37, 74
Writing (invented) 60, 143

Xanthippe 127

Xenophanes 52
Xenophon 53

Yabneh 154
Yehudah ha-Nasi (Judah the Prince, "Rabbi") 13, 111, 113, 124, 134
Yehuda(h) the Baker (Judah, Tanna) 12, 35

Yoḥanan (R., Amora) 133
Yoḥanan b. Zakkai 110
Yose b. Yehudah (Tanna) 116

Zeno (the Stoic) 53, 72, 103, 120, 148, 151
Zeno of Sidon (*OCD* 5, Epicurean) 1, 101, 117
Zeus 55, 118, 137, 146

INDEX OF MODERN AUTHORS

[An asterisk (*) preceding an entry signifies an additional and different work or essay of the same author]

Abel, K. 100
Abrahams, I. 1, 111, 160
Albeck, C. (or H.) 105, *105, cf. also Theodor, J.
Allen, W., Jr. (and P. deLacy) 100, 110
Altaner, B. 103
Altmann, A. 106, *111, 154
Aptowitzer, V. 158
Armstrong, A. H. 125
Arnaldez, R. 130
Arnim, v., see von Arnim
Arrighetti, G. 103, 109, 127, 156
Avi-Yonah, M. 105, 126

Bacher, W. 8, 76, *105, *105, *105, 108, 112, 115f., *122, 126, 144, *145f., 152, 157f., 159f., 164f.
Bagnani, G. 101
Bailey, C. 99, *100, *103, 109, 119, 123, *124, *135, 149, 156, *157
Barigazzi, A. 117
Baron, S. W. 105, 159
Basore, J. W. 147
Bendavid, A. 118
Bergmann, J. 150
Bignone, E. 103, *103, 118, 135
Bornstein, D. J. 110
Boyancé, P. 99, *119, *123
Brann, M. 154
Brink, K. O. 99
Buber S. 133, 135, *138
Buchheit, V. 142
Büchler, A. 112, *116, 121
Burnet, J. 155

Cançik, H. 100
Cary, M. (and Haarhoff, T. J.) 100
Chadwick, H. 103
Chartraine, P. 144
Chilton, C. W. 103, 136

Chroust, A.-H. 91
Clarke, H. L. 100, *104
Classen, C. J. 155
Cohen, H. 150
Cole, T. 140
Colson, F. H. 102, 124
Cornford, F. M. 123
Courcelle, P. 158
Crönert, W. 99, 100, 102, 117

Davidson, I. 128
DeLacy, P. H. 99, *99, (and —, E. A.) *99, *100, *111, *111, *124, 125, *137
Delatte, A. 162
Dessau, H. 136
DeWitt, N. W. 99, *100, 101, *103, 117, *119, 125, 137, 153
Diano, C. 103
Diels, H. 102, *137
Dill, S. 99, 100, *117
Dörrie, H. 140
Dudley, D. R. 126
Duff, J. W. 100

Eddy, S. K. 110
Edelstein, L. 99, *140, *159
Efros, I. I. 111
Ehrentreu, H. 105
Einarson, B. (and DeLacy, P. H.) 104, 109, 117
Elbogen, I. (J.) 154
Elder, J. P. 99, *121
Enk, P. J. 145
Epstein, Y. (J.) N. 105, *105

Feldman, L. H. 117
Ferguson, J. 150
Festugière, A. J. 111f., 121, *121, 125, 127
Finkelstein, L. 107

Fischel, H. A. 102, *102, *102, *107, *126, *128, *135, *162, and *passim*, Cyn., EJ, Story
Fraenkel, E. 100
Frank, T. 100, *100
Freymuth, G. 111
Friedländer, L. 100, 101, 105, 110
Friedländer, M. 110, *130
Friedmann, M. 109, *133
Fuchs, H. 135

Geffcken, J. 105
Gerhard, G. A. 122
Getty, R. C. 100
Gigon, O. 111, *120, 121
Ginzberg, L. 112, 116, *144
Goldschmidt, E. D. 159
Goldschmidt, L. 105
Goodenough, E. R. 102
Gow, A. S. F. 112
Green, P. 100, 101
Grelot, P. 129
Grilli, A. 103, 136
Grossfeld, B. 129
Grube, G. M. A. 104, 122
Grünbaum, M. 145
Grünhut, L. 108
Guthrie, W. K. C. 140, *164
Guttmann, A. 105

Hadot, I. 159
Häsler, B. 99, 103
Hagendahl, H. 111
Haines, C. R. 101f.
Halporn, J. W. (and Ostwald, M., Rosenmeyer, T. G.) 132
Hausleiter, J. 145
Heidel, W. A. 28, 123, 125
Heinemann, I. 130, *141
Heinze, R. 101
Heller, B. 146
Hemelrijk, J. 143
Hengel, M. 120
Hense, O. 149, 155
Hercher, R. 104
Hicks, R. D. 102, 103, 109, 119
Higger, M. 105
Highet, G. 101, *101, *101, 122

Hobein, H. 135
Holtzmann, O. 141
Hommel, H. 143
Horovitz, H. S. 110

Jaeger, W. 155
Jastrow, M. 19, 108, 114, 118, 119, 121f., 126, 160
Jellinek, A. 146
Jensen, C. 125
Jungkuntz, 111, 116, 130

Kaempf, M. 115
Kaibel, G. 136
Kaminka, A. 141
Kas(s)owski, (C)H. J. 106
Katsh, I. A. 152
Kennedy, G. 104
Kerényi, K. 123
Kittel, R. - Kahle, P. 130
Klauser, T. 99
Kleingünther, A. 140
Kleinknecht, H. 122
Kleve, K. 111
Knight, W. F. Jackson 100
Koch, C. 100, 123, 125
Kohl, R. 138
Krauss, S. 154, *162
Krohn, K. 140

Lämmli, F. 140
Lattimore, R. 109
Lausberg, H. 131
Lauterbach, J. Z. 164
Leslie, R. J. 100
Levy, J. 108f., 115, 118, 119, 121f., 137, 146, 156
Liddell, H. G. (-Scott, R., -Jones, H. S.) 118, 127, 145, 157
Lieberman, S. 106, *106, *106, 111, 138f., *145, 154, 156, *162
Long, H. S. 102, 109, 156
Lovejoy, A. O. (-Boas, G.) 140

Margulies, M. 133
Marmorstein, A. 106, 111, 115, *129, 130
Marrou, H. I. 105
Meineke, A. 155

Merlan, P. 99, *111, *125
Meyer, R. 125
Meyer, W. 143
Michel, A. 130
Mielziner, M. 105
Migne, J. P. 155
Momigliano, A. 100, 126
Mommsen, T. 101
Müller, R. 140
Murmelstein, B. 144
Mutschmann, H. 100, 103

Nauck, (J.) A. 155
Neher, A. 126
Neubauer, A. 154
Neubecker, A. J. 117
Neusner, J. 102, *105
Nock, A. D. 90, *121
Norden, E. 104, 132
Nota (signed without initial) 162
Olivieri, A. 119
Opelt, I. 118

Packer, M. N. 101
Panichas, G. A. 99
Paschell, D. M. 118
Pauly, W. (- Wissowa, G., et al.) 99, 127, and passim (P.-W.)
Peek, W. 110
Perry, B. E. 109
Philippson, R. 99, *99, *100, *101, *103

Quasten, J. 103

Rab(b)inowicz (—tz), R. N. 105, 139
Radermacher, I. 136
Rappaport, S. 141
Ratner, B. 106, *116, 157
Regenbogen, O. 99, 125
Reinhardt, K. 141, *141
Reitzenstein, R. 28, 31, 124, 125
Ronconi, A. 162
Roscher, W. 135
Rose, H. J. 100, *132, *135f.
Rosenthal, F. 149
Rostovtzeff, M. 102
Rudberg, G. 140

Ruether, R. R. 103

Sbordone, F. 127
Schanz, M. (-Hosius, C., -Krüger, G.) 100
Schechter, S., see AdRN, 164
Schmid, W. 99, *99, *99, *99, *100, *100, 111, *117, 117, 124, and passim (RAC)
Schmidt, J. 147
Scholem, G. G. 106, 107, *111, 121, 122, 124
Schwabe, M. 139
Schwartz, E. 152
Sigsbee, D. L. 147, 149
Simpson, A. 111, 126
Sinor, D. 102
Solmsen, F. 111, *125, *125
Sophocles, E. A. 109
Spaeth, J. W. 106
Spanier, A. 160
Spoerri, W. 140, *140, 146
Stark, R. 132
Steckel, H. 99
Stein E. (M.) 106
Stella, S. 147
Sternbach, L. 155
Strack, H. L. 105, 144, (-Billerbeck, P.) *164
Stückelberger, A. 145
Süss, W. 155
Sullivan, J. P. 101
Syme, R. 100

Tait, J. I. M. 100
Taylor, C. 116
Theodor, J. (-Albeck, C. or H.) 110, 134, 154, 160
Thraede, K. 123, 140ff. and passim (RAC), *140
Townsend, G. 126
Tschizewskij, D. 155

Ueberweg, F. (-Praechter, K.) 99, 101, 102, 117
Urbach, E. E. 107, 121, *154
Usener, H. 101-104, 109, 112, 117, 124f., 156f.
Uxkull-Gyllenband, W. 140

Vermès, G. 37, 129
Vischer, R. 109, 143
Vogliano, A. 99
Volkmann, R. 131, 136, 147
von Arnim, H. (latinized, I.) 99, *134, 141, 147f.
von Wilamowitz-Moellendorff, U. 103, *132
von der Muehll, P. 104, *129

Wacholder, B. Z. 102
Wachsmuth, K. (C.) -Hense, O., 149, 155
Wagner, S. M. 106, 111, 114

Wallach, L. 151f.
Weinstein, N. I. 160
Wechsler, T. 112, 119, 121, 125
Weiss, H.-F. 160
Weiss, I. H. 110
Wendland, P. 130, *130, *134
William, I. 103
Wolfson, H. A. 106, *165

Zeitlin, S. 105
Ziegler, H. 135
Ziegler, K. 18, 104, 118, 137
Zuckermandel, M. S. 106